THE SECRET SERVICE

KINGSMAN

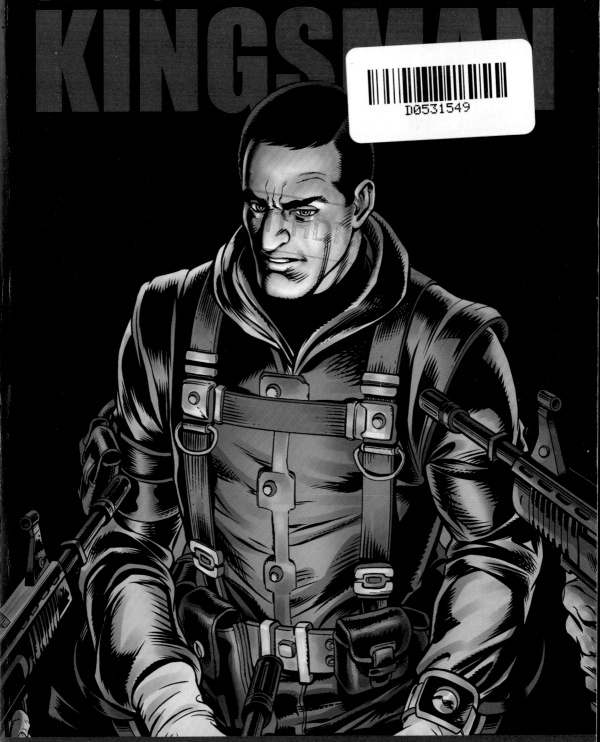

KINGSMAN: THE SECRET SERVICE (MOVIE TIE-IN EDITION) ISBN 978 7832933676. First edition January 2015.

Published by Titan Books, a division of Titan Publishing Group Ltd., 144 Southwark St, London, SE1 0UP. Copyright © 2012, 2013, 2014, 2015 Millarworld Limited, Dave Gibbons, LLC, and Marv Films Limited. All rights reserved. THE SECRET SERVICE, the The Secret Service logo, and all characters featured in this comics issue and the distinctive names and likenesses thereof and all related indicia are trademarks of Millarworld Limited and Dave Gibbons LLC. "MILLARWORLD" and the Millarworld logo are trademarks of Millarworld Limited. No similarity between any of the names, characters, persons, and/or institutions in this title and those of any person or institution is intended and any such similarity that may seem to exist is purely coincidental. No part of this publication may be reproduced, stored in a retrieval system, or transmitted, in any form or by any means, without the prior written consent from the authors and the publisher.

Contains material originally published in magazine form as THE SECRET SERVICE #1-6. Kingsman: The Secret Service film artwork © 2014 Twentieth Century Fox Film Corporation. All rights reserved.

A CIP catalogue record for this title is available from the British Library.

3 5 7 9 10 8 6 4 2

Printed in Spain.

For my old school friend Eggsy, who cannot believe he's about to become the next James Bond, and for Russ, who helped me with so many wonderful set pieces for this story, most of which were inspired by his military experiences.

—Mark Millar

For the young Mark Millar, whose boyish ambition to work with me led, many years later, to such an enjoyable collaboration, and for Andy and Angus with thanks for all their help.

—Dave Gibbons

THE SECRET SERVICE
KINGSMAN

WRITER
MARK MILLAR

ARTIST
DAVE GIBBONS

CO-PLOTTER
MATTHEW VAUGHN

INKERS
DAVE GIBBONS (ISSUE 1)
ANDY LANNING (ISSUES 2-6)

COLOURIST
ANGUS MCKIE

LETTERERS
DAVE GIBBONS
AND ANGUS MCKIE

ISSUE 1 VARIANT COVER
LEINIL FRANCIS YU
AND SUNNY GHO

THE SECRET SERVICE CREATED BY

ONE

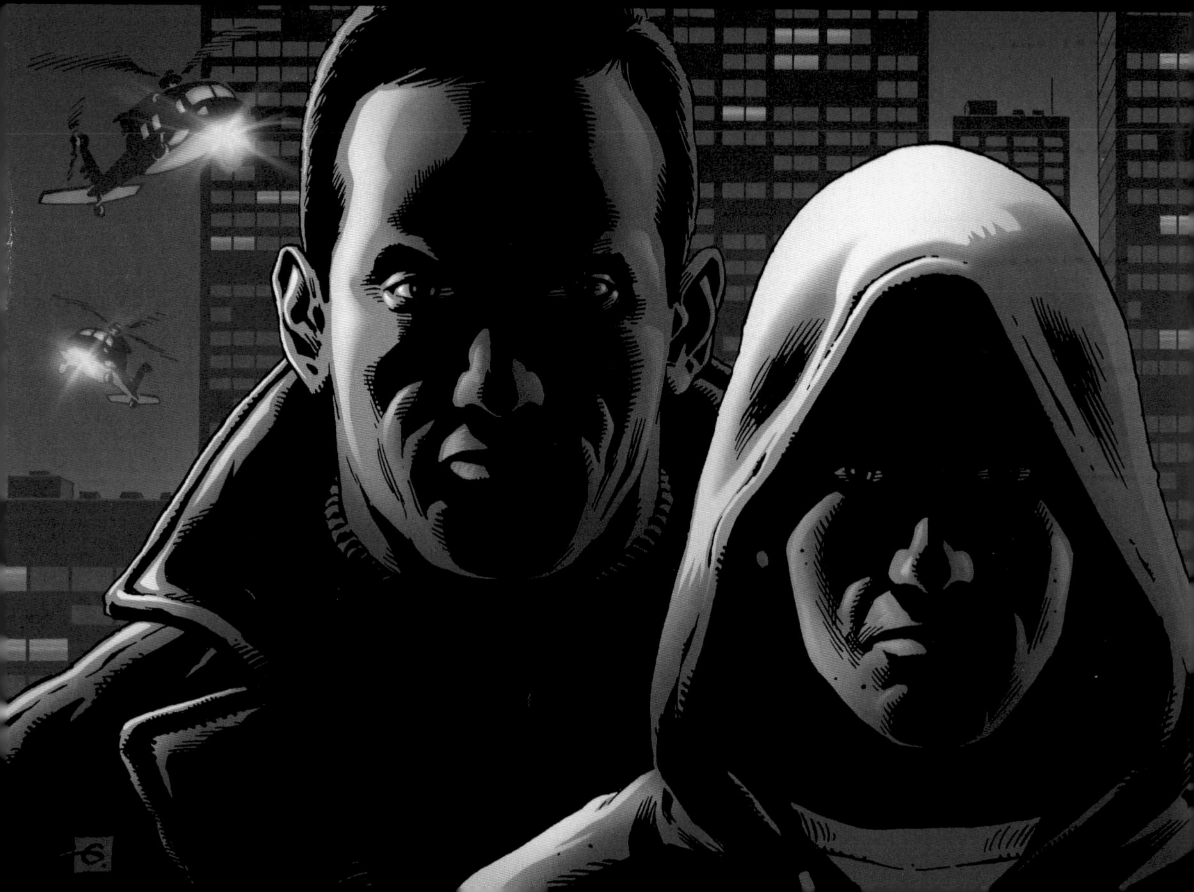

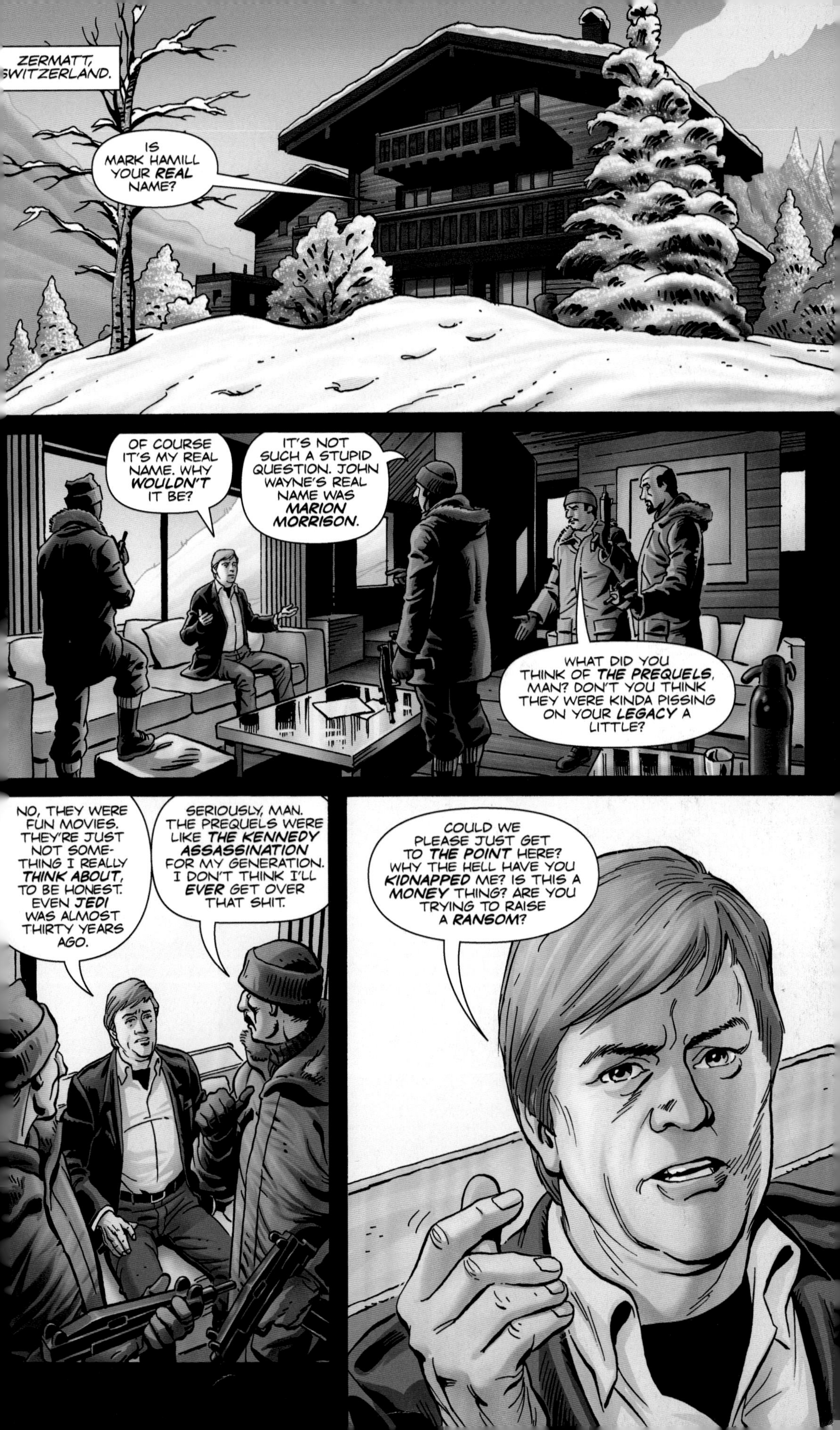
ZERMATT, SWITZERLAND.
IS MARK HAMILL YOUR REAL NAME?
OF COURSE IT'S MY REAL NAME. WHY WOULDN'T IT BE?
IT'S NOT SUCH A STUPID QUESTION. JOHN WAYNE'S REAL NAME WAS MARION MORRISON.
WHAT DID YOU THINK OF THE PREQUELS, MAN? DON'T YOU THINK THEY WERE KINDA PISSING ON YOUR LEGACY A LITTLE?
NO, THEY WERE FUN MOVIES. THEY'RE JUST NOT SOME-THING I REALLY THINK ABOUT, TO BE HONEST. EVEN JEDI WAS ALMOST THIRTY YEARS AGO.
SERIOUSLY, MAN. THE PREQUELS WERE LIKE THE KENNEDY ASSASSINATION FOR MY GENERATION. I DON'T THINK I'LL EVER GET OVER THAT SHIT.
COULD WE PLEASE JUST GET TO THE POINT HERE? WHY THE HELL HAVE YOU KIDNAPPED ME? IS THIS A MONEY THING? ARE YOU TRYING TO RAISE A RANSOM?

NO, MONEY IS SOMETHING OUR PEOPLE HAVE PLENTY OF, SIR.
I'M AFRAID YOU'LL HAVE TO WAIT UNTIL WE REACH THE MIDDLE EAST BEFORE YOU FIND OUT WHERE YOU FIT INTO ALL THIS.
HUH?
OH JESUS...

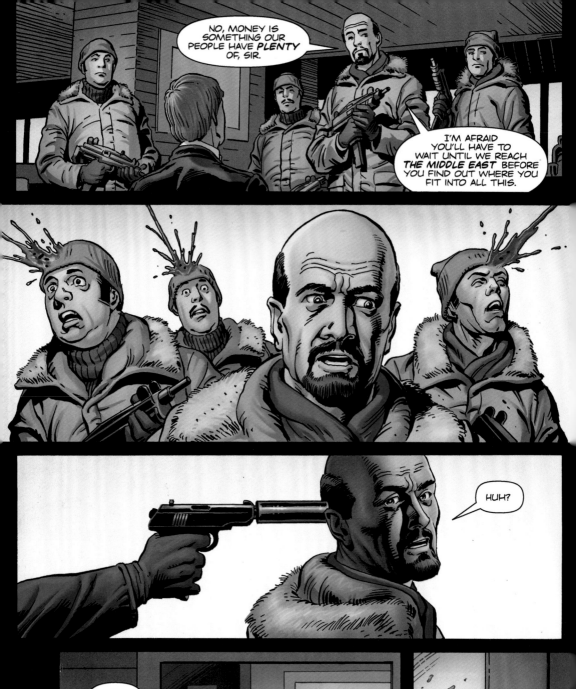

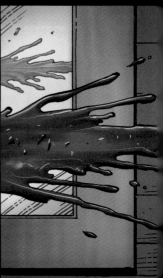

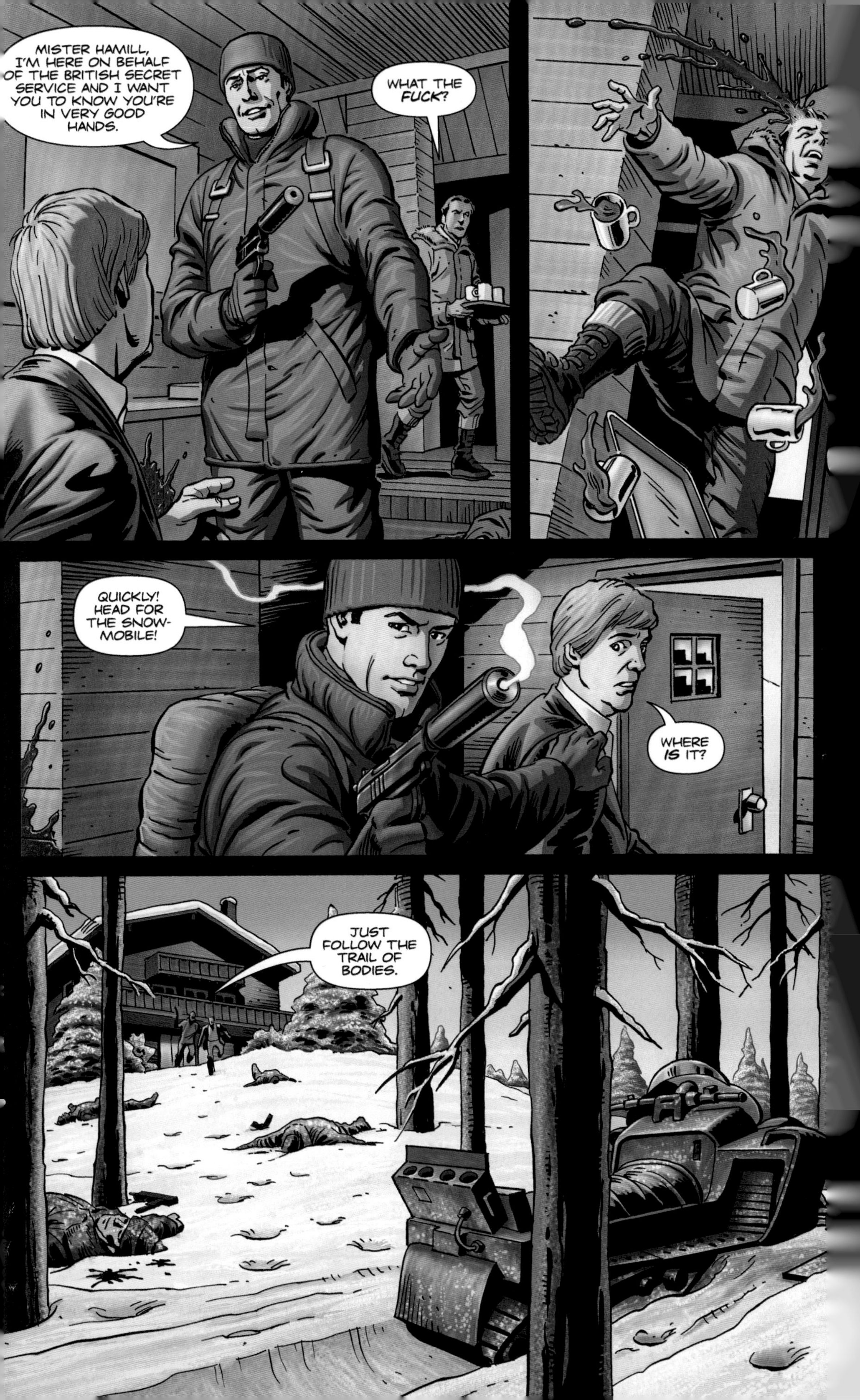
MISTER HAMILL, I'M HERE ON BEHALF OF THE BRITISH SECRET SERVICE AND I WANT YOU TO KNOW YOU'RE IN VERY GOOD HANDS.
WHAT THE *FUCK*?
QUICKLY! HEAD FOR THE SNOW-MOBILE!
WHERE *IS* IT?
JUST FOLLOW THE TRAIL OF BODIES.

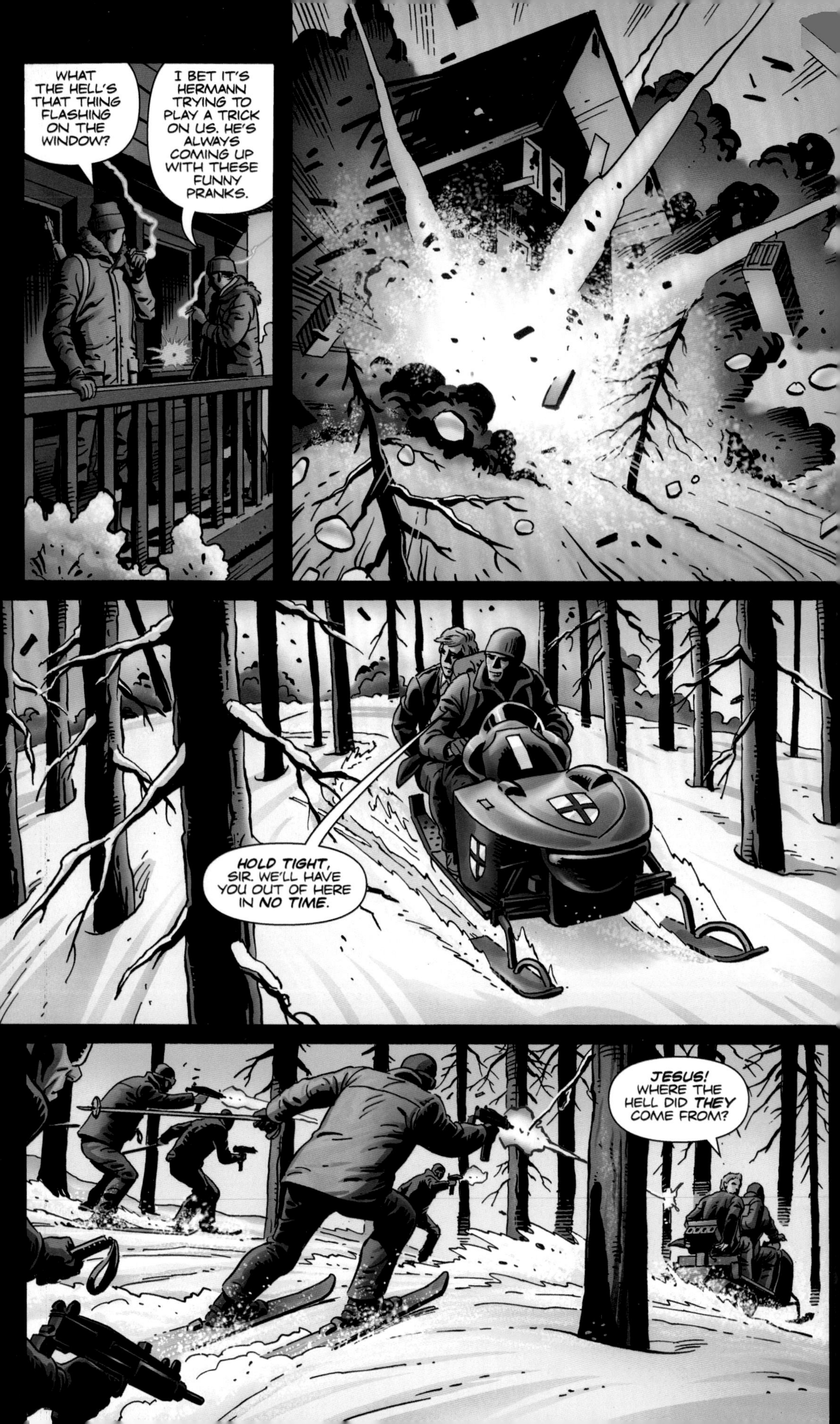
WHAT THE HELL'S THAT THING FLASHING ON THE WINDOW?
I BET IT'S HERMANN TRYING TO PLAY A TRICK ON US. HE'S ALWAYS COMING UP WITH THESE FUNNY PRANKS.
HOLD TIGHT, SIR. WE'LL HAVE YOU OUT OF HERE IN NO TIME.
JESUS! WHERE THE HELL DID THEY COME FROM?

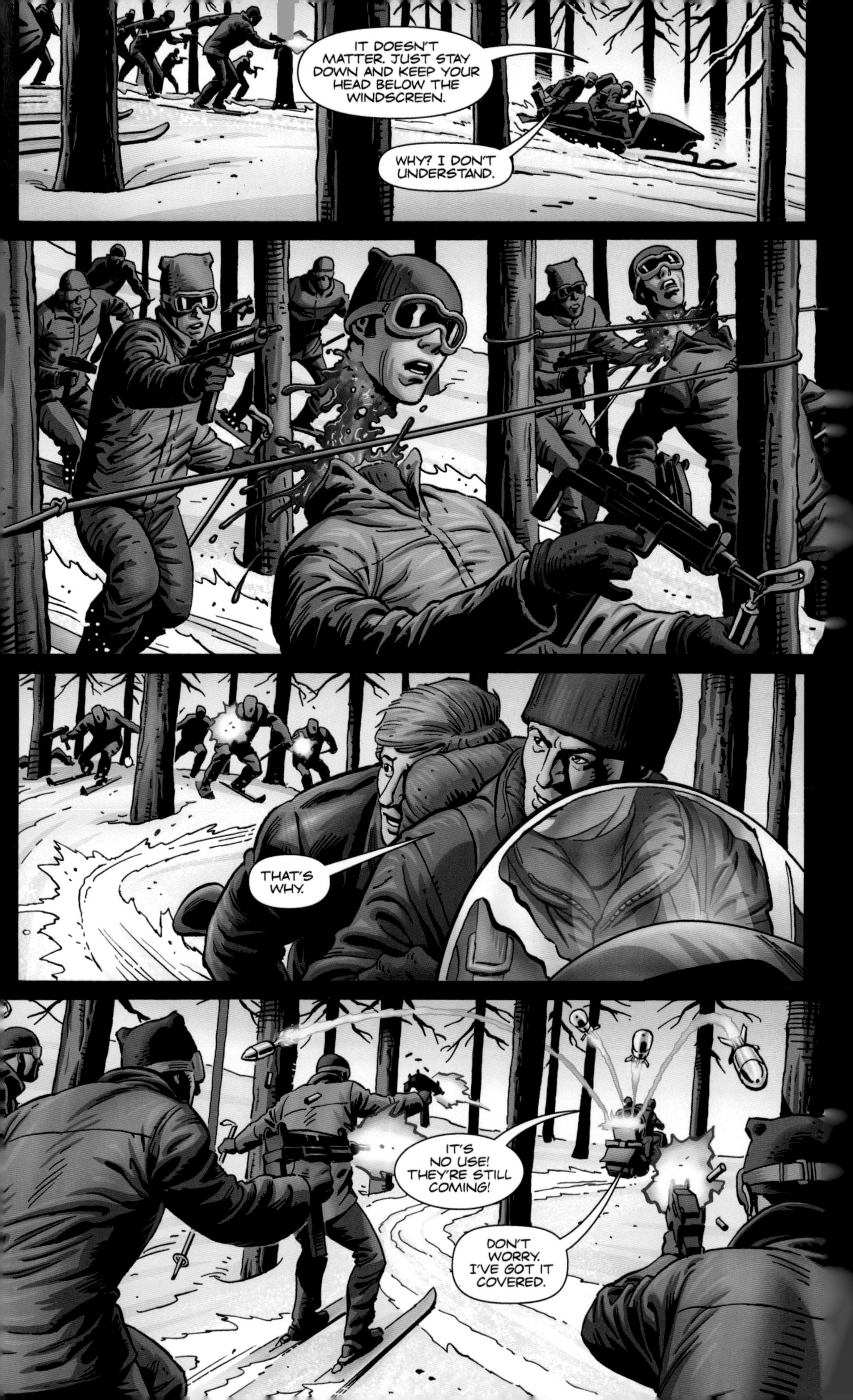
IT DOESN'T MATTER. JUST STAY DOWN AND KEEP YOUR HEAD BELOW THE WINDSCREEN.
WHY? I DON'T UNDERSTAND.
THAT'S WHY.
IT'S NO USE! THEY'RE STILL COMING!
DON'T WORRY. I'VE GOT IT COVERED.

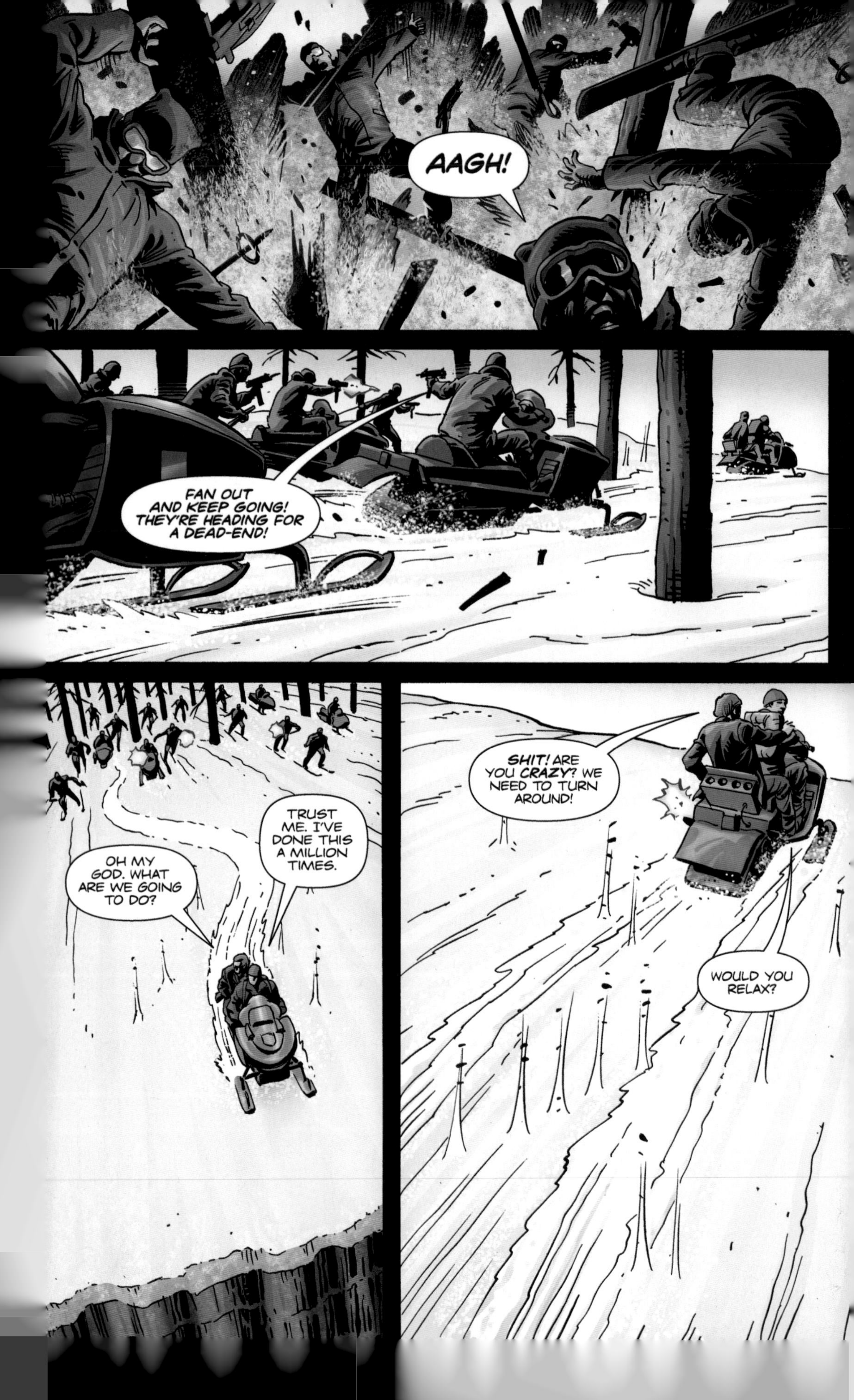
AAGH!
FAN OUT AND KEEP GOING! THEY'RE HEADING FOR A DEAD-END!
OH MY GOD. WHAT ARE WE GOING TO DO?
TRUST ME. I'VE DONE THIS A MILLION TIMES.
SHIT! ARE YOU CRAZY? WE NEED TO TURN AROUND!
WOULD YOU RELAX?

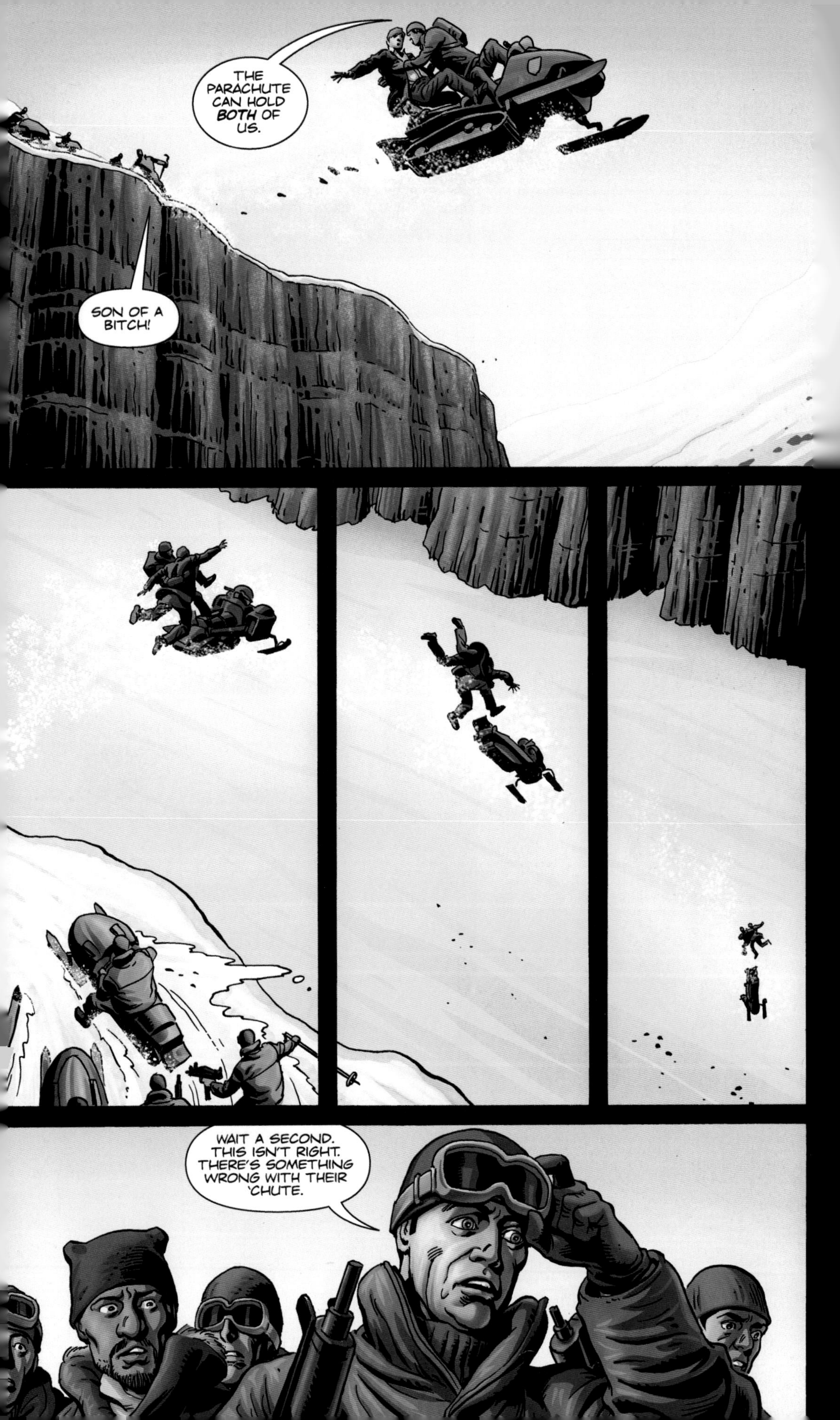
THE PARACHUTE CAN HOLD BOTH OF US.
SON OF A BITCH!
WAIT A SECOND. THIS ISN'T RIGHT. THERE'S SOMETHING WRONG WITH THEIR 'CHUTE.

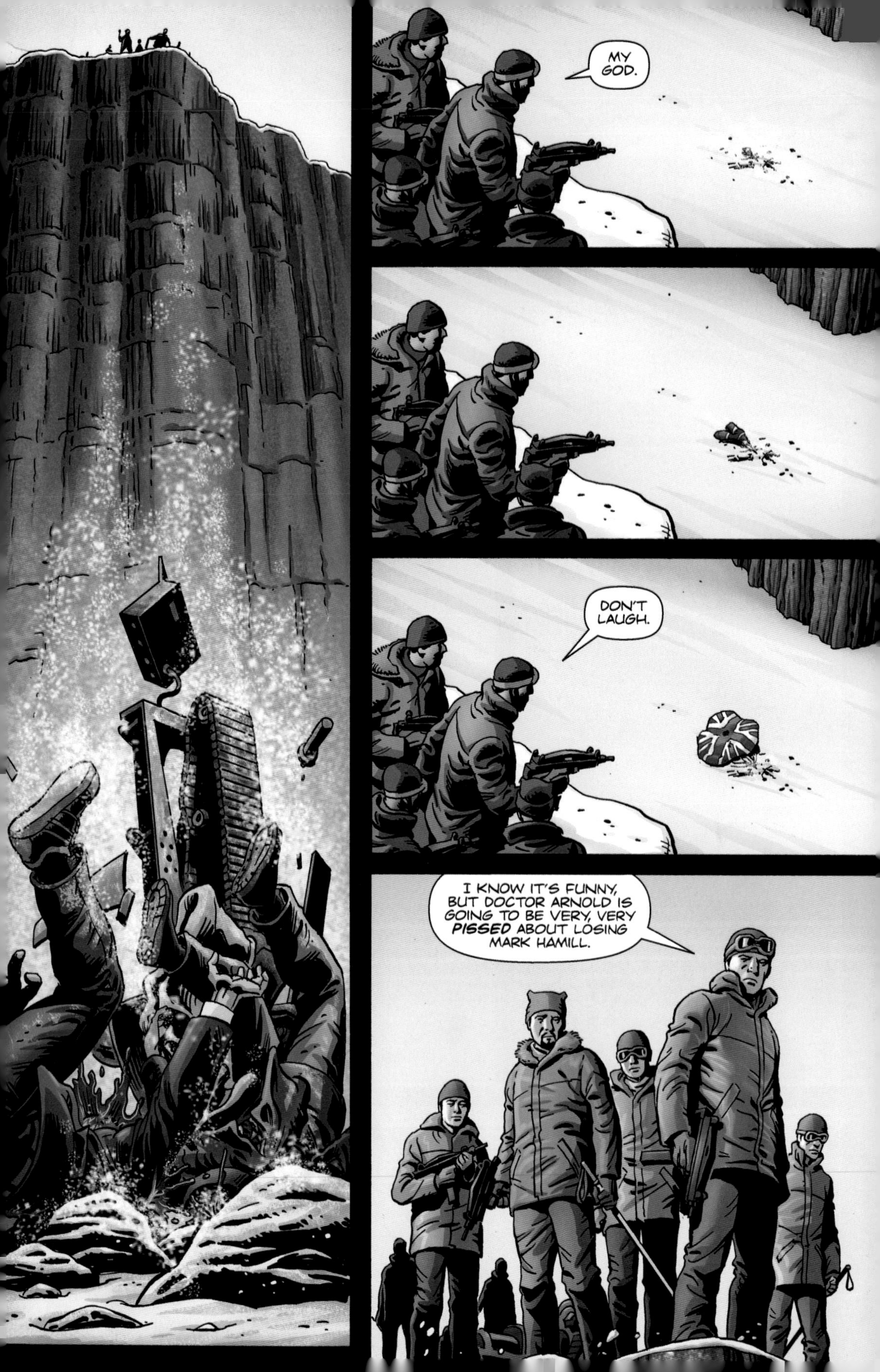
MY GOD.
DON'T LAUGH.
I KNOW IT'S FUNNY, BUT DOCTOR ARNOLD IS GOING TO BE VERY, VERY ***PISSED*** ABOUT LOSING MARK HAMILL.

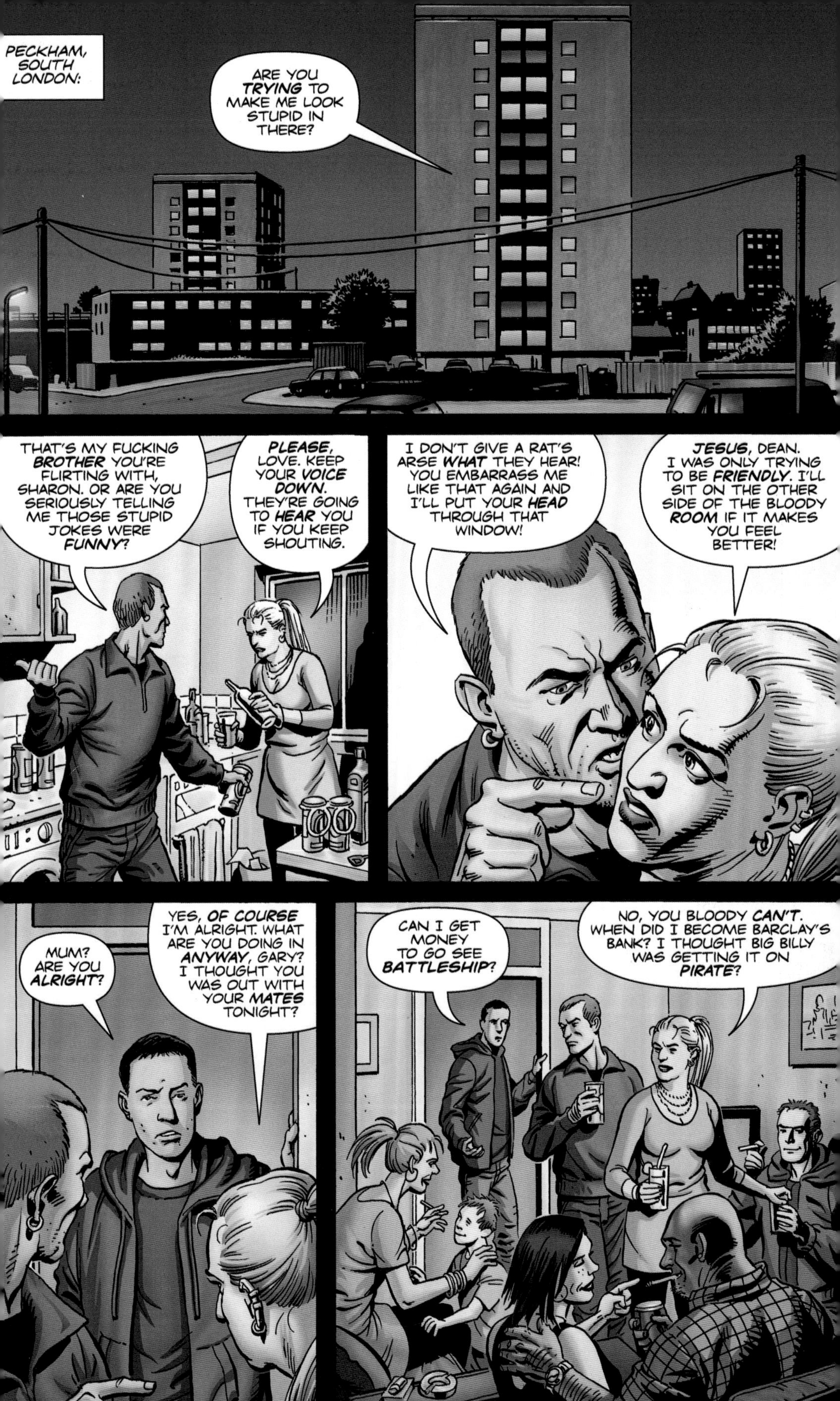
PECKHAM, SOUTH LONDON:
ARE YOU TRYING TO MAKE ME LOOK STUPID IN THERE?
THAT'S MY FUCKING BROTHER YOU'RE FLIRTING WITH, SHARON. OR ARE YOU SERIOUSLY TELLING ME THOSE STUPID JOKES WERE FUNNY?
PLEASE, LOVE. KEEP YOUR VOICE DOWN. THEY'RE GOING TO HEAR YOU IF YOU KEEP SHOUTING.
I DON'T GIVE A RAT'S ARSE WHAT THEY HEAR! YOU EMBARRASS ME LIKE THAT AGAIN AND I'LL PUT YOUR HEAD THROUGH THAT WINDOW!
JESUS, DEAN. I WAS ONLY TRYING TO BE FRIENDLY. I'LL SIT ON THE OTHER SIDE OF THE BLOODY ROOM IF IT MAKES YOU FEEL BETTER!
MUM? ARE YOU ALRIGHT?
YES, OF COURSE I'M ALRIGHT. WHAT ARE YOU DOING IN ANYWAY, GARY? I THOUGHT YOU WAS OUT WITH YOUR MATES TONIGHT?
CAN I GET MONEY TO GO SEE BATTLESHIP?
NO, YOU BLOODY CAN'T. WHEN DID I BECOME BARCLAY'S BANK? I THOUGHT BIG BILLY WAS GETTING IT ON PIRATE?

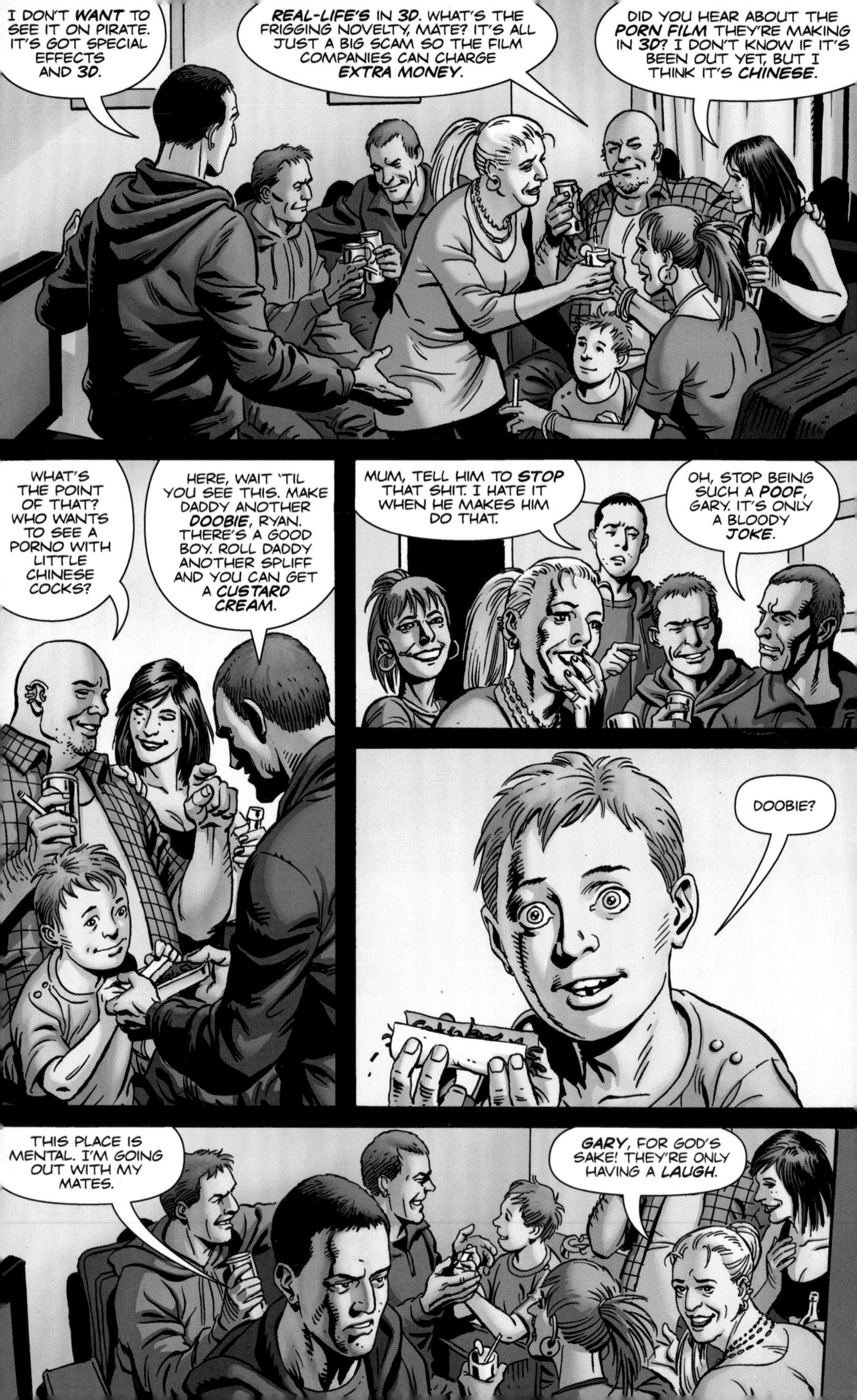
I DON'T **WANT** TO SEE IT ON PIRATE. IT'S GOT SPECIAL EFFECTS AND **3D**.
REAL-LIFE'S IN **3D**. WHAT'S THE FRIGGING NOVELTY, MATE? IT'S ALL JUST A BIG SCAM SO THE FILM COMPANIES CAN CHARGE **EXTRA MONEY**.
DID YOU HEAR ABOUT THE **PORN FILM** THEY'RE MAKING IN **3D**? I DON'T KNOW IF IT'S BEEN OUT YET, BUT I THINK IT'S **CHINESE**.
WHAT'S THE POINT OF THAT? WHO WANTS TO SEE A PORNO WITH LITTLE CHINESE COCKS?
HERE, WAIT 'TIL YOU SEE THIS. MAKE DADDY ANOTHER **DOOBIE**, RYAN. THERE'S A GOOD BOY. ROLL DADDY ANOTHER SPLIFF AND YOU CAN GET A **CUSTARD CREAM**.
MUM, TELL HIM TO **STOP** THAT SHIT. I HATE IT WHEN HE MAKES HIM DO THAT.
OH, STOP BEING SUCH A **POOF**, GARY. IT'S ONLY A BLOODY **JOKE**.
DOOBIE?
THIS PLACE IS MENTAL. I'M GOING OUT WITH MY MATES.
GARY, FOR GOD'S SAKE! THEY'RE ONLY HAVING A **LAUGH**.

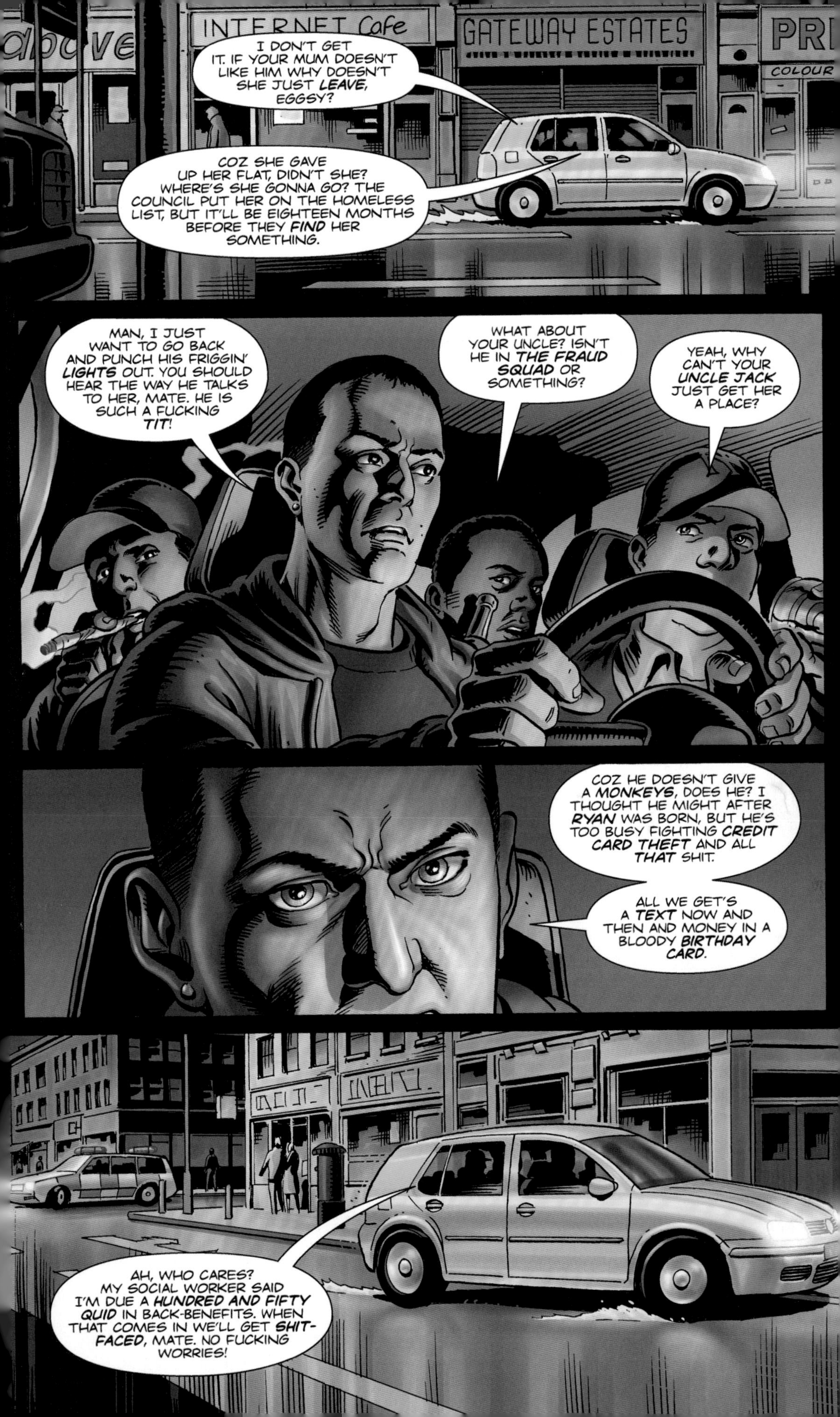
INTERNET Cafe
GATEWAY ESTATES
I DON'T GET IT. IF YOUR MUM DOESN'T LIKE HIM WHY DOESN'T SHE JUST LEAVE, EGGSY?
COZ SHE GAVE UP HER FLAT, DIDN'T SHE? WHERE'S SHE GONNA GO? THE COUNCIL PUT HER ON THE HOMELESS LIST, BUT IT'LL BE EIGHTEEN MONTHS BEFORE THEY FIND HER SOMETHING.
MAN, I JUST WANT TO GO BACK AND PUNCH HIS FRIGGIN' LIGHTS OUT. YOU SHOULD HEAR THE WAY HE TALKS TO HER, MATE. HE IS SUCH A FUCKING TIT!
WHAT ABOUT YOUR UNCLE? ISN'T HE IN THE FRAUD SQUAD OR SOMETHING?
YEAH, WHY CAN'T YOUR UNCLE JACK JUST GET HER A PLACE?
COZ HE DOESN'T GIVE A MONKEYS, DOES HE? I THOUGHT HE MIGHT AFTER RYAN WAS BORN, BUT HE'S TOO BUSY FIGHTING CREDIT CARD THEFT AND ALL THAT SHIT.
ALL WE GET'S A TEXT NOW AND THEN AND MONEY IN A BLOODY BIRTHDAY CARD.
AH, WHO CARES? MY SOCIAL WORKER SAID I'M DUE A HUNDRED AND FIFTY QUID IN BACK-BENEFITS. WHEN THAT COMES IN WE'LL GET SHIT-FACED, MATE. NO FUCKING WORRIES!

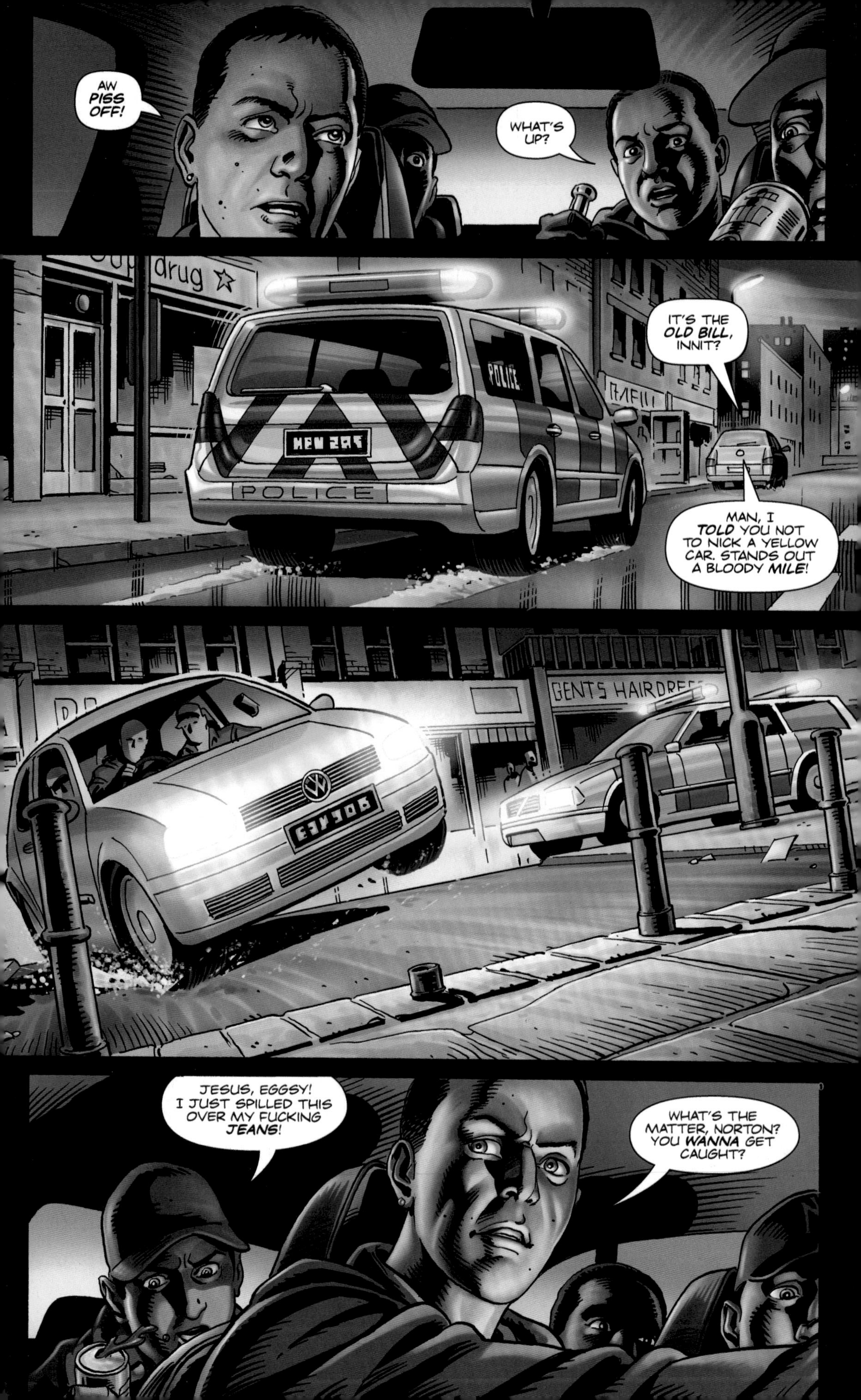
AW PISS OFF!
WHAT'S UP?
drug
POLICE
POLICE
IT'S THE OLD BILL, INNIT?
MAN, I TOLD YOU NOT TO NICK A YELLOW CAR. STANDS OUT A BLOODY MILE!
GENTS HAIRDRE
JESUS, EGGSY! I JUST SPILLED THIS OVER MY FUCKING JEANS!
WHAT'S THE MATTER, NORTON? YOU WANNA GET CAUGHT?

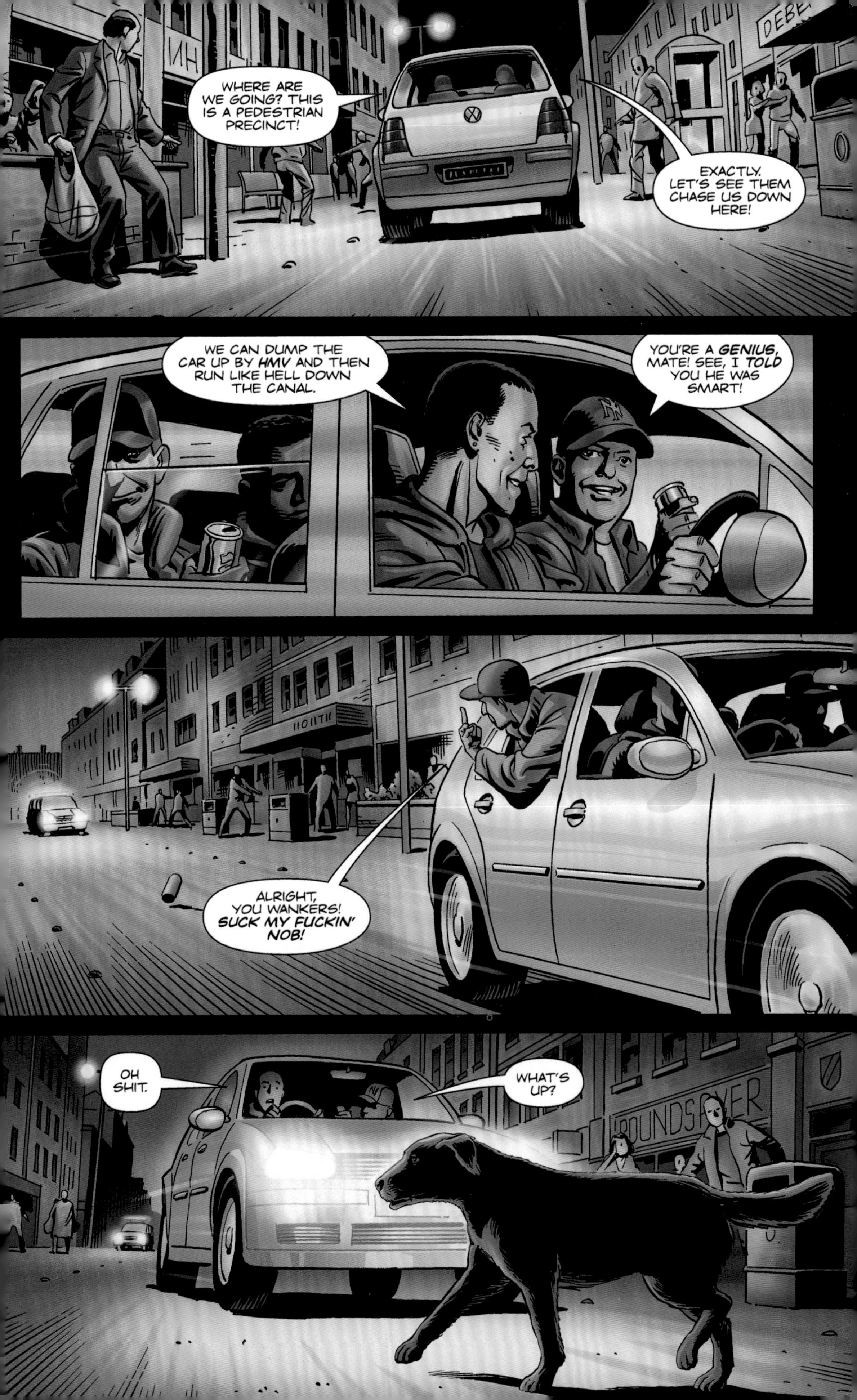
WHERE ARE WE GOING? THIS IS A PEDESTRIAN PRECINCT!
EXACTLY. LET'S SEE THEM CHASE US DOWN HERE!
WE CAN DUMP THE CAR UP BY HMV AND THEN RUN LIKE HELL DOWN THE CANAL.
YOU'RE A GENIUS, MATE! SEE, I TOLD YOU HE WAS SMART!
ALRIGHT, YOU WANKERS! SUCK MY FUCKIN' NOB!
OH SHIT.
WHAT'S UP?

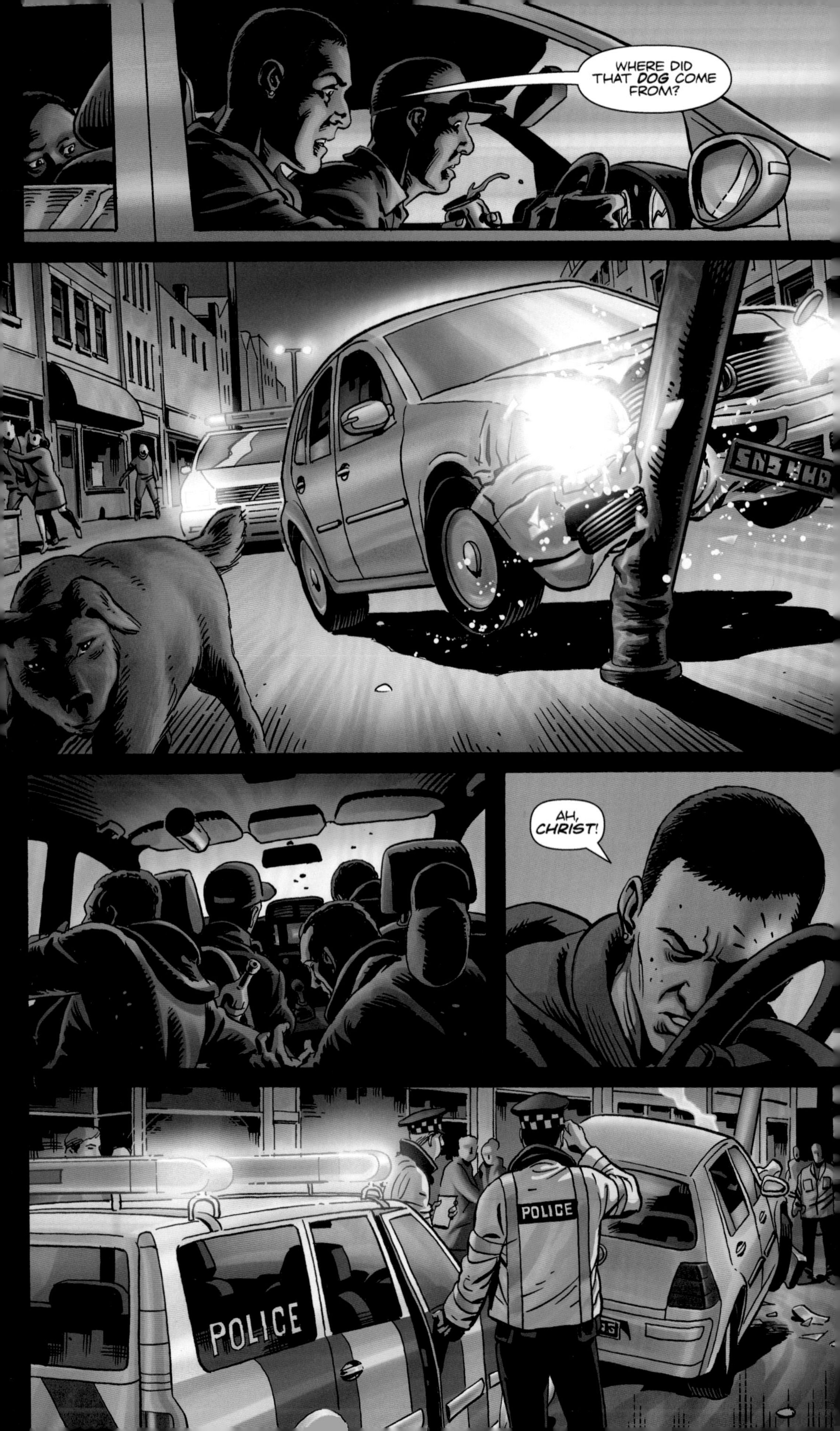
WHERE DID THAT DOG COME FROM?
AH, CHRIST!
POLICE
POLICE

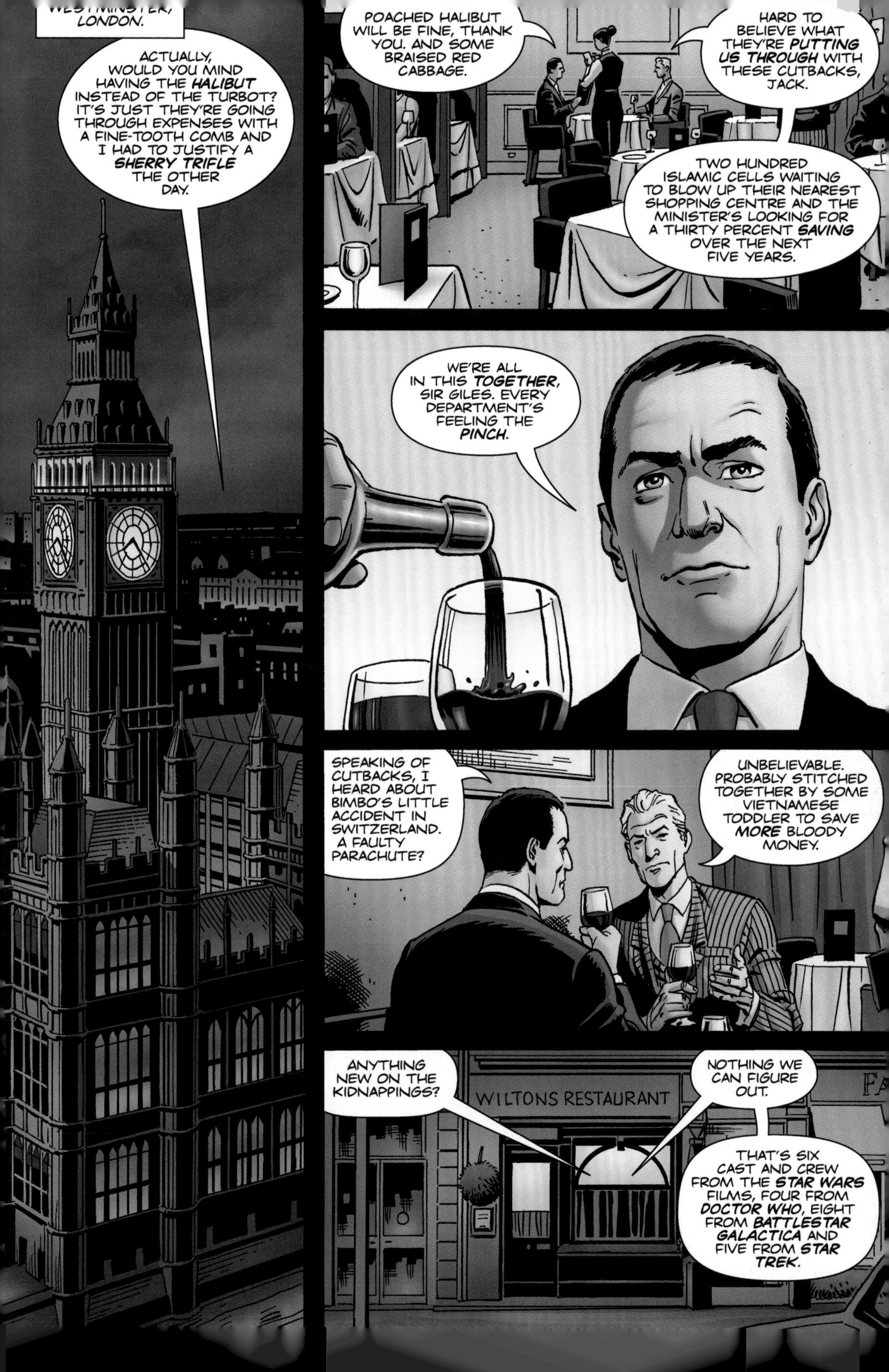
LONDON.
ACTUALLY, WOULD YOU MIND HAVING THE HALIBUT INSTEAD OF THE TURBOT? IT'S JUST THEY'RE GOING THROUGH EXPENSES WITH A FINE-TOOTH COMB AND I HAD TO JUSTIFY A SHERRY TRIFLE THE OTHER DAY.
POACHED HALIBUT WILL BE FINE, THANK YOU. AND SOME BRAISED RED CABBAGE.
HARD TO BELIEVE WHAT THEY'RE PUTTING US THROUGH WITH THESE CUTBACKS, JACK.
TWO HUNDRED ISLAMIC CELLS WAITING TO BLOW UP THEIR NEAREST SHOPPING CENTRE AND THE MINISTER'S LOOKING FOR A THIRTY PERCENT SAVING OVER THE NEXT FIVE YEARS.
WE'RE ALL IN THIS TOGETHER, SIR GILES. EVERY DEPARTMENT'S FEELING THE PINCH.
SPEAKING OF CUTBACKS, I HEARD ABOUT BIMBO'S LITTLE ACCIDENT IN SWITZERLAND. A FAULTY PARACHUTE?
UNBELIEVABLE. PROBABLY STITCHED TOGETHER BY SOME VIETNAMESE TODDLER TO SAVE MORE BLOODY MONEY.
ANYTHING NEW ON THE KIDNAPPINGS?
WILTONS RESTAURANT
NOTHING WE CAN FIGURE OUT.
THAT'S SIX CAST AND CREW FROM THE STAR WARS FILMS, FOUR FROM DOCTOR WHO, EIGHT FROM BATTLESTAR GALACTICA AND FIVE FROM STAR TREK.

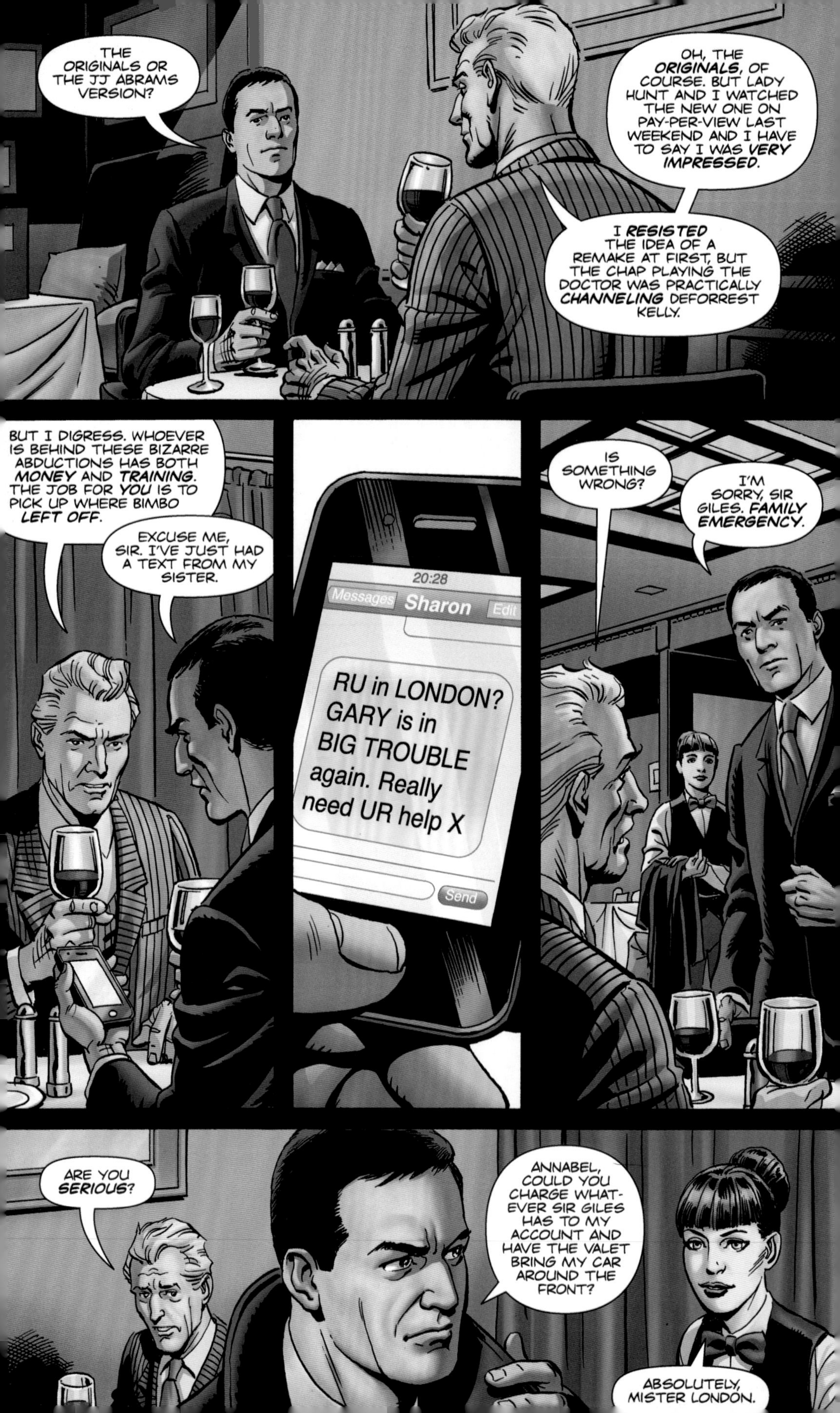

THE ORIGINALS OR THE JJ ABRAMS VERSION?
OH, THE ORIGINALS, OF COURSE. BUT LADY HUNT AND I WATCHED THE NEW ONE ON PAY-PER-VIEW LAST WEEKEND AND I HAVE TO SAY I WAS VERY IMPRESSED.
I RESISTED THE IDEA OF A REMAKE AT FIRST, BUT THE CHAP PLAYING THE DOCTOR WAS PRACTICALLY CHANNELING DEFORREST KELLY.
BUT I DIGRESS. WHOEVER IS BEHIND THESE BIZARRE ABDUCTIONS HAS BOTH MONEY AND TRAINING. THE JOB FOR YOU IS TO PICK UP WHERE BIMBO LEFT OFF.
EXCUSE ME, SIR. I'VE JUST HAD A TEXT FROM MY SISTER.
20:28
Messages
Sharon
Edit
RU in LONDON? GARY is in BIG TROUBLE again. Really need UR help X
Send
IS SOMETHING WRONG?
I'M SORRY, SIR GILES. FAMILY EMERGENCY.
ARE YOU SERIOUS?
ANNABEL, COULD YOU CHARGE WHAT-EVER SIR GILES HAS TO MY ACCOUNT AND HAVE THE VALET BRING MY CAR AROUND THE FRONT?
ABSOLUTELY, MISTER LONDON.

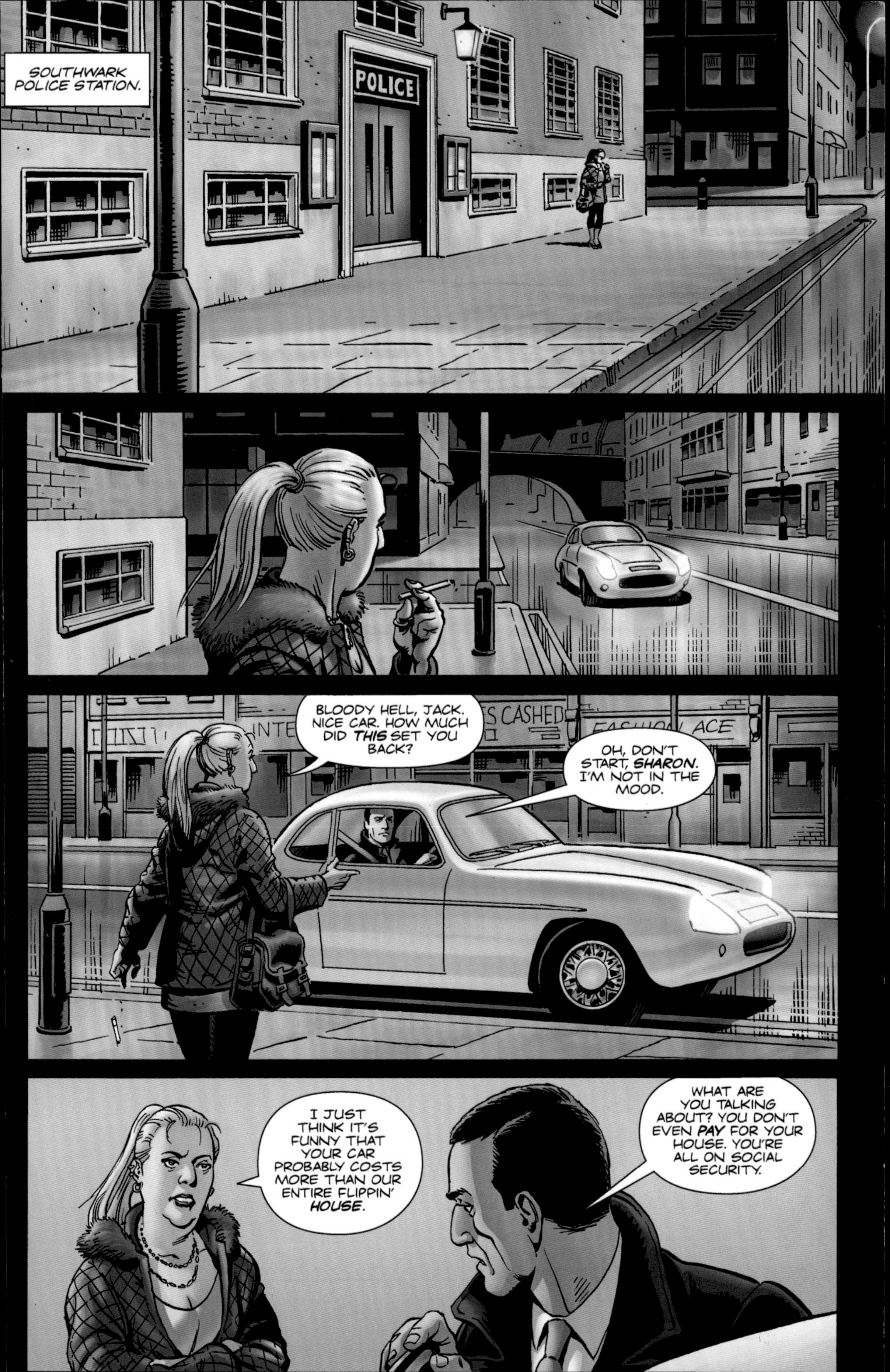
SOUTHWARK POLICE STATION.
POLICE
BLOODY HELL, JACK. NICE CAR. HOW MUCH DID THIS SET YOU BACK?
OH, DON'T START, SHARON. I'M NOT IN THE MOOD.
I JUST THINK IT'S FUNNY THAT YOUR CAR PROBABLY COSTS MORE THAN OUR ENTIRE FLIPPIN' HOUSE.
WHAT ARE YOU TALKING ABOUT? YOU DON'T EVEN PAY FOR YOUR HOUSE. YOU'RE ALL ON SOCIAL SECURITY.

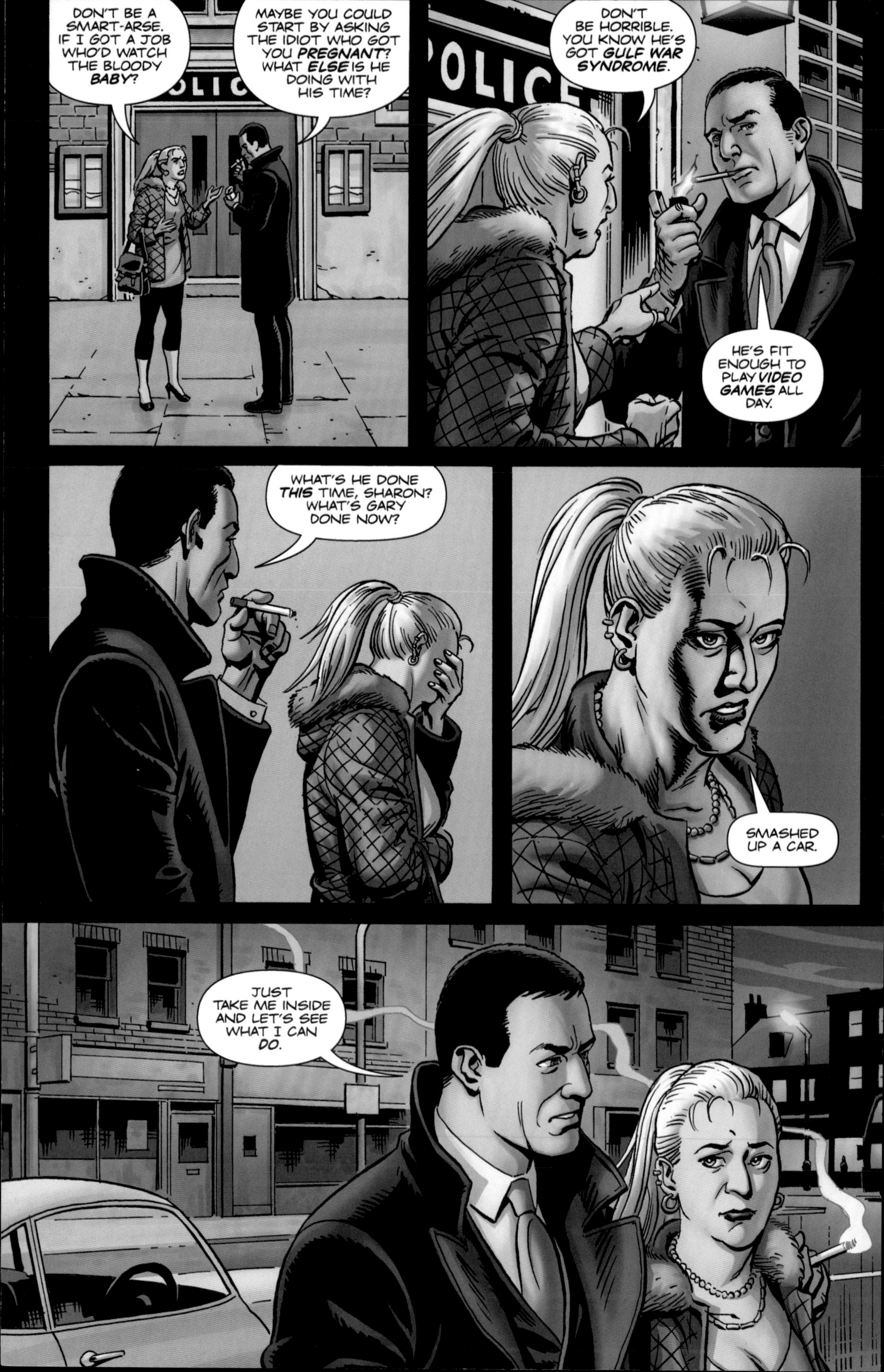
DON'T BE A SMART-ARSE. IF I GOT A JOB WHO'D WATCH THE BLOODY BABY?
MAYBE YOU COULD START BY ASKING THE IDIOT WHO GOT YOU PREGNANT? WHAT ELSE IS HE DOING WITH HIS TIME?
POLICE
DON'T BE HORRIBLE. YOU KNOW HE'S GOT GULF WAR SYNDROME.
HE'S FIT ENOUGH TO PLAY VIDEO GAMES ALL DAY.
WHAT'S HE DONE THIS TIME, SHARON? WHAT'S GARY DONE NOW?
SMASHED UP A CAR.
JUST TAKE ME INSIDE AND LET'S SEE WHAT I CAN DO.

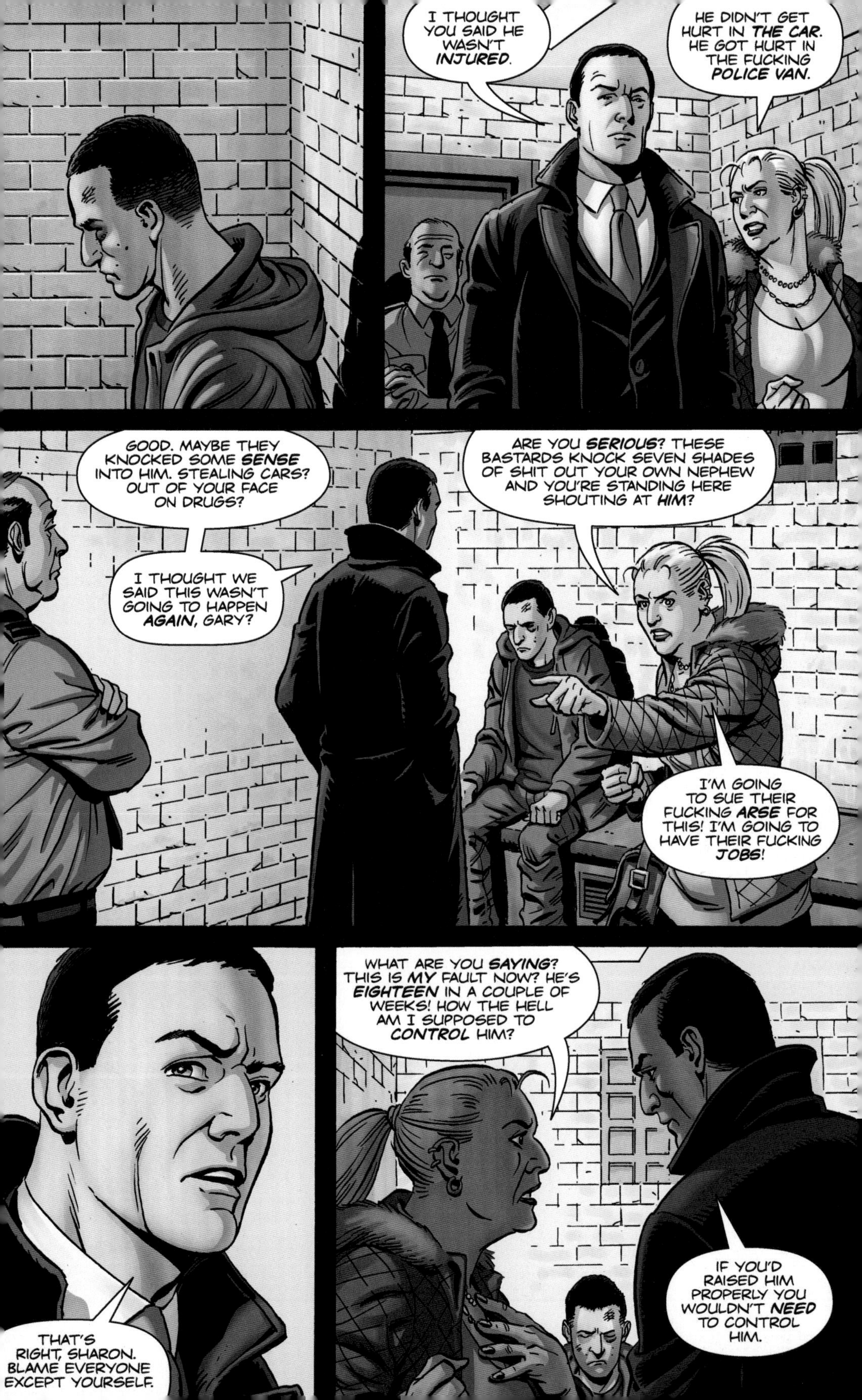
I THOUGHT YOU SAID HE WASN'T *INJURED*.
HE DIDN'T GET HURT IN *THE CAR*. HE GOT HURT IN THE FUCKING *POLICE VAN*.
GOOD. MAYBE THEY KNOCKED SOME *SENSE* INTO HIM. STEALING CARS? OUT OF YOUR FACE ON DRUGS?
I THOUGHT WE SAID THIS WASN'T GOING TO HAPPEN *AGAIN*, GARY?
ARE YOU *SERIOUS*? THESE BASTARDS KNOCK SEVEN SHADES OF SHIT OUT YOUR OWN NEPHEW AND YOU'RE STANDING HERE SHOUTING AT *HIM*?
I'M GOING TO SUE THEIR FUCKING *ARSE* FOR THIS! I'M GOING TO HAVE THEIR FUCKING *JOBS*!
WHAT ARE YOU *SAYING*? THIS IS *MY* FAULT NOW? HE'S *EIGHTEEN* IN A COUPLE OF WEEKS! HOW THE HELL AM I SUPPOSED TO *CONTROL* HIM?
THAT'S RIGHT, SHARON. BLAME EVERYONE EXCEPT YOURSELF.
IF YOU'D RAISED HIM PROPERLY YOU WOULDN'T *NEED* TO CONTROL HIM.

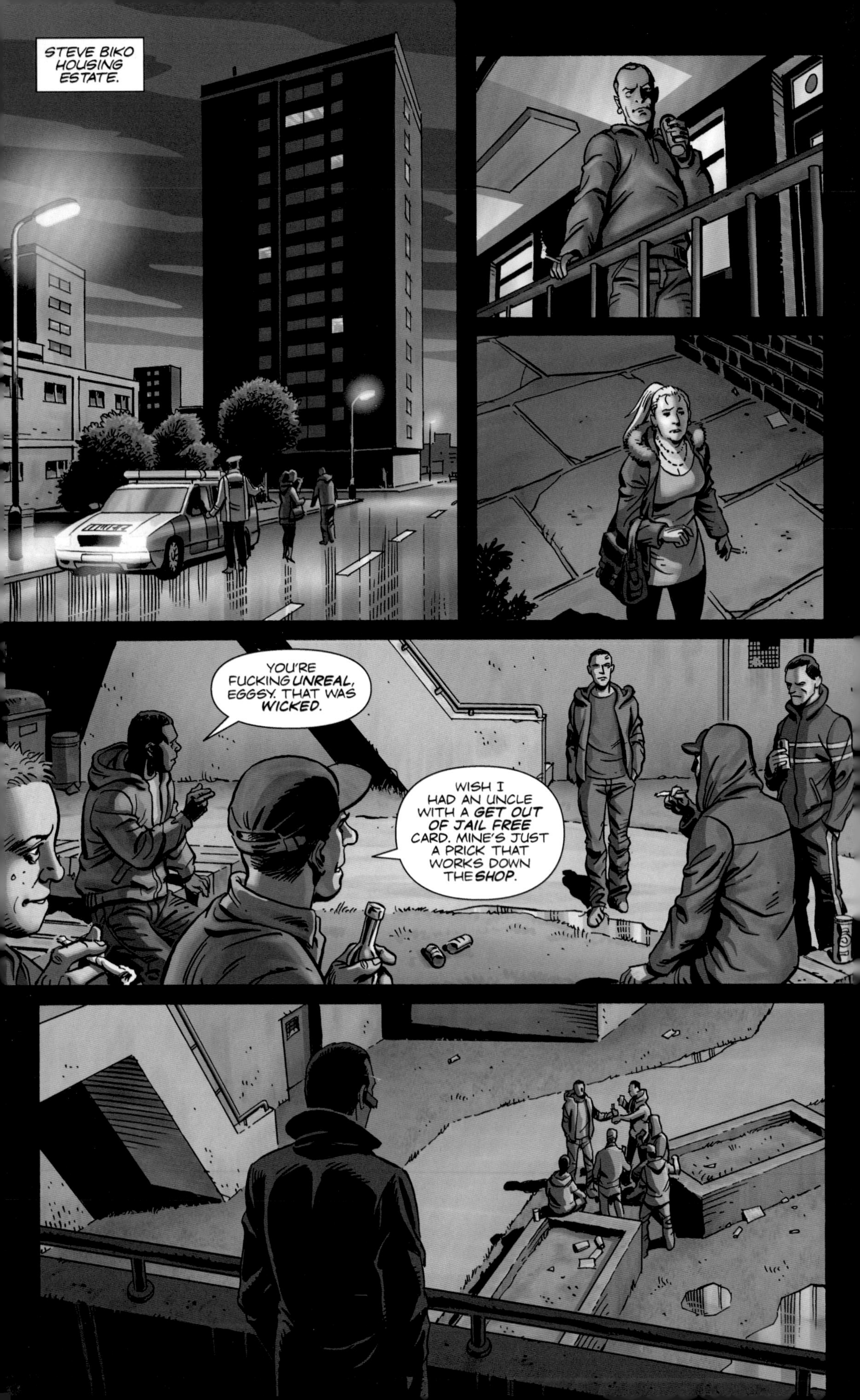
STEVE BIKO HOUSING ESTATE.
YOU'RE FUCKING UNREAL, EGGSY. THAT WAS WICKED.
WISH I HAD AN UNCLE WITH A GET OUT OF JAIL FREE CARD. MINE'S JUST A PRICK THAT WORKS DOWN THE SHOP.

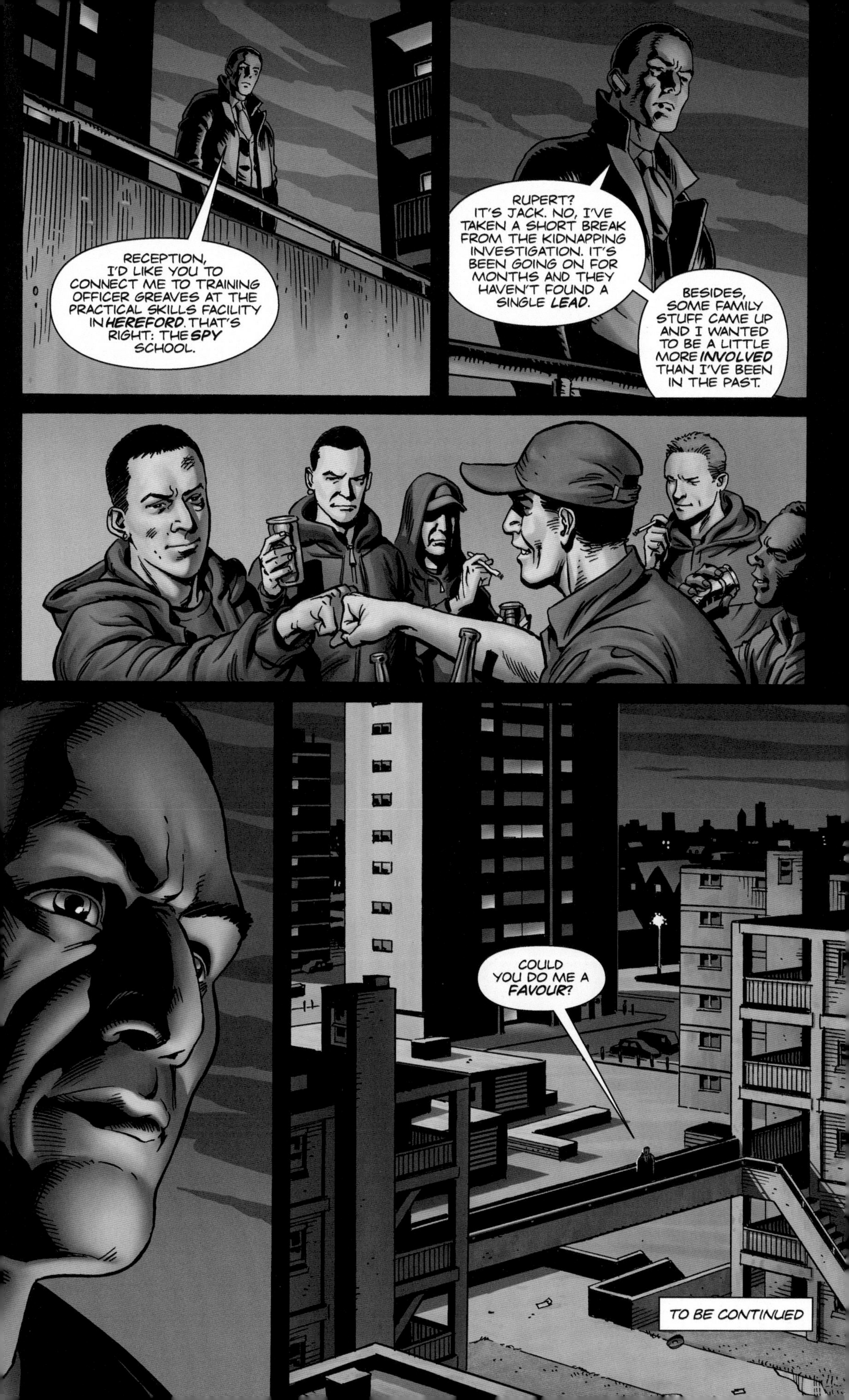
RECEPTION, I'D LIKE YOU TO CONNECT ME TO TRAINING OFFICER GREAVES AT THE PRACTICAL SKILLS FACILITY IN HEREFORD. THAT'S RIGHT: THE SPY SCHOOL.
RUPERT? IT'S JACK. NO, I'VE TAKEN A SHORT BREAK FROM THE KIDNAPPING INVESTIGATION. IT'S BEEN GOING ON FOR MONTHS AND THEY HAVEN'T FOUND A SINGLE LEAD.
BESIDES, SOME FAMILY STUFF CAME UP AND I WANTED TO BE A LITTLE MORE INVOLVED THAN I'VE BEEN IN THE PAST.
COULD YOU DO ME A FAVOUR?
TO BE CONTINUED

TWO

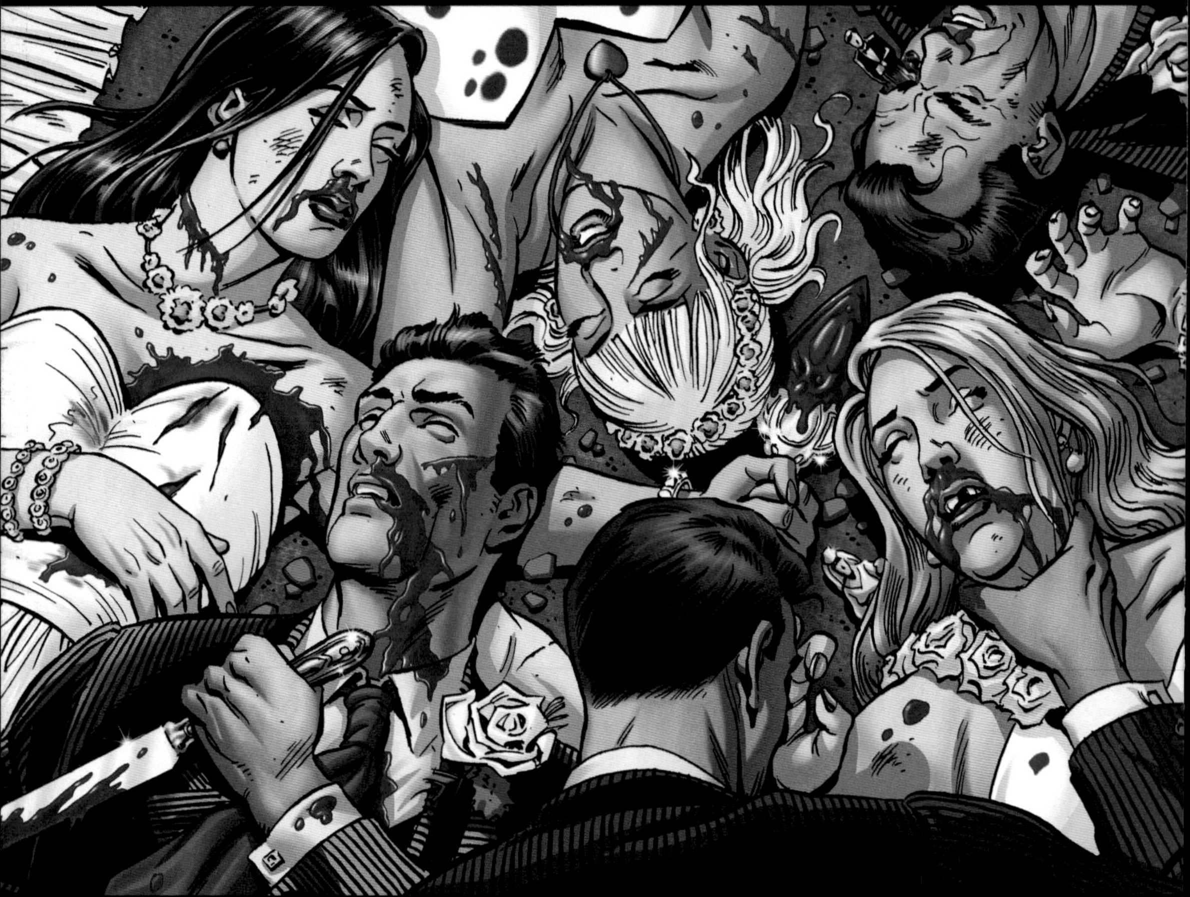

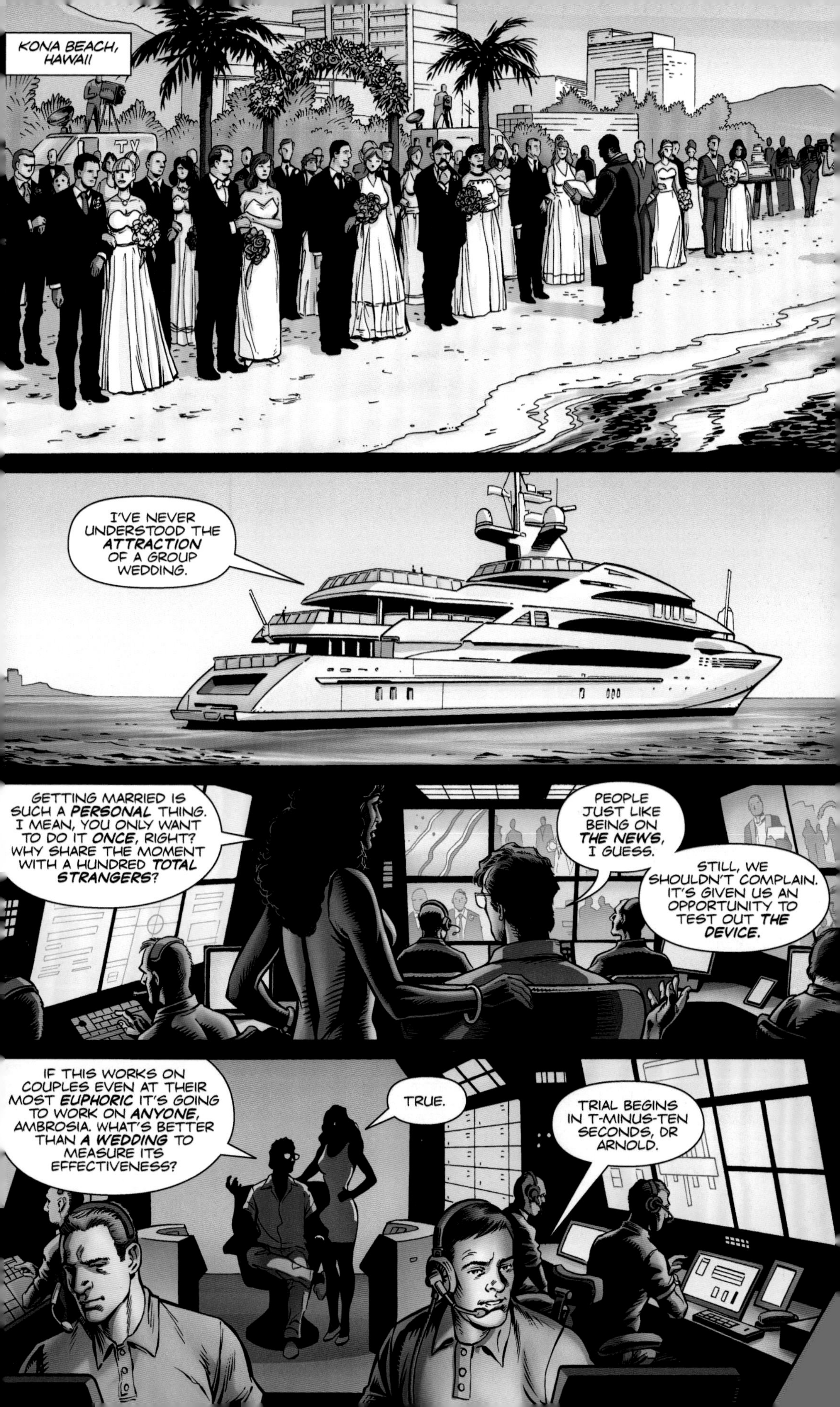
KONA BEACH, HAWAII
I'VE NEVER UNDERSTOOD THE ATTRACTION OF A GROUP WEDDING.
GETTING MARRIED IS SUCH A PERSONAL THING. I MEAN, YOU ONLY WANT TO DO IT ONCE, RIGHT? WHY SHARE THE MOMENT WITH A HUNDRED TOTAL STRANGERS?
PEOPLE JUST LIKE BEING ON THE NEWS, I GUESS.
STILL, WE SHOULDN'T COMPLAIN. IT'S GIVEN US AN OPPORTUNITY TO TEST OUT THE DEVICE.
IF THIS WORKS ON COUPLES EVEN AT THEIR MOST EUPHORIC IT'S GOING TO WORK ON ANYONE, AMBROSIA. WHAT'S BETTER THAN A WEDDING TO MEASURE ITS EFFECTIVENESS?
TRUE.
TRIAL BEGINS IN T-MINUS-TEN SECONDS, DR ARNOLD.

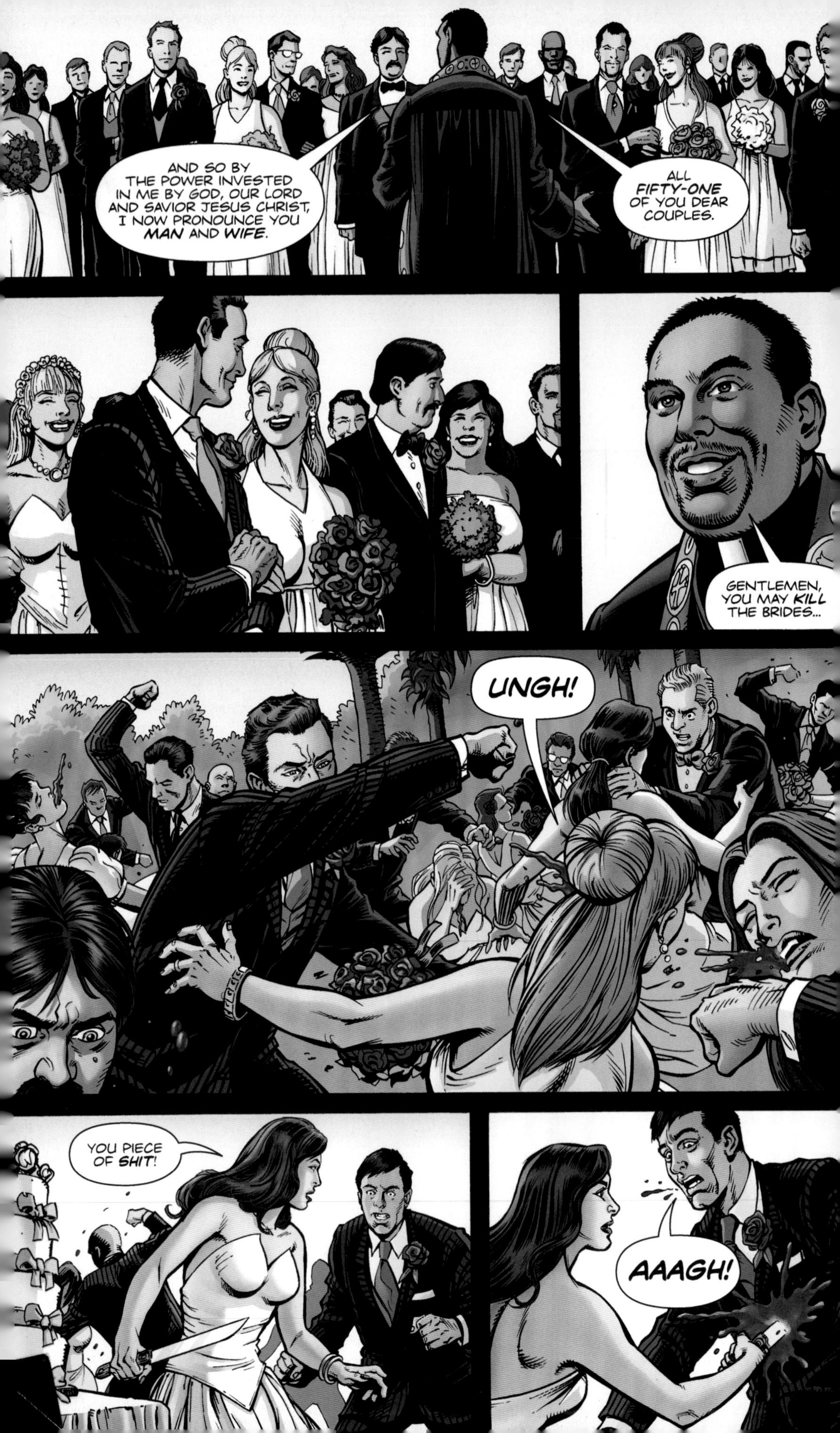
AND SO BY THE POWER INVESTED IN ME BY GOD, OUR LORD AND SAVIOR JESUS CHRIST, I NOW PRONOUNCE YOU MAN AND WIFE.
ALL FIFTY-ONE OF YOU DEAR COUPLES.
GENTLEMEN, YOU MAY KILL THE BRIDES...
UNGH!
YOU PIECE OF SHIT!
AAAGH!

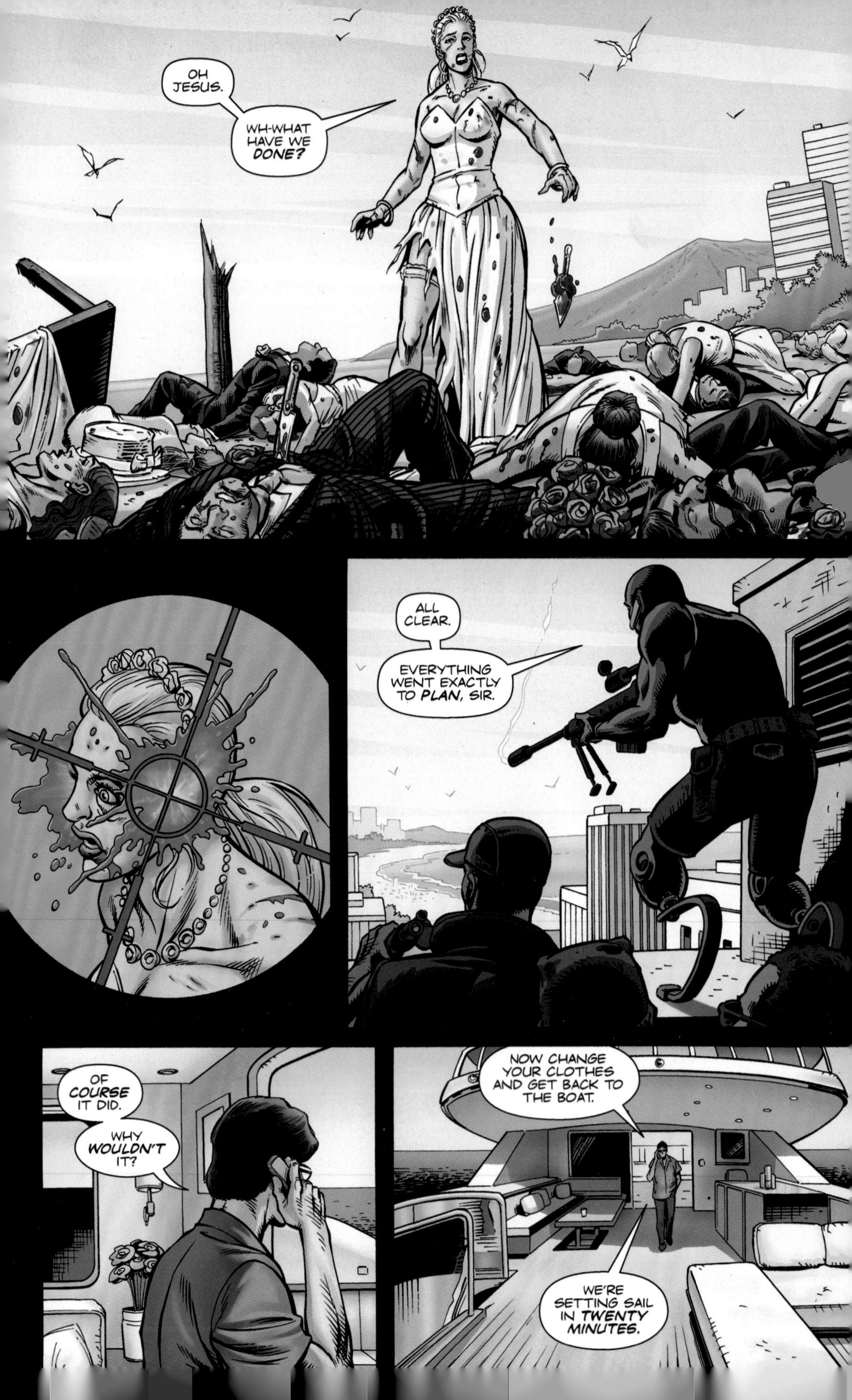

OH JESUS.
WH-WHAT HAVE WE DONE?
ALL CLEAR.
EVERYTHING WENT EXACTLY TO PLAN, SIR.
OF COURSE IT DID.
WHY WOULDN'T IT?
NOW CHANGE YOUR CLOTHES AND GET BACK TO THE BOAT.
WE'RE SETTING SAIL IN TWENTY MINUTES.

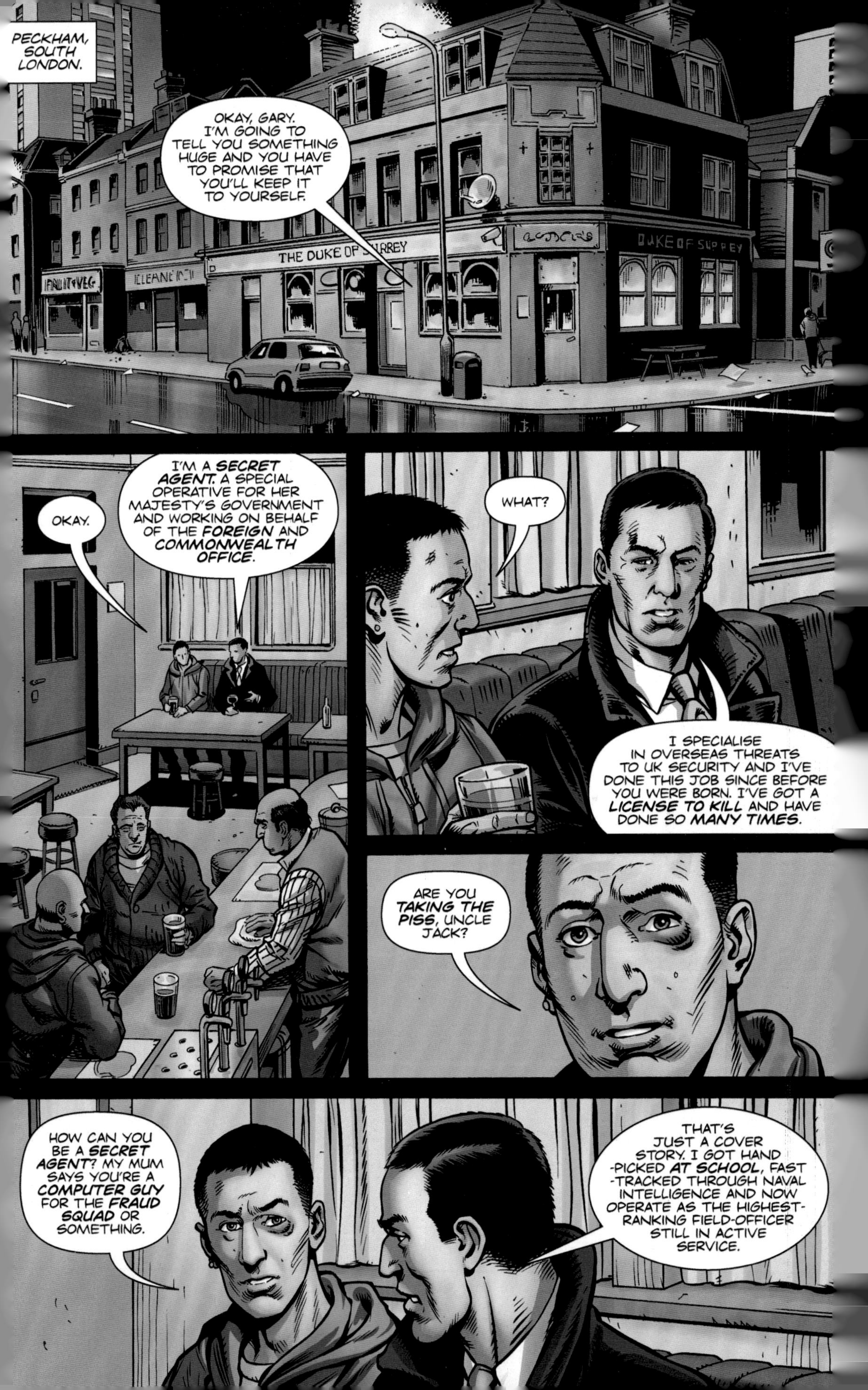
PECKHAM, SOUTH LONDON.
OKAY, GARY. I'M GOING TO TELL YOU SOMETHING HUGE AND YOU HAVE TO PROMISE THAT YOU'LL KEEP IT TO YOURSELF.
THE DUKE OF SURREY
DUKE OF SURREY
OKAY.
I'M A SECRET AGENT. A SPECIAL OPERATIVE FOR HER MAJESTY'S GOVERNMENT AND WORKING ON BEHALF OF THE FOREIGN AND COMMONWEALTH OFFICE.
WHAT?
I SPECIALISE IN OVERSEAS THREATS TO UK SECURITY AND I'VE DONE THIS JOB SINCE BEFORE YOU WERE BORN. I'VE GOT A LICENSE TO KILL AND HAVE DONE SO MANY TIMES.
ARE YOU TAKING THE PISS, UNCLE JACK?
HOW CAN YOU BE A SECRET AGENT? MY MUM SAYS YOU'RE A COMPUTER GUY FOR THE FRAUD SQUAD OR SOMETHING.
THAT'S JUST A COVER STORY. I GOT HAND-PICKED AT SCHOOL, FAST-TRACKED THROUGH NAVAL INTELLIGENCE AND NOW OPERATE AS THE HIGHEST-RANKING FIELD-OFFICER STILL IN ACTIVE SERVICE.

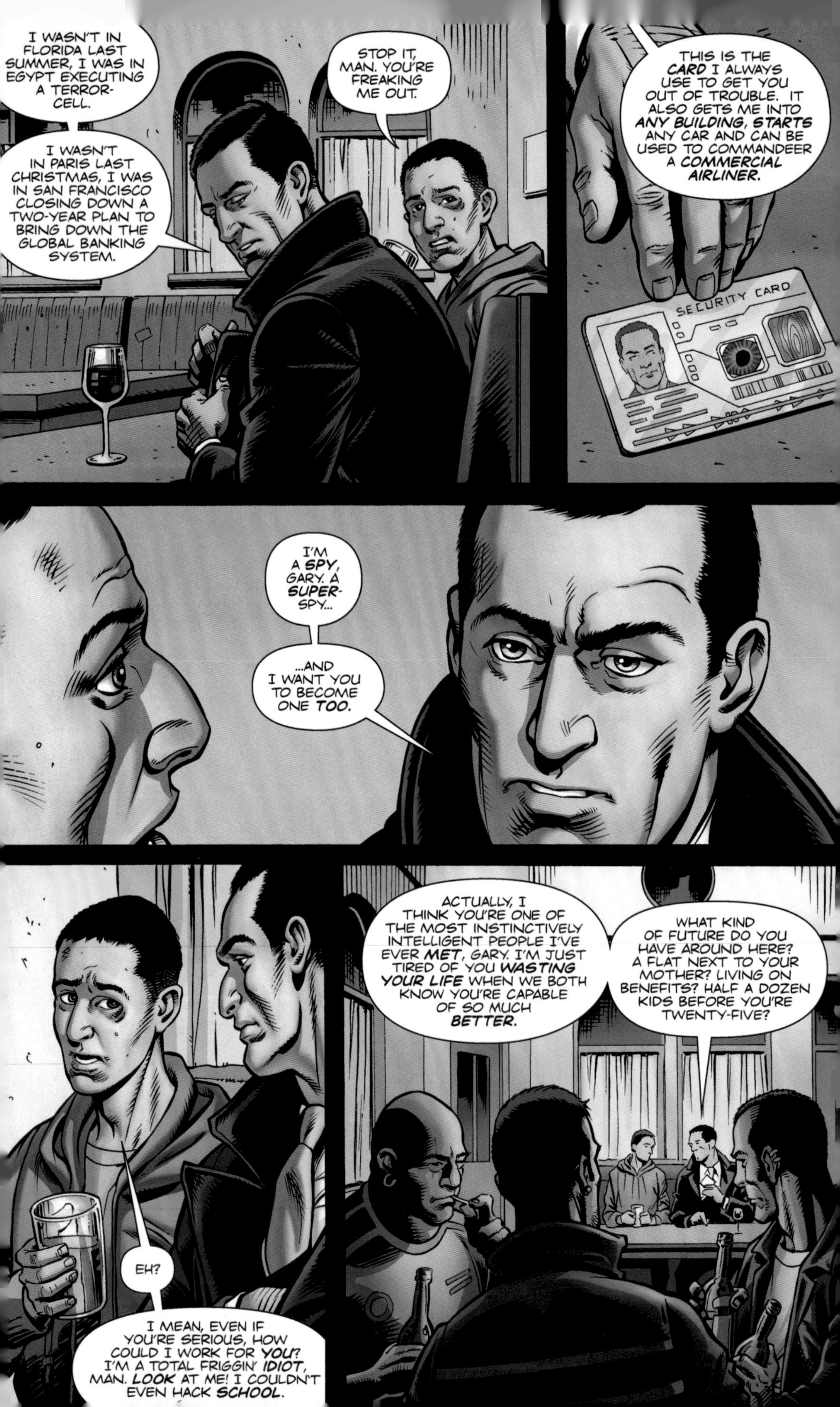
I WASN'T IN FLORIDA LAST SUMMER, I WAS IN EGYPT EXECUTING A TERROR-CELL.
I WASN'T IN PARIS LAST CHRISTMAS, I WAS IN SAN FRANCISCO CLOSING DOWN A TWO-YEAR PLAN TO BRING DOWN THE GLOBAL BANKING SYSTEM.
STOP IT, MAN. YOU'RE FREAKING ME OUT.
THIS IS THE **CARD** I ALWAYS USE TO GET YOU OUT OF TROUBLE. IT ALSO GETS ME INTO **ANY BUILDING, STARTS** ANY CAR AND CAN BE USED TO COMMANDEER A **COMMERCIAL AIRLINER.**
SECURITY CARD
I'M A **SPY**, GARY. A **SUPER**-SPY...
...AND I WANT YOU TO BECOME ONE **TOO.**
EH?
I MEAN, EVEN IF YOU'RE SERIOUS, HOW COULD I WORK FOR **YOU**? I'M A TOTAL FRIGGIN' **IDIOT**, MAN. **LOOK** AT ME! I COULDN'T EVEN HACK **SCHOOL**.
ACTUALLY, I THINK YOU'RE ONE OF THE MOST INSTINCTIVELY INTELLIGENT PEOPLE I'VE EVER **MET**, GARY. I'M JUST TIRED OF YOU **WASTING YOUR LIFE** WHEN WE BOTH KNOW YOU'RE CAPABLE OF SO MUCH **BETTER.**
WHAT KIND OF FUTURE DO YOU HAVE AROUND HERE? A FLAT NEXT TO YOUR MOTHER? LIVING ON BENEFITS? HALF A DOZEN KIDS BEFORE YOU'RE TWENTY-FIVE?

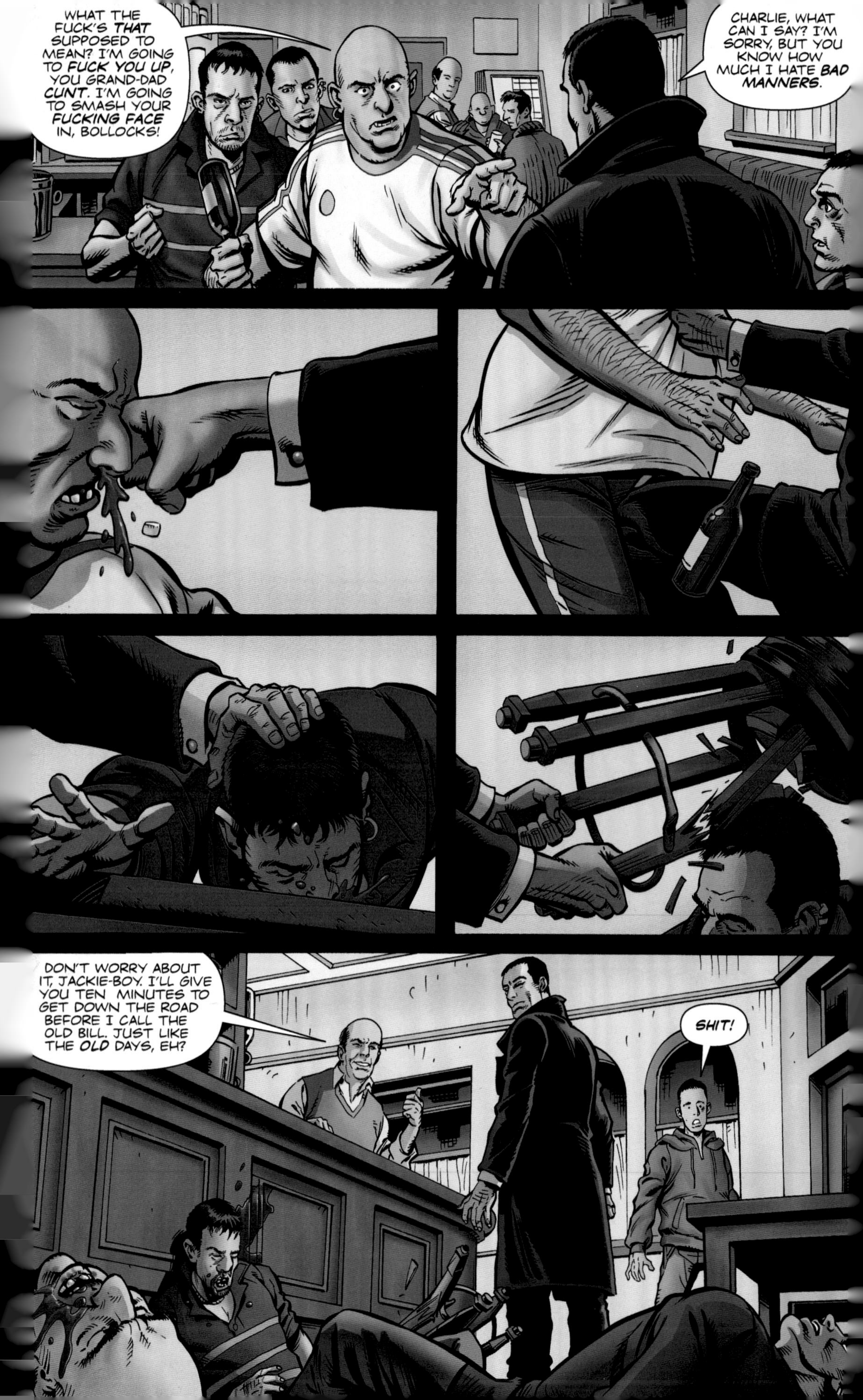
WHAT THE FUCK'S THAT SUPPOSED TO MEAN? I'M GOING TO FUCK YOU UP, YOU GRAND-DAD CUNT. I'M GOING TO SMASH YOUR FUCKING FACE IN, BOLLOCKS!
CHARLIE, WHAT CAN I SAY? I'M SORRY, BUT YOU KNOW HOW MUCH I HATE BAD MANNERS.
DON'T WORRY ABOUT IT, JACKIE-BOY. I'LL GIVE YOU TEN MINUTES TO GET DOWN THE ROAD BEFORE I CALL THE OLD BILL. JUST LIKE THE OLD DAYS, EH?
SHIT!

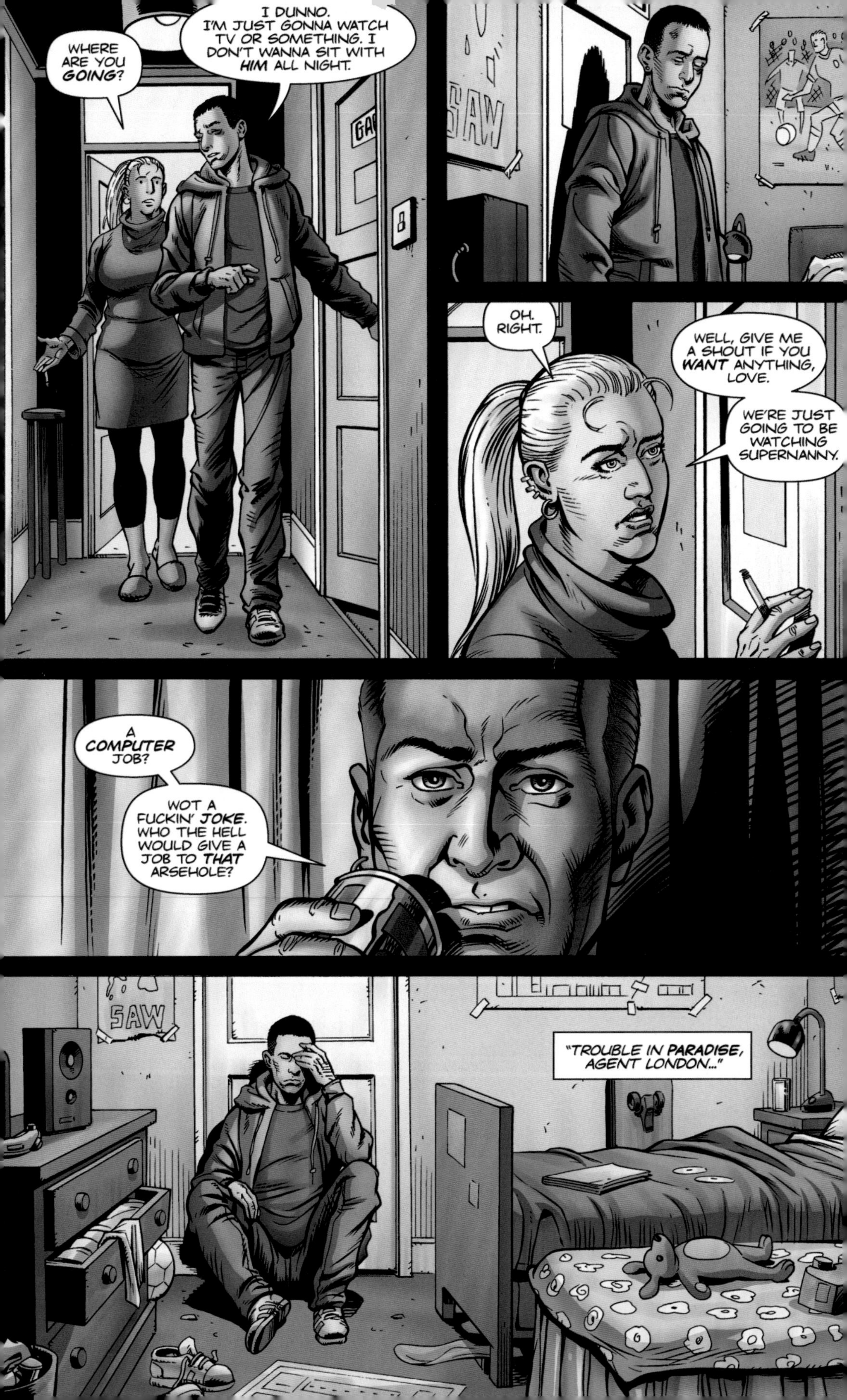
WHERE ARE YOU GOING?
I DUNNO. I'M JUST GONNA WATCH TV OR SOMETHING. I DON'T WANNA SIT WITH HIM ALL NIGHT.
SAW
OH. RIGHT.
WELL, GIVE ME A SHOUT IF YOU WANT ANYTHING, LOVE.
WE'RE JUST GOING TO BE WATCHING SUPERNANNY.
A COMPUTER JOB?
WOT A FUCKIN' JOKE. WHO THE HELL WOULD GIVE A JOB TO THAT ARSEHOLE?
SAW
"TROUBLE IN PARADISE, AGENT LONDON..."

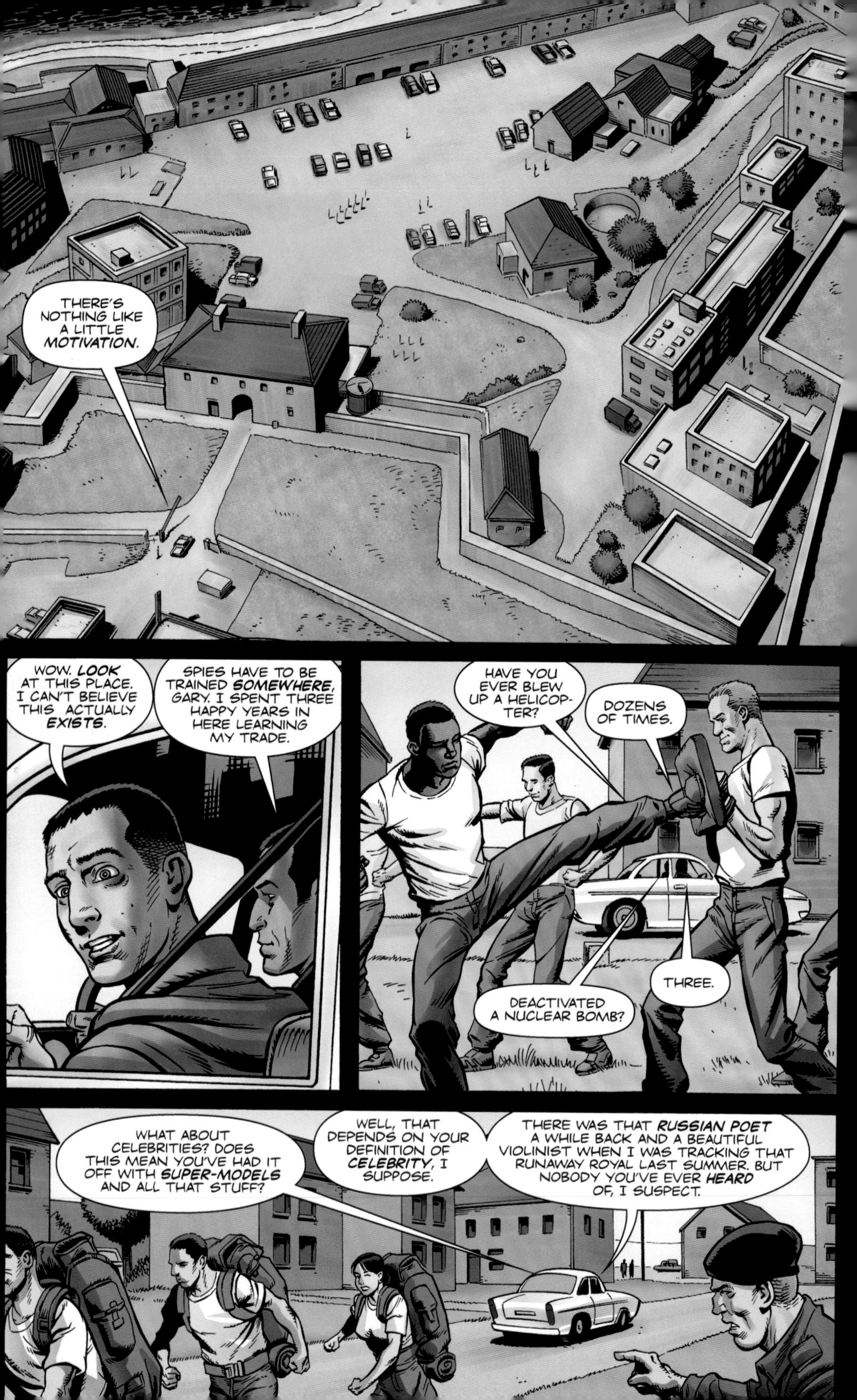
THERE'S NOTHING LIKE A LITTLE MOTIVATION.
WOW. LOOK AT THIS PLACE. I CAN'T BELIEVE THIS ACTUALLY EXISTS.
SPIES HAVE TO BE TRAINED SOMEWHERE, GARY. I SPENT THREE HAPPY YEARS IN HERE LEARNING MY TRADE.
HAVE YOU EVER BLEW UP A HELICOPTER?
DOZENS OF TIMES.
DEACTIVATED A NUCLEAR BOMB?
THREE.
WHAT ABOUT CELEBRITIES? DOES THIS MEAN YOU'VE HAD IT OFF WITH SUPER-MODELS AND ALL THAT STUFF?
WELL, THAT DEPENDS ON YOUR DEFINITION OF CELEBRITY, I SUPPOSE.
THERE WAS THAT RUSSIAN POET A WHILE BACK AND A BEAUTIFUL VIOLINIST WHEN I WAS TRACKING THAT RUNAWAY ROYAL LAST SUMMER. BUT NOBODY YOU'VE EVER HEARD OF, I SUSPECT.

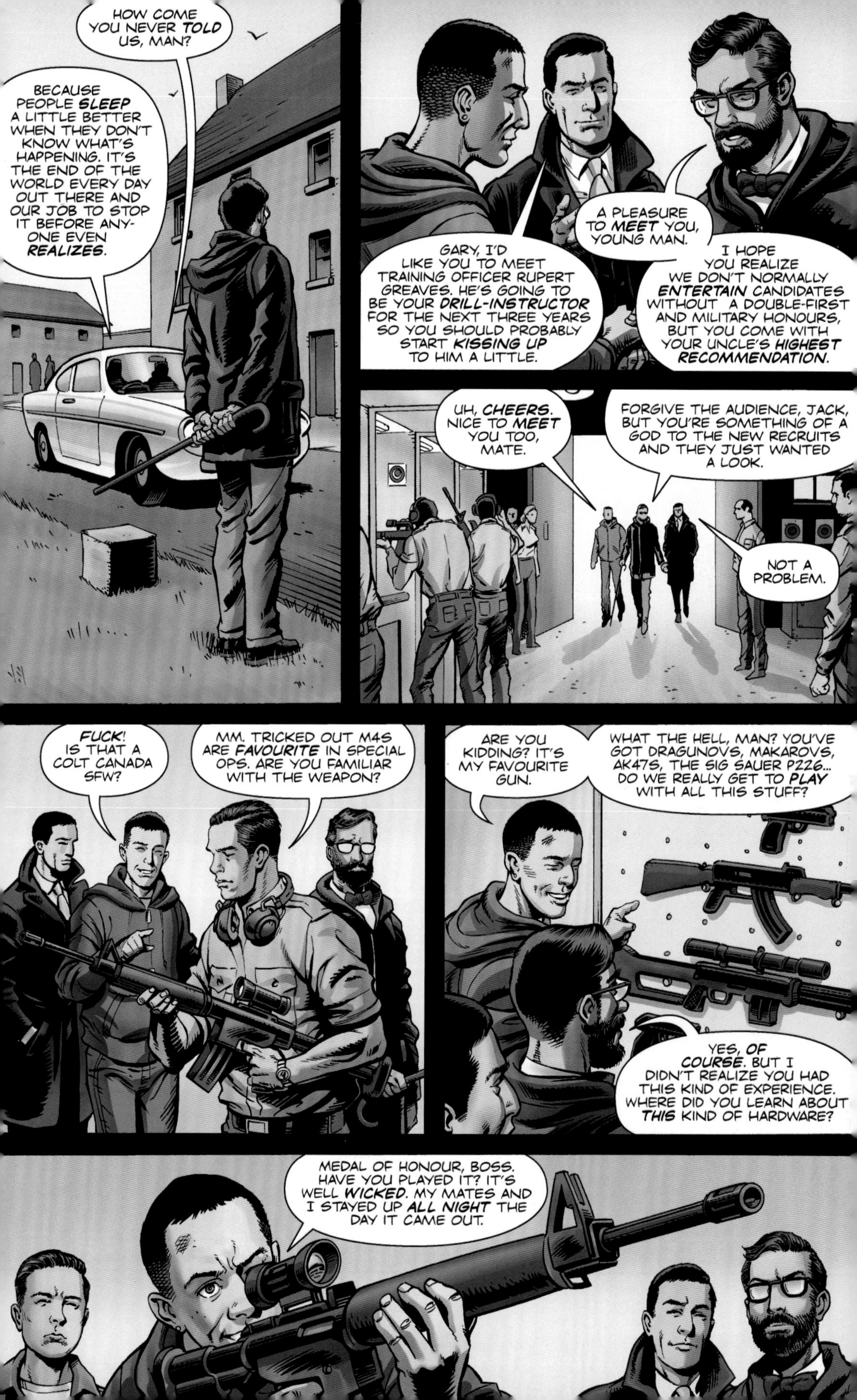
HOW COME YOU NEVER TOLD US, MAN?
BECAUSE PEOPLE SLEEP A LITTLE BETTER WHEN THEY DON'T KNOW WHAT'S HAPPENING. IT'S THE END OF THE WORLD EVERY DAY OUT THERE AND OUR JOB TO STOP IT BEFORE ANYONE EVEN REALIZES.
GARY, I'D LIKE YOU TO MEET TRAINING OFFICER RUPERT GREAVES. HE'S GOING TO BE YOUR DRILL-INSTRUCTOR FOR THE NEXT THREE YEARS SO YOU SHOULD PROBABLY START KISSING UP TO HIM A LITTLE.
A PLEASURE TO MEET YOU, YOUNG MAN.
I HOPE YOU REALIZE WE DON'T NORMALLY ENTERTAIN CANDIDATES WITHOUT A DOUBLE-FIRST AND MILITARY HONOURS, BUT YOU COME WITH YOUR UNCLE'S HIGHEST RECOMMENDATION.
UH, CHEERS. NICE TO MEET YOU TOO, MATE.
FORGIVE THE AUDIENCE, JACK, BUT YOU'RE SOMETHING OF A GOD TO THE NEW RECRUITS AND THEY JUST WANTED A LOOK.
NOT A PROBLEM.
FUCK! IS THAT A COLT CANADA SFW?
MM. TRICKED OUT M4S ARE FAVOURITE IN SPECIAL OPS. ARE YOU FAMILIAR WITH THE WEAPON?
ARE YOU KIDDING? IT'S MY FAVOURITE GUN.
WHAT THE HELL, MAN? YOU'VE GOT DRAGUNOVS, MAKAROVS, AK47S, THE SIG SAUER P226... DO WE REALLY GET TO PLAY WITH ALL THIS STUFF?
YES, OF COURSE. BUT I DIDN'T REALIZE YOU HAD THIS KIND OF EXPERIENCE. WHERE DID YOU LEARN ABOUT THIS KIND OF HARDWARE?
MEDAL OF HONOUR, BOSS. HAVE YOU PLAYED IT? IT'S WELL WICKED. MY MATES AND I STAYED UP ALL NIGHT THE DAY IT CAME OUT.

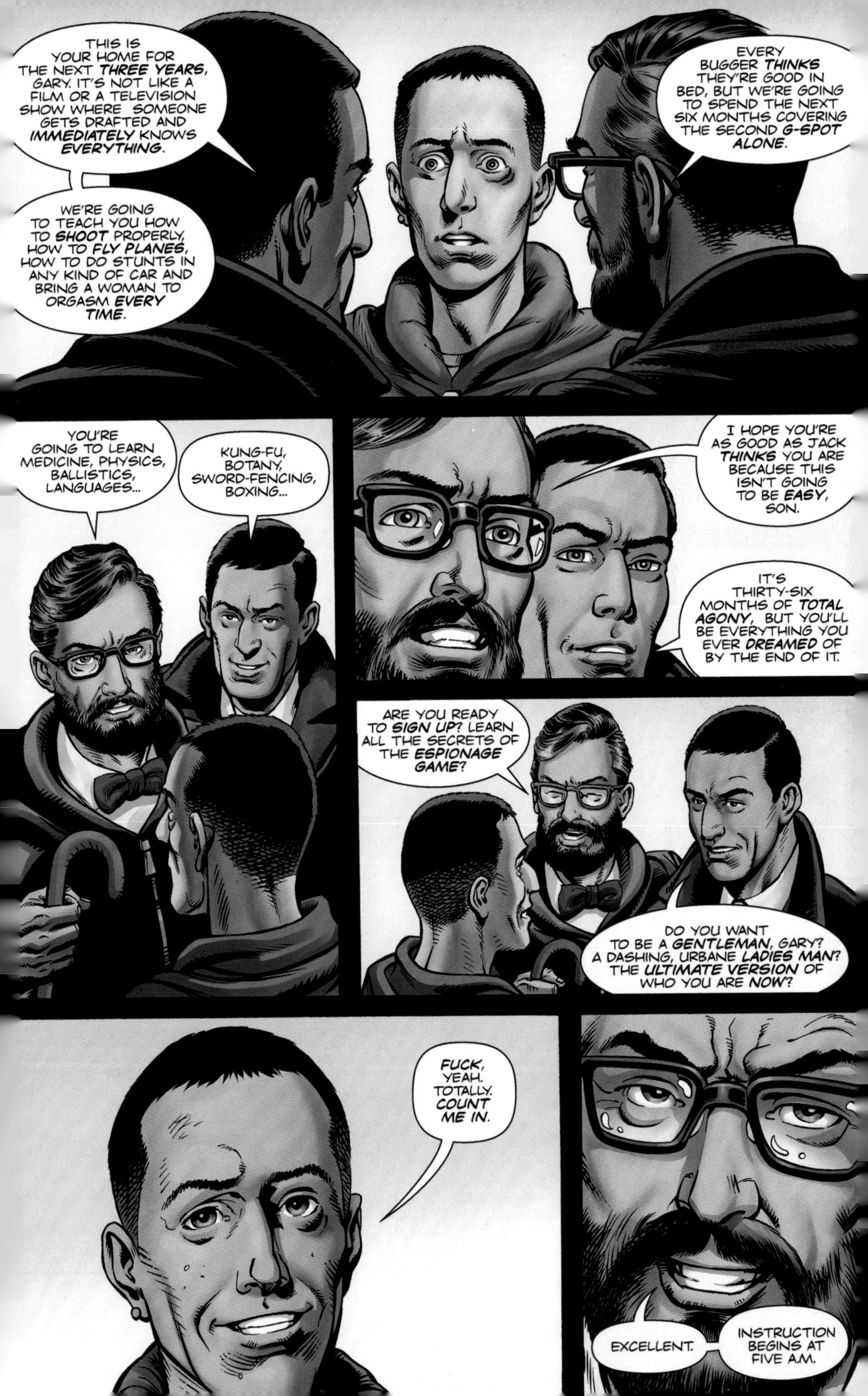
THIS IS YOUR HOME FOR THE NEXT THREE YEARS, GARY. IT'S NOT LIKE A FILM OR A TELEVISION SHOW WHERE SOMEONE GETS DRAFTED AND IMMEDIATELY KNOWS EVERYTHING.
WE'RE GOING TO TEACH YOU HOW TO SHOOT PROPERLY, HOW TO FLY PLANES, HOW TO DO STUNTS IN ANY KIND OF CAR AND BRING A WOMAN TO ORGASM EVERY TIME.
EVERY BUGGER THINKS THEY'RE GOOD IN BED, BUT WE'RE GOING TO SPEND THE NEXT SIX MONTHS COVERING THE SECOND G-SPOT ALONE.
YOU'RE GOING TO LEARN MEDICINE, PHYSICS, BALLISTICS, LANGUAGES...
KUNG-FU, BOTANY, SWORD-FENCING, BOXING...
I HOPE YOU'RE AS GOOD AS JACK THINKS YOU ARE BECAUSE THIS ISN'T GOING TO BE EASY, SON.
IT'S THIRTY-SIX MONTHS OF TOTAL AGONY, BUT YOU'LL BE EVERYTHING YOU EVER DREAMED OF BY THE END OF IT.
ARE YOU READY TO SIGN UP? LEARN ALL THE SECRETS OF THE ESPIONAGE GAME?
DO YOU WANT TO BE A GENTLEMAN, GARY? A DASHING, URBANE LADIES MAN? THE ULTIMATE VERSION OF WHO YOU ARE NOW?
FUCK, YEAH. TOTALLY. COUNT ME IN.
EXCELLENT.
INSTRUCTION BEGINS AT FIVE A.M.

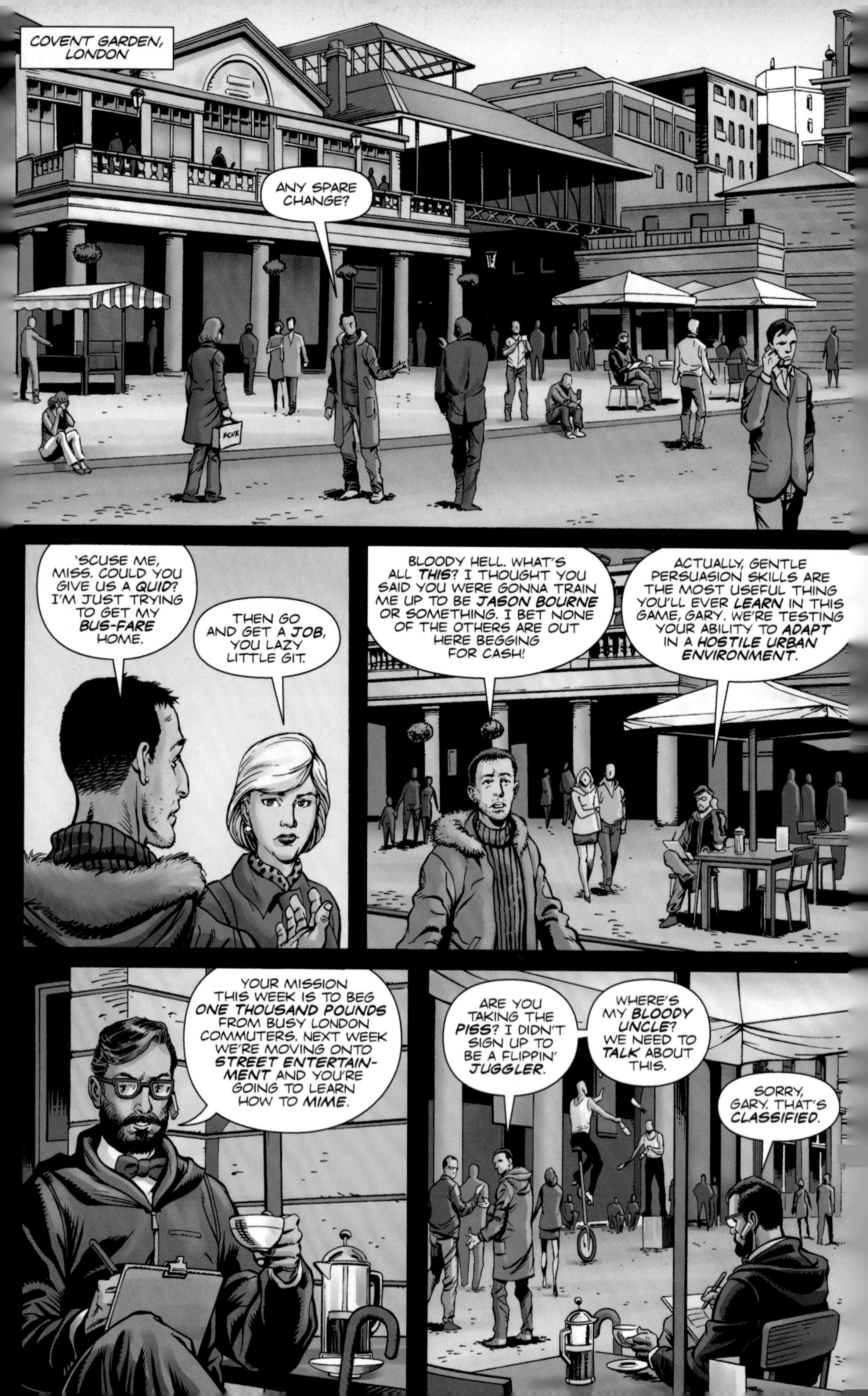
COVENT GARDEN, LONDON
ANY SPARE CHANGE?
FCUK
'SCUSE ME, MISS. COULD YOU GIVE US A QUID? I'M JUST TRYING TO GET MY BUS-FARE HOME.
THEN GO AND GET A JOB, YOU LAZY LITTLE GIT.
BLOODY HELL. WHAT'S ALL THIS? I THOUGHT YOU SAID YOU WERE GONNA TRAIN ME UP TO BE JASON BOURNE OR SOMETHING. I BET NONE OF THE OTHERS ARE OUT HERE BEGGING FOR CASH!
ACTUALLY, GENTLE PERSUASION SKILLS ARE THE MOST USEFUL THING YOU'LL EVER LEARN IN THIS GAME, GARY. WE'RE TESTING YOUR ABILITY TO ADAPT IN A HOSTILE URBAN ENVIRONMENT.
YOUR MISSION THIS WEEK IS TO BEG ONE THOUSAND POUNDS FROM BUSY LONDON COMMUTERS. NEXT WEEK WE'RE MOVING ONTO STREET ENTERTAINMENT AND YOU'RE GOING TO LEARN HOW TO MIME.
ARE YOU TAKING THE PISS? I DIDN'T SIGN UP TO BE A FLIPPIN' JUGGLER.
WHERE'S MY BLOODY UNCLE? WE NEED TO TALK ABOUT THIS.
SORRY, GARY. THAT'S CLASSIFIED.

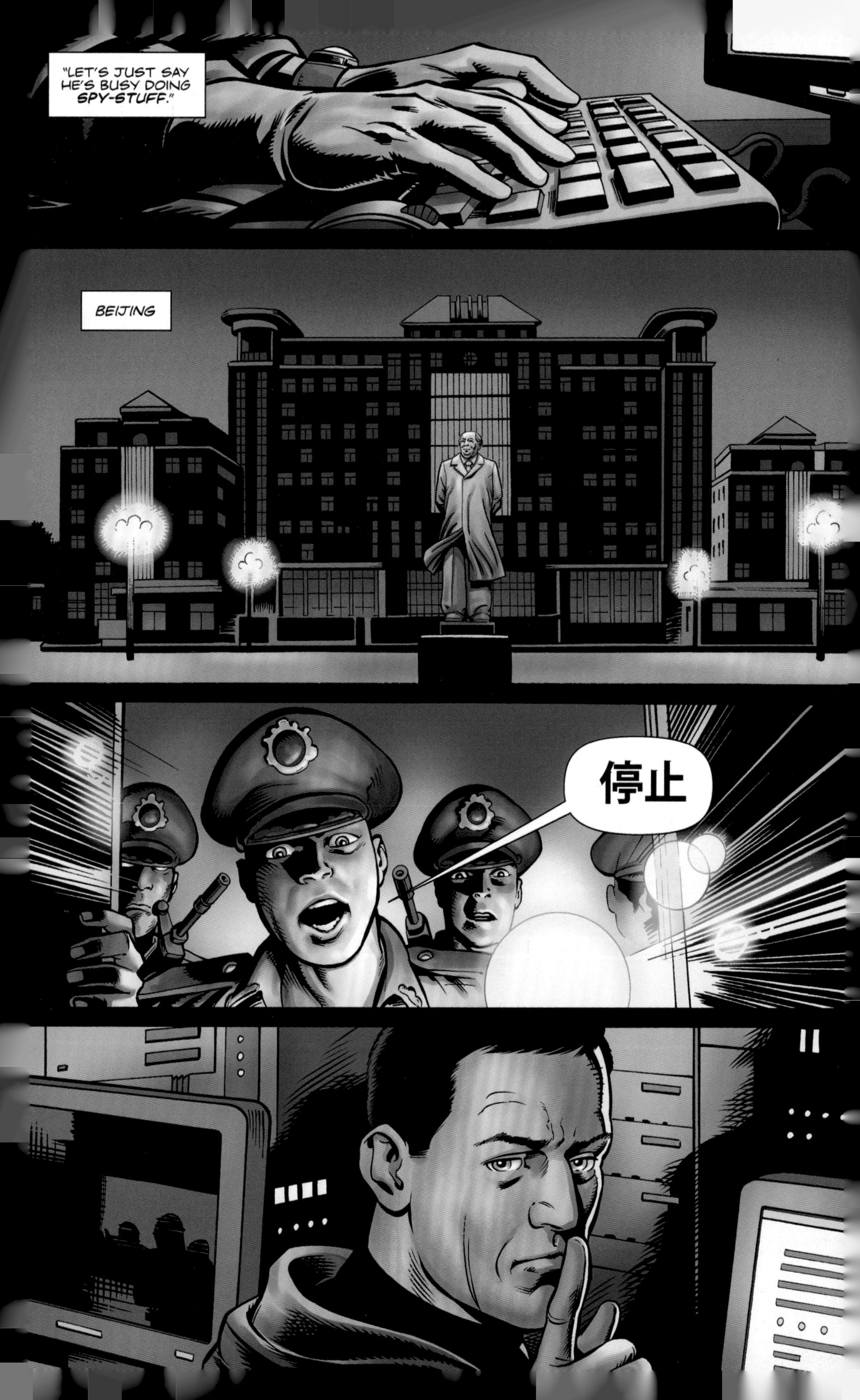
"LET'S JUST SAY HE'S BUSY DOING SPY-STUFF."
BEIJING
停止

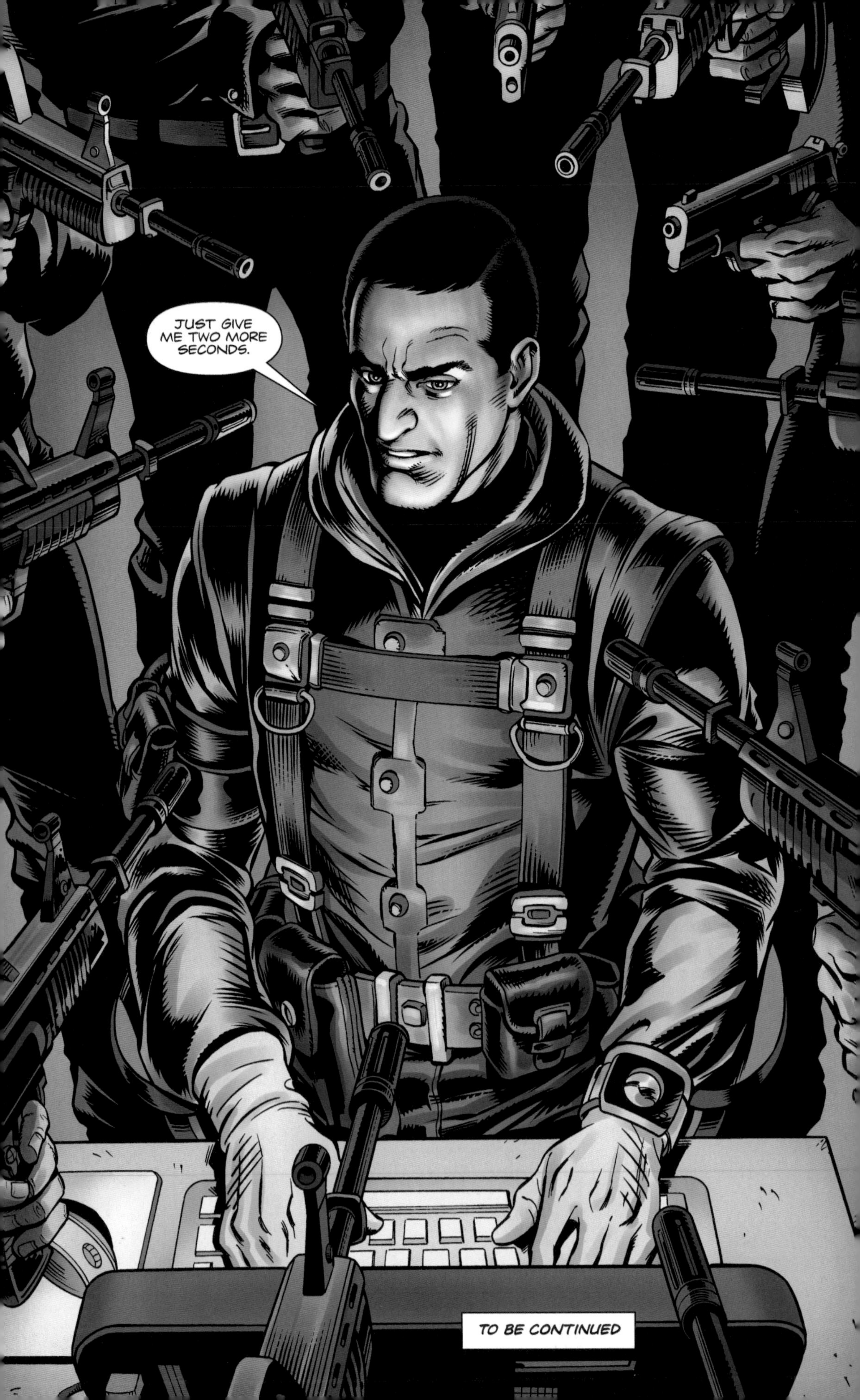
JUST GIVE ME TWO MORE SECONDS.
TO BE CONTINUED

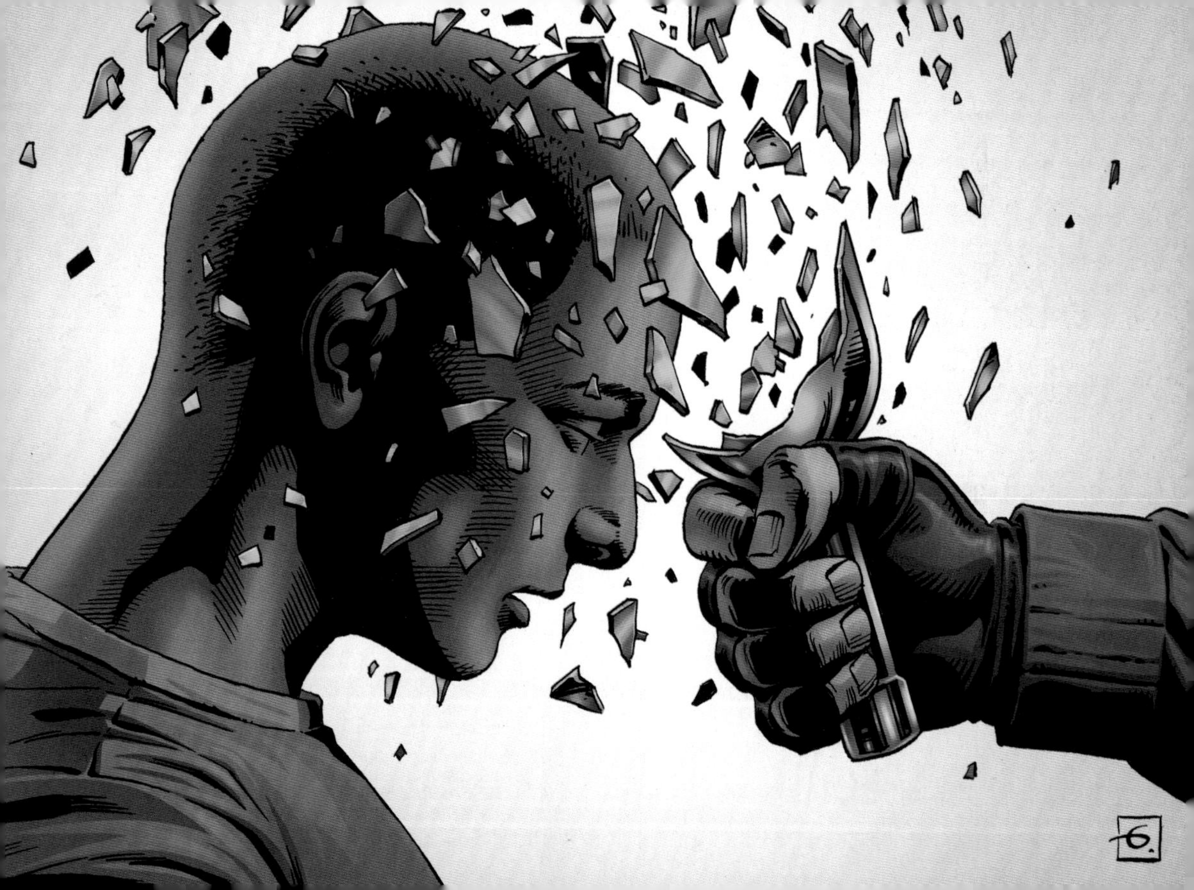
6.

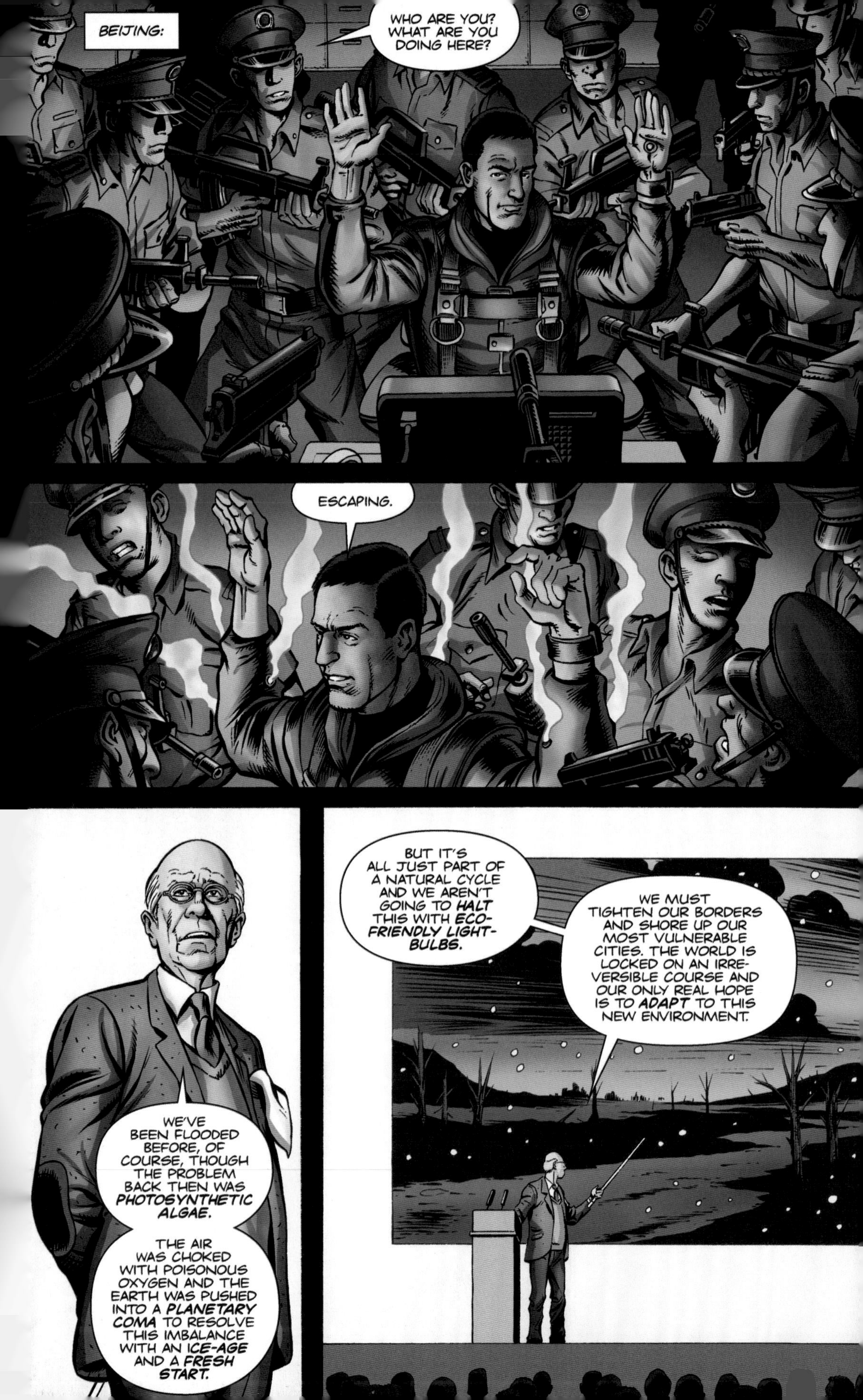
BEIJING:
WHO ARE YOU? WHAT ARE YOU DOING HERE?
ESCAPING.
WE'VE BEEN FLOODED BEFORE, OF COURSE, THOUGH THE PROBLEM BACK THEN WAS PHOTOSYNTHETIC ALGAE.
THE AIR WAS CHOKED WITH POISONOUS OXYGEN AND THE EARTH WAS PUSHED INTO A PLANETARY COMA TO RESOLVE THIS IMBALANCE WITH AN ICE-AGE AND A FRESH START.
BUT IT'S ALL JUST PART OF A NATURAL CYCLE AND WE AREN'T GOING TO HALT THIS WITH ECO-FRIENDLY LIGHT-BULBS.
WE MUST TIGHTEN OUR BORDERS AND SHORE UP OUR MOST VULNERABLE CITIES. THE WORLD IS LOCKED ON AN IRREVERSIBLE COURSE AND OUR ONLY REAL HOPE IS TO ADAPT TO THIS NEW ENVIRONMENT.

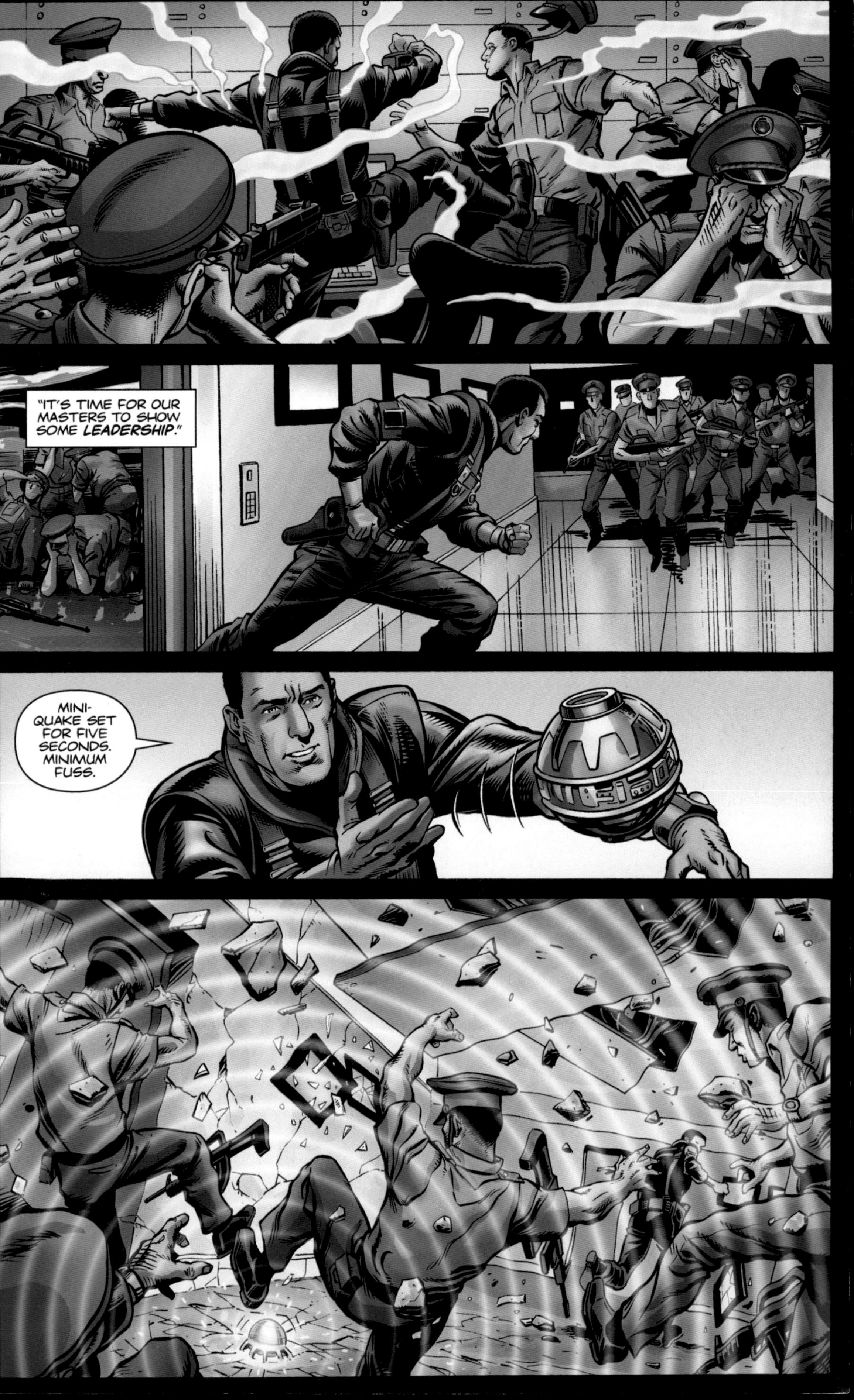
"IT'S TIME FOR OUR MASTERS TO SHOW SOME LEADERSHIP."
MINI-QUAKE SET FOR FIVE SECONDS. MINIMUM FUSS.

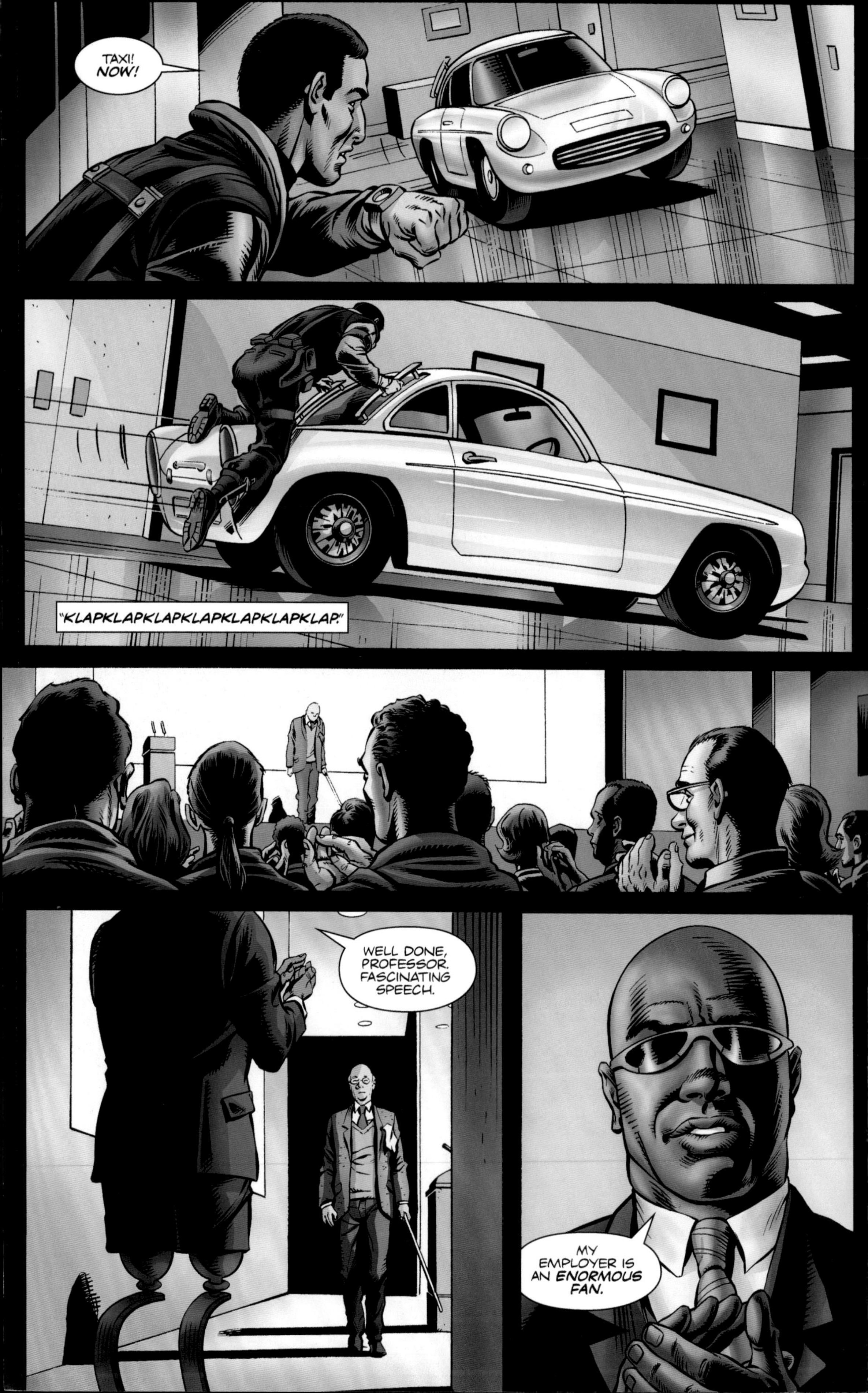
TAXI! NOW!
"KLAPKLAPKLAPKLAPKLAPKLAPKLAP."
WELL DONE, PROFESSOR. FASCINATING SPEECH.
MY EMPLOYER IS AN ENORMOUS FAN.

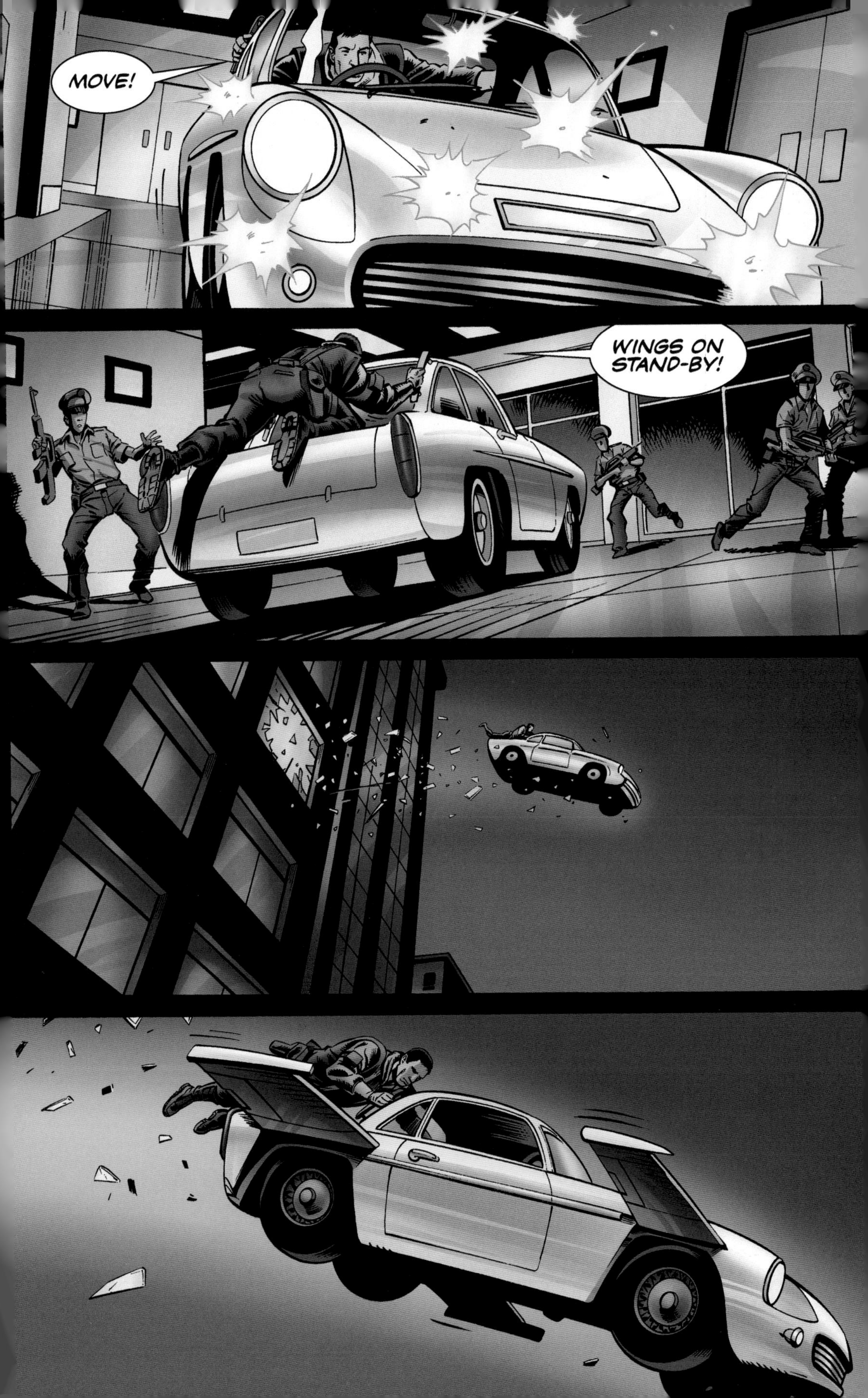
MOVE!
WINGS ON STAND-BY!

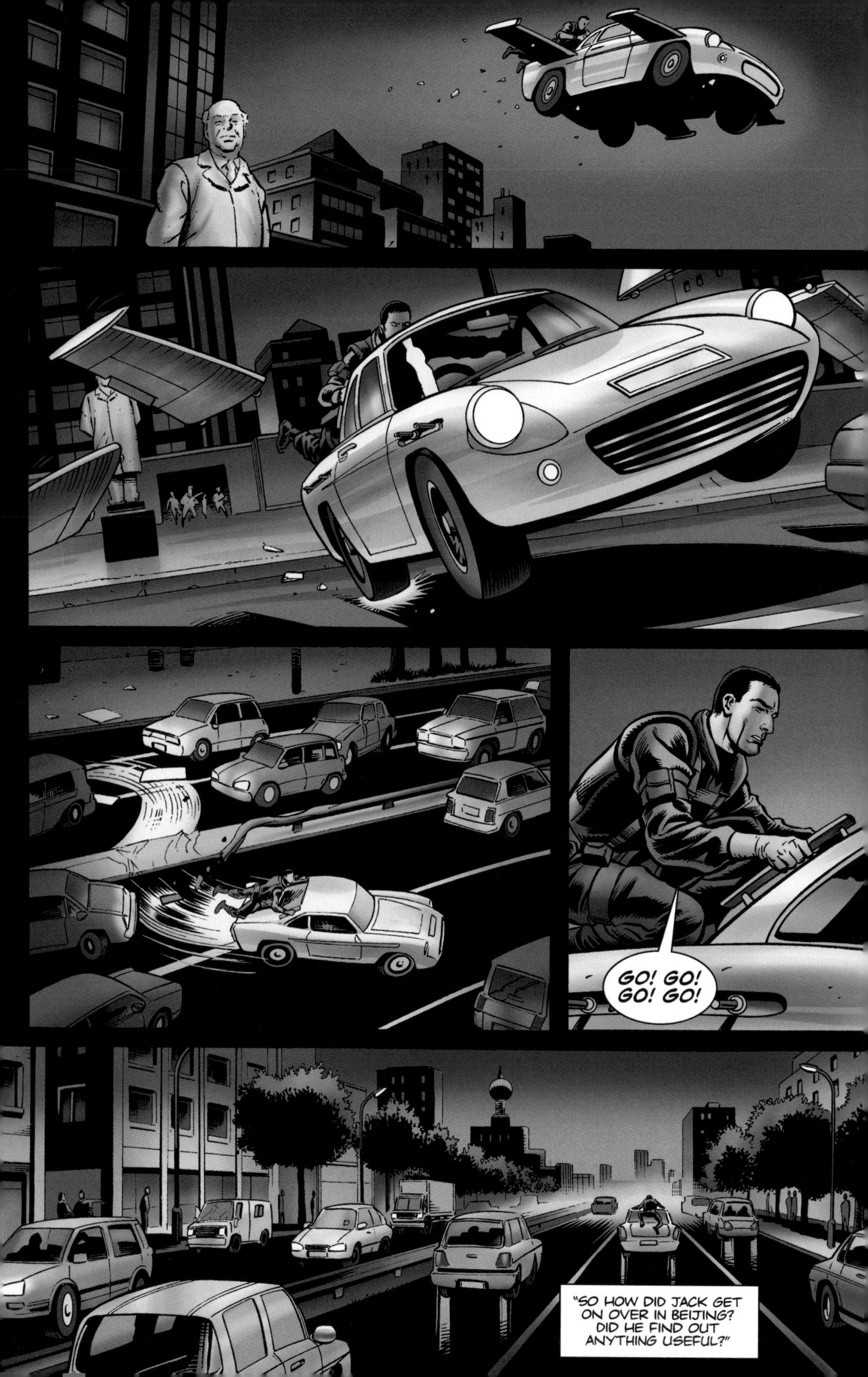
GO! GO! GO! GO!
"SO HOW DID JACK GET ON OVER IN BEIJING? DID HE FIND OUT ANYTHING USEFUL?"

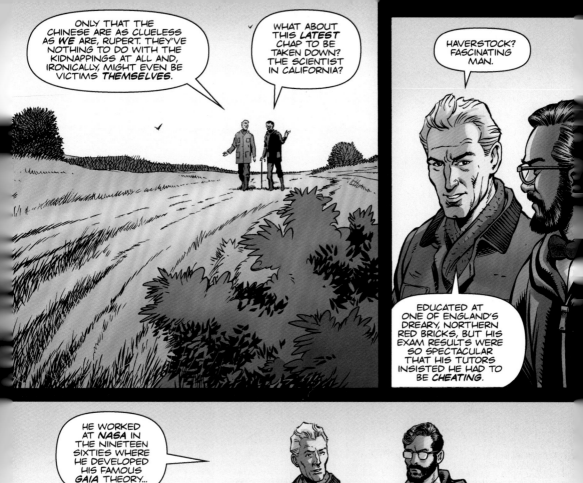

ONLY THAT THE CHINESE ARE AS CLUELESS AS **WE** ARE, RUPERT. THEY'VE NOTHING TO DO WITH THE KIDNAPPINGS AT ALL AND, IRONICALLY, MIGHT EVEN BE VICTIMS **THEMSELVES**.

WHAT ABOUT THIS **LATEST** CHAP TO BE TAKEN DOWN? THE SCIENTIST IN CALIFORNIA?

HAVERSTOCK? FASCINATING MAN.

EDUCATED AT ONE OF ENGLAND'S DREARY, NORTHERN RED BRICKS, BUT HIS EXAM RESULTS WERE SO SPECTACULAR THAT HIS TUTORS INSISTED HE HAD TO BE **CHEATING**.

HE WORKED AT **NASA** IN THE NINETEEN SIXTIES WHERE HE DEVELOPED HIS FAMOUS **GAIA** THEORY...

...THIS NOTION THAT THE EARTH IS A LIVING, SELF-REGULATING ORGANISM AND GLOBAL WARMING NOTHING MORE THAN A NATURAL PHENOMENON.

ABSOLVING MAN OF ALL OUR SINS HAS THE GREENS UP IN ARMS, BUT HE'S STARTING TO GET TAKEN VERY SERIOUSLY.

BASICALLY, HE WANTS A **COMPLETE REVERSE** OF OUR CURRENT THINKING AND A GLOBAL STRATEGY TO SIMPLY **COPE** WITH OUR NEW ENVIRONMENT.

WRITERS, MOVIE STARS, TECHNOLOGISTS AND NOW THIS: WHAT THE HELL **LINKS** ALL THESE PEOPLE, SIR GILES?

ONE VERY RICH **CRANK**, I SUSPECT.

I'LL NEVER **FORGIVE** TONY BLAIR FOR MAKING THIS COUNTRY A MAGNET FOR ALL THOSE **RUSSIAN OLIGARCHS** AND SEEDY **OIL-BARONS**.

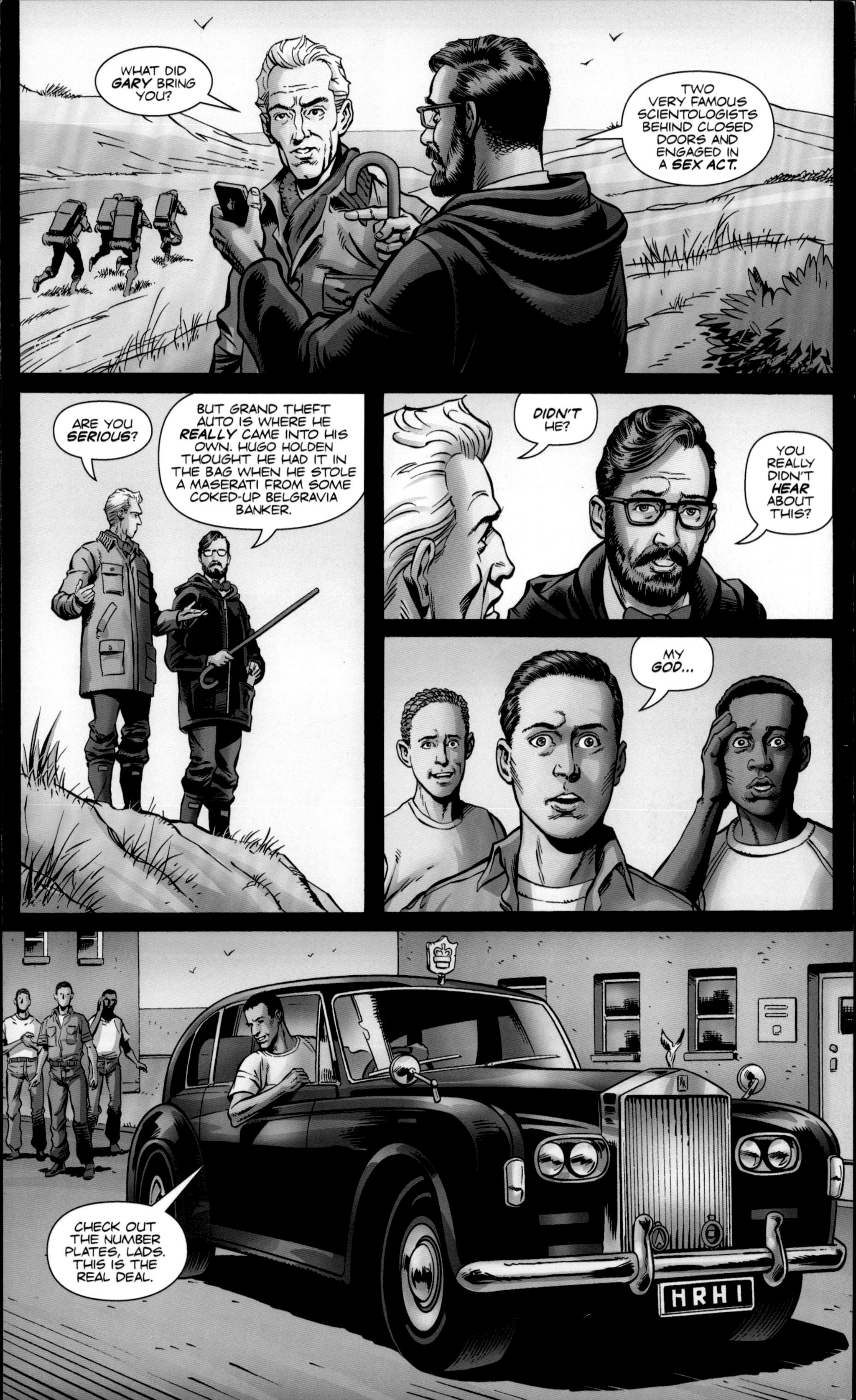
WHAT DID GARY BRING YOU?
TWO VERY FAMOUS SCIENTOLOGISTS BEHIND CLOSED DOORS AND ENGAGED IN A SEX ACT.
ARE YOU SERIOUS?
BUT GRAND THEFT AUTO IS WHERE HE REALLY CAME INTO HIS OWN. HUGO HOLDEN THOUGHT HE HAD IT IN THE BAG WHEN HE STOLE A MASERATI FROM SOME COKED-UP BELGRAVIA BANKER.
DIDN'T HE?
YOU REALLY DIDN'T HEAR ABOUT THIS?
MY GOD...
CHECK OUT THE NUMBER PLATES, LADS. THIS IS THE REAL DEAL.
HRH I

GARY'S STREET-SKILLS HAVE DEFINITELY GIVEN HIM AN *ADVANTAGE*. THE ETON BOXING CLUB HARDLY COMPARES TO FIGHTING THE LOCAL *POLICE* EVERY NIGHT.

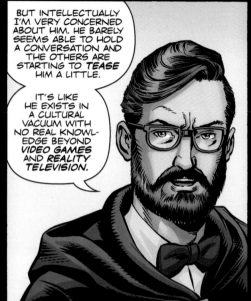

BUT INTELLECTUALLY I'M VERY CONCERNED ABOUT HIM. HE BARELY SEEMS ABLE TO HOLD A CONVERSATION AND THE OTHERS ARE STARTING TO *TEASE* HIM A LITTLE.

IT'S LIKE HE EXISTS IN A CULTURAL VACUUM WITH NO REAL KNOWLEDGE BEYOND *VIDEO GAMES* AND *REALITY TELEVISION*.

COME ON, UNWIN. GET A MOVE ON. LAUDATE DOMINUM BY FERREUS OPUS!

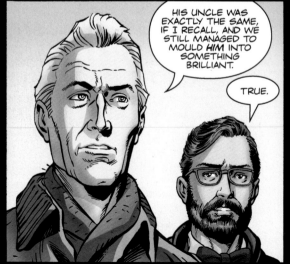

HIS UNCLE WAS EXACTLY THE SAME, IF I RECALL, AND WE STILL MANAGED TO MOULD *HIM* INTO SOMETHING BRILLIANT.

TRUE.

LET'S SEE HOW HIS FIRST *ASSASSINATION* GOES. MURDERING A TOTAL STRANGER ALWAYS SHOWS US WHAT THEY'RE *MADE OF*.

"AREN'T YOU A BIT *FREAKED OUT* BY ALL THIS, STUFF?"

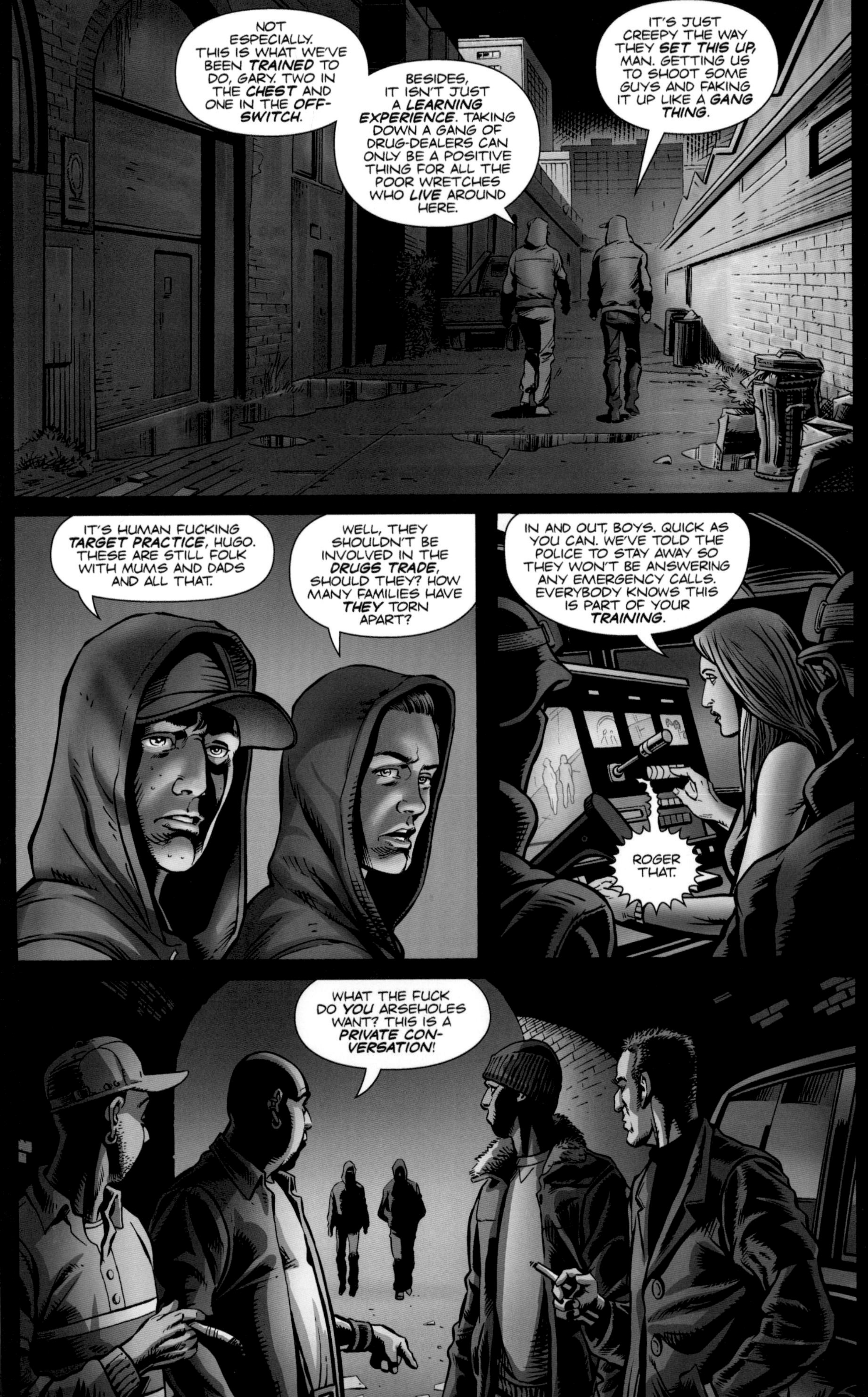
NOT ESPECIALLY. THIS IS WHAT WE'VE BEEN TRAINED TO DO, GARY. TWO IN THE CHEST AND ONE IN THE OFF-SWITCH.
BESIDES, IT ISN'T JUST A LEARNING EXPERIENCE. TAKING DOWN A GANG OF DRUG-DEALERS CAN ONLY BE A POSITIVE THING FOR ALL THE POOR WRETCHES WHO LIVE AROUND HERE.
IT'S JUST CREEPY THE WAY THEY SET THIS UP, MAN. GETTING US TO SHOOT SOME GUYS AND FAKING IT UP LIKE A GANG THING.
IT'S HUMAN FUCKING TARGET PRACTICE, HUGO. THESE ARE STILL FOLK WITH MUMS AND DADS AND ALL THAT.
WELL, THEY SHOULDN'T BE INVOLVED IN THE DRUGS TRADE, SHOULD THEY? HOW MANY FAMILIES HAVE THEY TORN APART?
IN AND OUT, BOYS. QUICK AS YOU CAN. WE'VE TOLD THE POLICE TO STAY AWAY SO THEY WON'T BE ANSWERING ANY EMERGENCY CALLS. EVERYBODY KNOWS THIS IS PART OF YOUR TRAINING.
ROGER THAT.
WHAT THE FUCK DO YOU ARSEHOLES WANT? THIS IS A PRIVATE CONVERSATION!

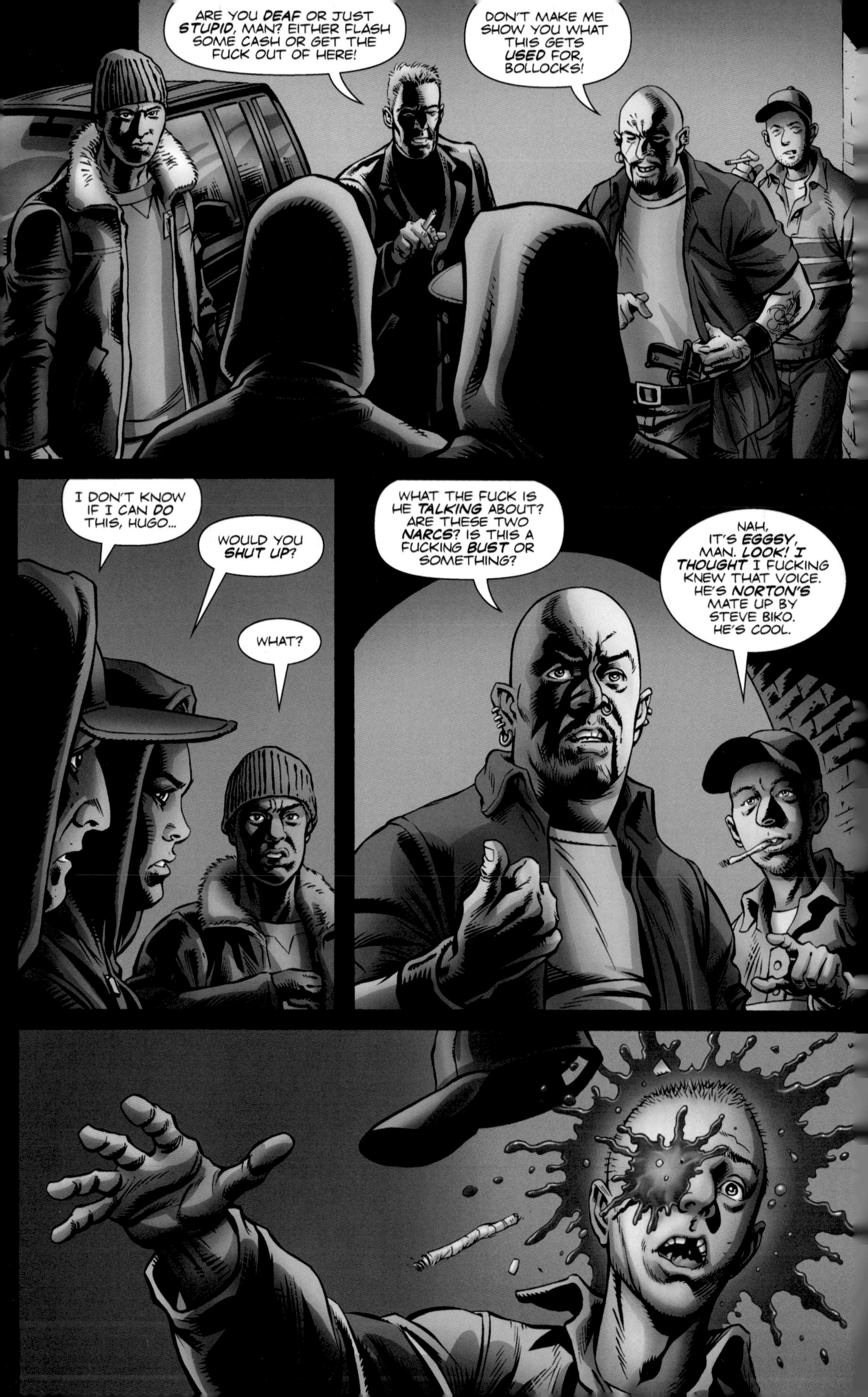
ARE YOU DEAF OR JUST STUPID, MAN? EITHER FLASH SOME CASH OR GET THE FUCK OUT OF HERE!
DON'T MAKE ME SHOW YOU WHAT THIS GETS USED FOR, BOLLOCKS!
I DON'T KNOW IF I CAN DO THIS, HUGO...
WOULD YOU SHUT UP?
WHAT?
WHAT THE FUCK IS HE TALKING ABOUT? ARE THESE TWO NARCS? IS THIS A FUCKING BUST OR SOMETHING?
NAH, IT'S EGGSY, MAN. LOOK! I THOUGHT I FUCKING KNEW THAT VOICE. HE'S NORTON'S MATE UP BY STEVE BIKO. HE'S COOL.

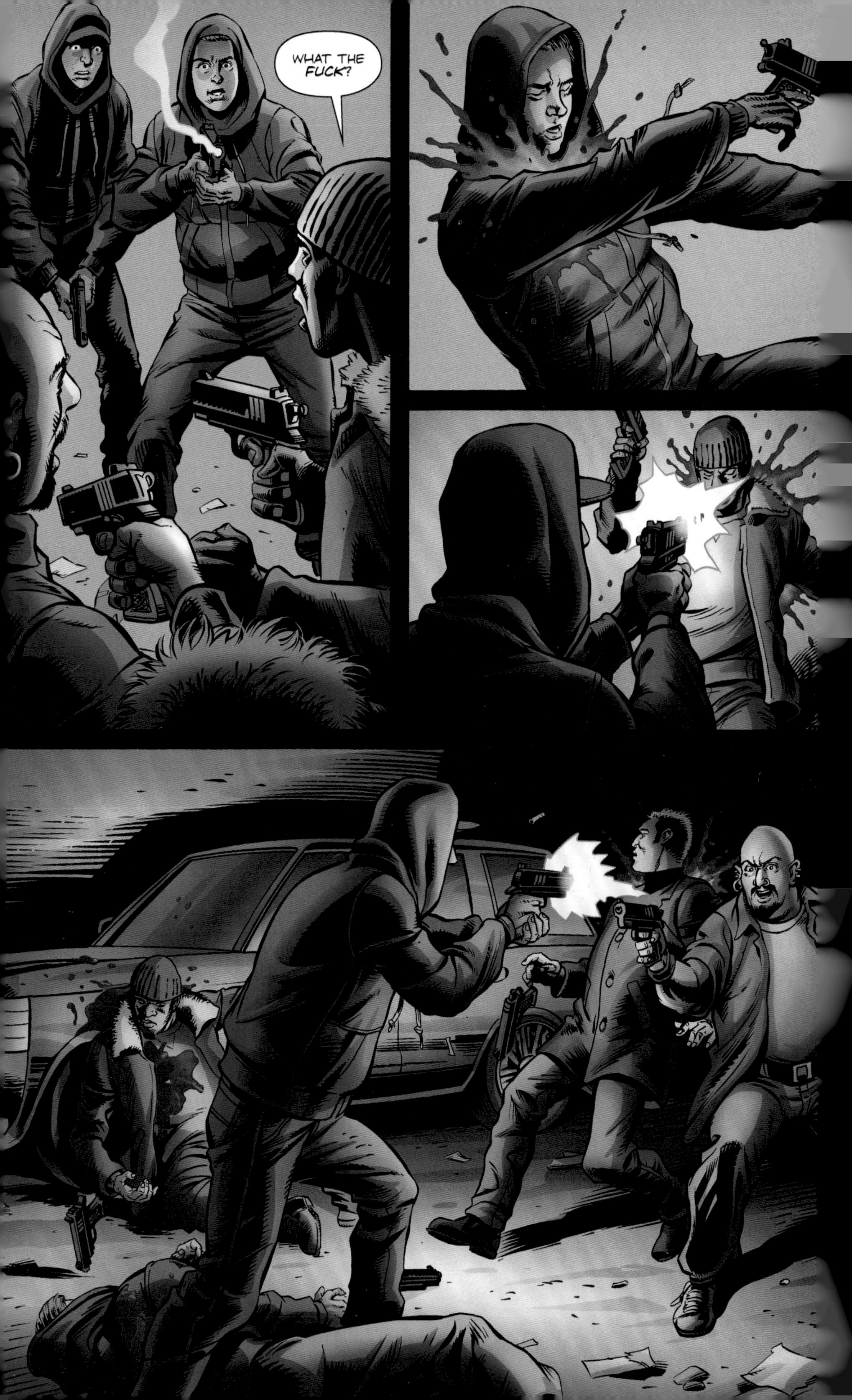
WHAT THE FUCK?

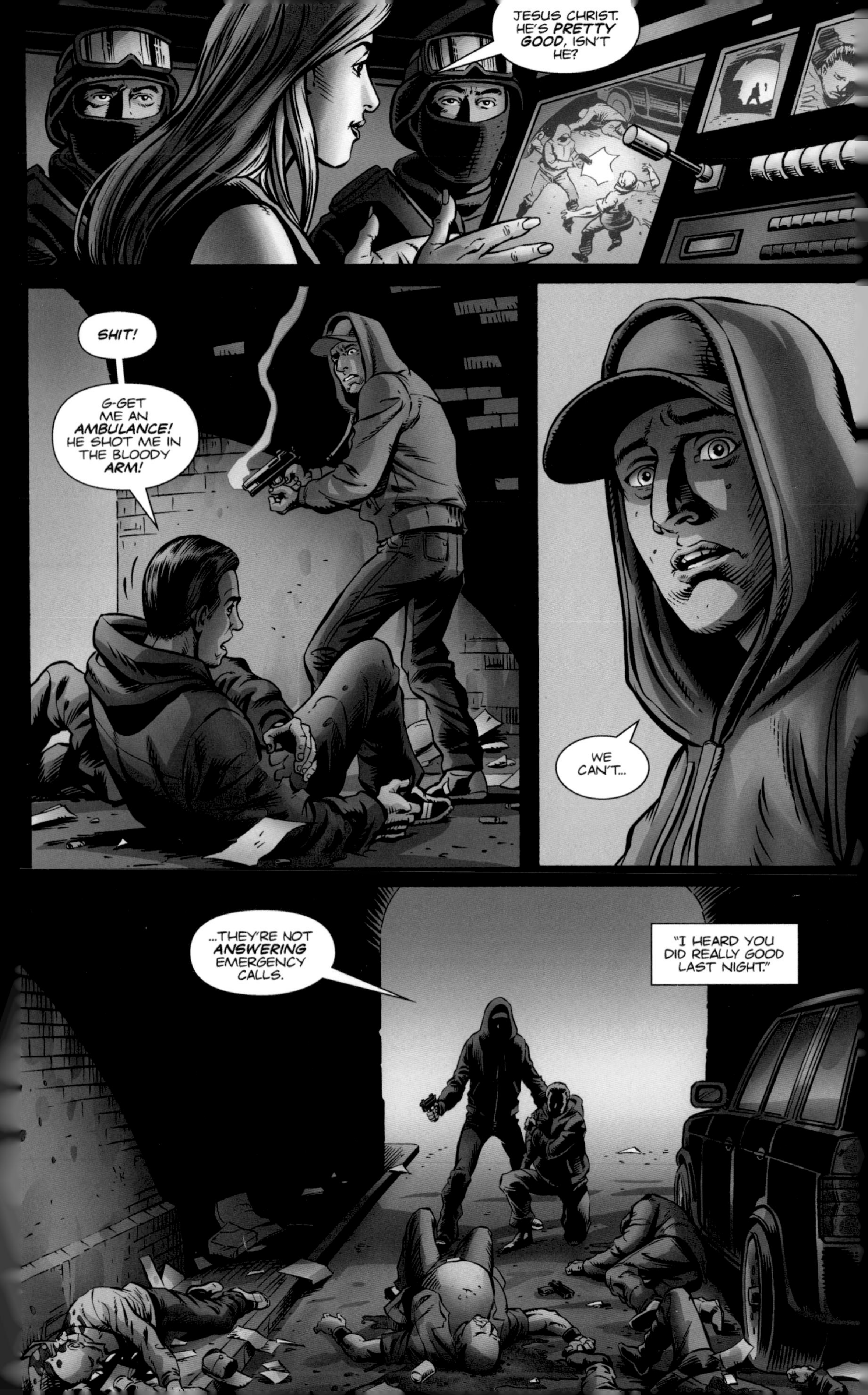
JESUS CHRIST. HE'S PRETTY GOOD, ISN'T HE?
SHIT!
G-GET ME AN AMBULANCE! HE SHOT ME IN THE BLOODY ARM!
WE CAN'T...
...THEY'RE NOT ANSWERING EMERGENCY CALLS.
"I HEARD YOU DID REALLY GOOD LAST NIGHT."

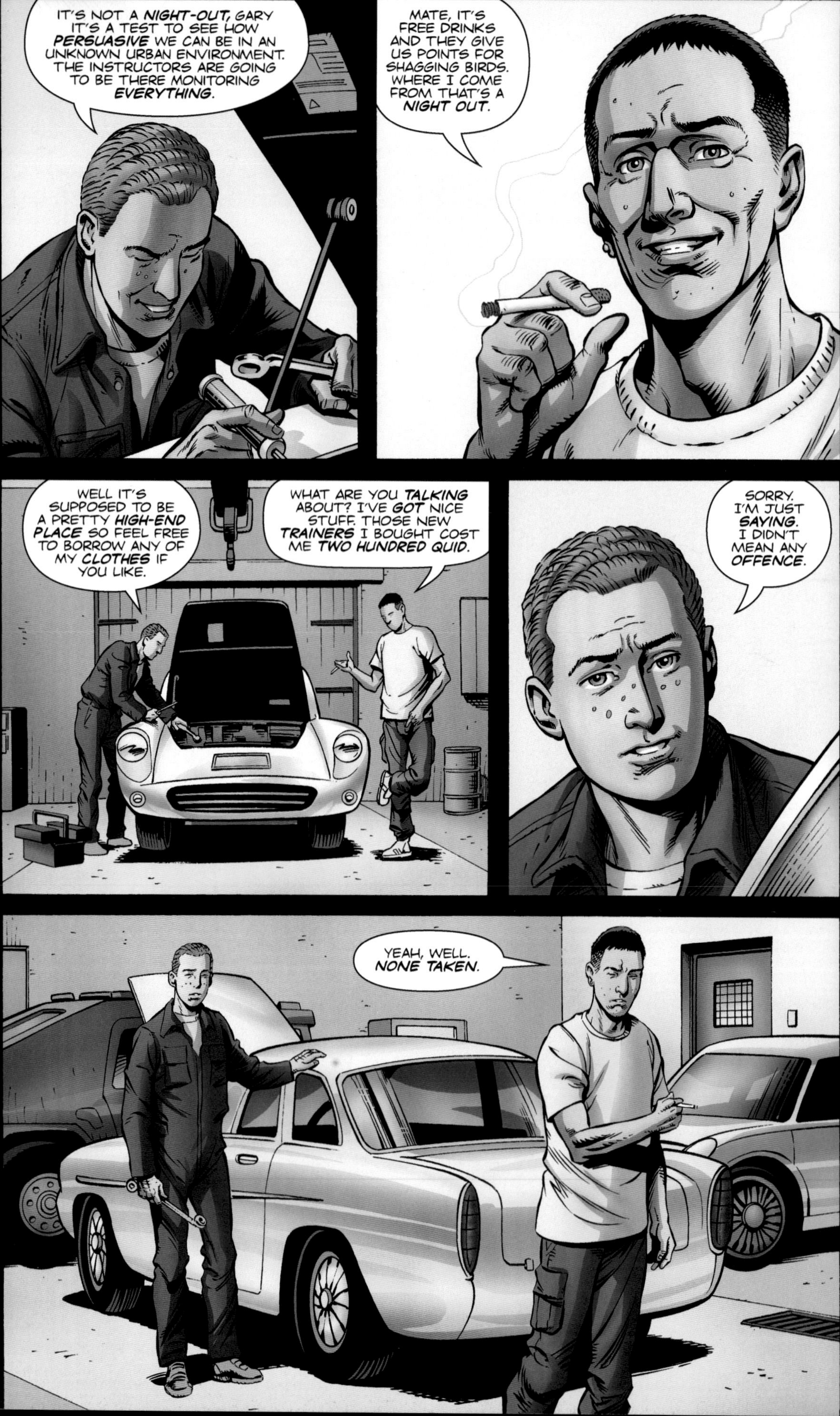
IT'S NOT A **NIGHT-OUT,** GARY IT'S A TEST TO SEE HOW **PERSUASIVE** WE CAN BE IN AN UNKNOWN URBAN ENVIRONMENT. THE INSTRUCTORS ARE GOING TO BE THERE MONITORING **EVERYTHING**.
MATE, IT'S FREE DRINKS AND THEY GIVE US POINTS FOR SHAGGING BIRDS. WHERE I COME FROM THAT'S A **NIGHT OUT**.
WELL IT'S SUPPOSED TO BE A PRETTY **HIGH-END PLACE** SO FEEL FREE TO BORROW ANY OF MY **CLOTHES** IF YOU LIKE.
WHAT ARE YOU **TALKING** ABOUT? I'VE **GOT** NICE STUFF. THOSE NEW **TRAINERS** I BOUGHT COST ME **TWO HUNDRED QUID**.
SORRY. I'M JUST **SAYING**. I DIDN'T MEAN ANY **OFFENCE**.
YEAH, WELL. **NONE TAKEN**.

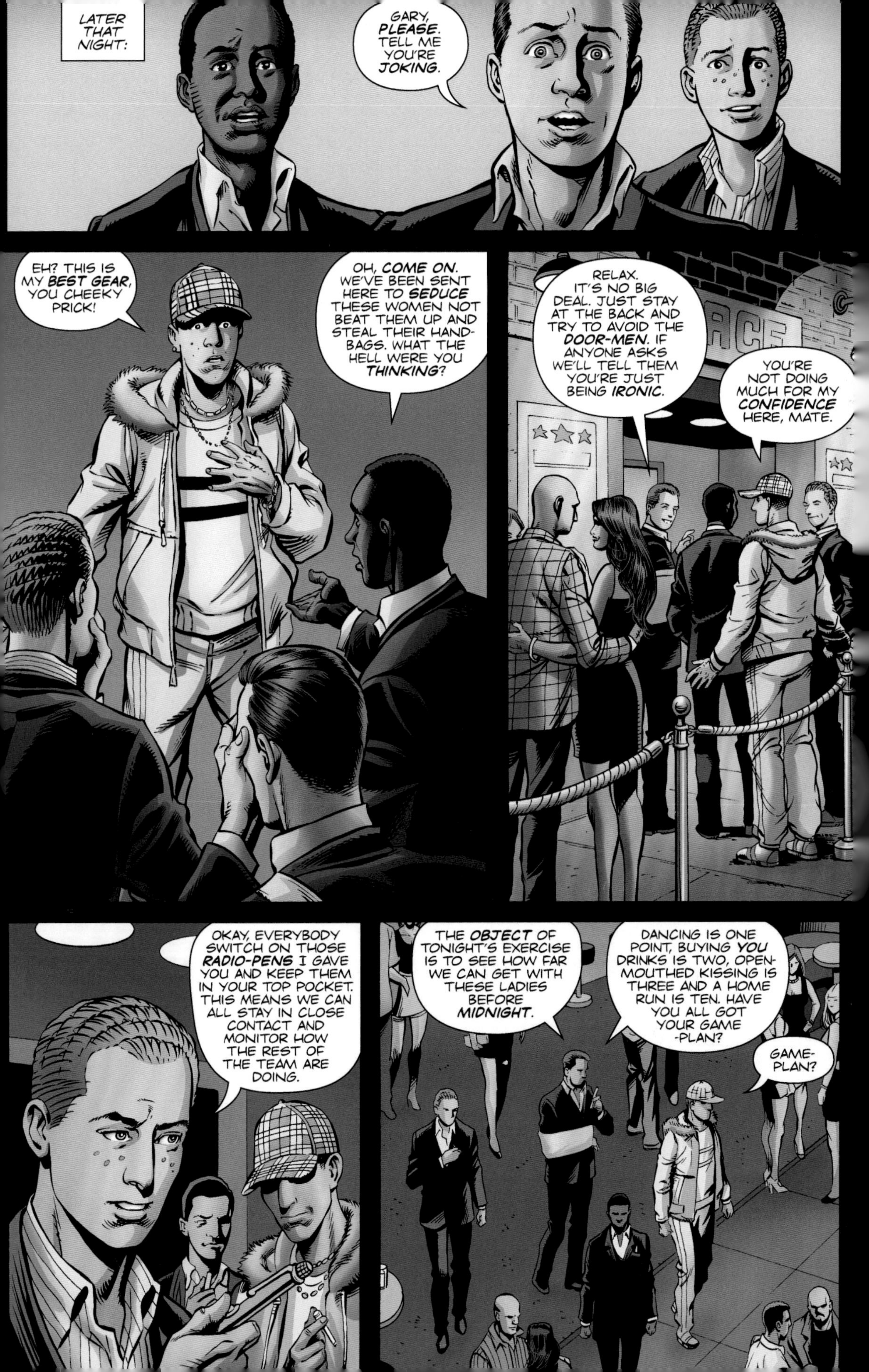
LATER THAT NIGHT:
GARY, PLEASE. TELL ME YOU'RE JOKING.
EH? THIS IS MY BEST GEAR, YOU CHEEKY PRICK!
OH, COME ON. WE'VE BEEN SENT HERE TO SEDUCE THESE WOMEN NOT BEAT THEM UP AND STEAL THEIR HAND-BAGS. WHAT THE HELL WERE YOU THINKING?
RELAX. IT'S NO BIG DEAL. JUST STAY AT THE BACK AND TRY TO AVOID THE DOOR-MEN. IF ANYONE ASKS WE'LL TELL THEM YOU'RE JUST BEING IRONIC.
YOU'RE NOT DOING MUCH FOR MY CONFIDENCE HERE, MATE.
OKAY, EVERYBODY SWITCH ON THOSE RADIO-PENS I GAVE YOU AND KEEP THEM IN YOUR TOP POCKET. THIS MEANS WE CAN ALL STAY IN CLOSE CONTACT AND MONITOR HOW THE REST OF THE TEAM ARE DOING.
THE OBJECT OF TONIGHT'S EXERCISE IS TO SEE HOW FAR WE CAN GET WITH THESE LADIES BEFORE MIDNIGHT.
DANCING IS ONE POINT, BUYING YOU DRINKS IS TWO, OPEN-MOUTHED KISSING IS THREE AND A HOME RUN IS TEN. HAVE YOU ALL GOT YOUR GAME -PLAN?
GAME-PLAN?

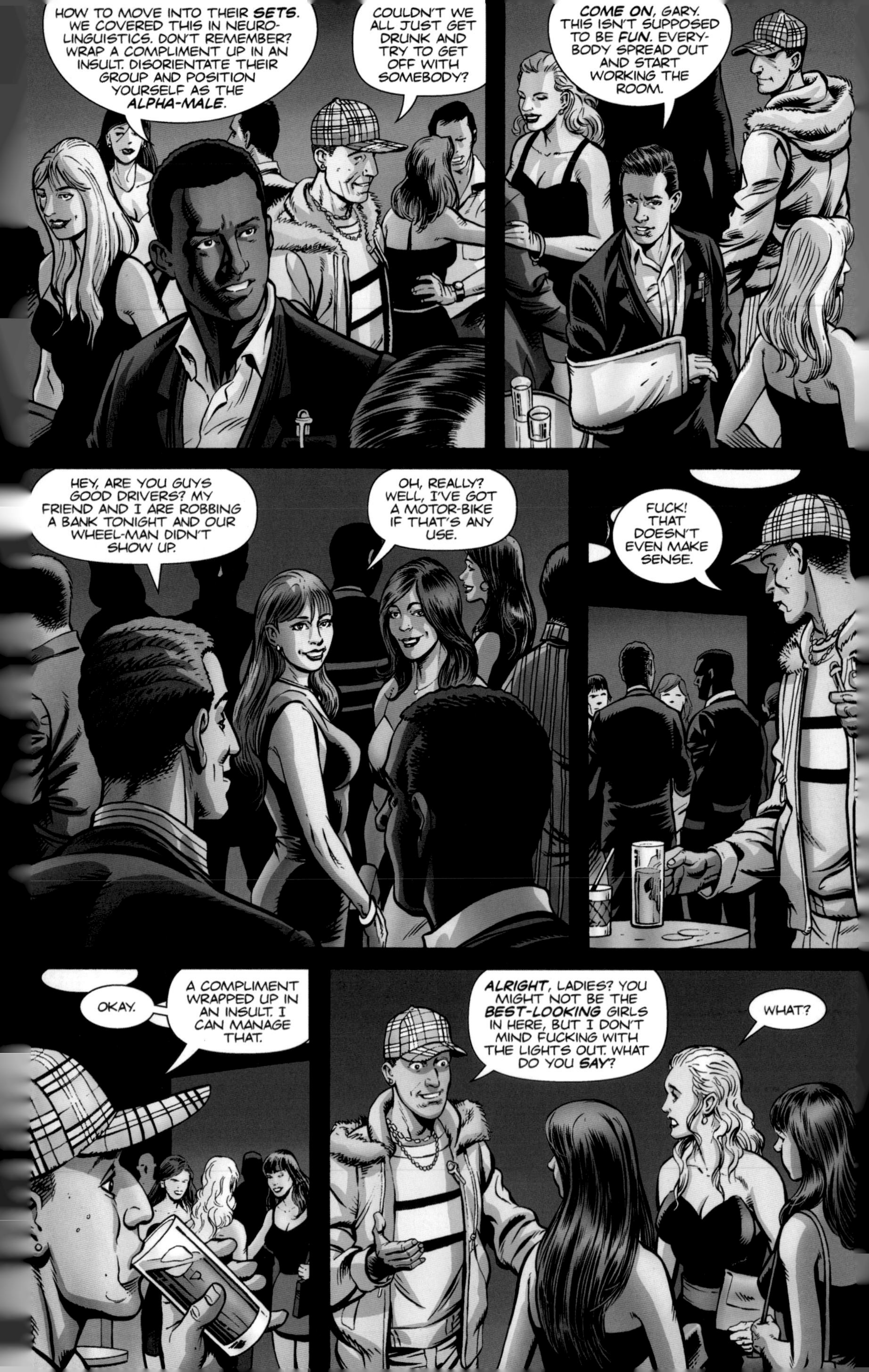
HOW TO MOVE INTO THEIR SETS. WE COVERED THIS IN NEURO-LINGUISTICS. DON'T REMEMBER? WRAP A COMPLIMENT UP IN AN INSULT. DISORIENTATE THEIR GROUP AND POSITION YOURSELF AS THE ALPHA-MALE.
COULDN'T WE ALL JUST GET DRUNK AND TRY TO GET OFF WITH SOMEBODY?
COME ON, GARY. THIS ISN'T SUPPOSED TO BE FUN. EVERY-BODY SPREAD OUT AND START WORKING THE ROOM.
HEY, ARE YOU GUYS GOOD DRIVERS? MY FRIEND AND I ARE ROBBING A BANK TONIGHT AND OUR WHEEL-MAN DIDN'T SHOW UP.
OH, REALLY? WELL, I'VE GOT A MOTOR-BIKE IF THAT'S ANY USE.
FUCK! THAT DOESN'T EVEN MAKE SENSE.
OKAY.
A COMPLIMENT WRAPPED UP IN AN INSULT. I CAN MANAGE THAT.
ALRIGHT, LADIES? YOU MIGHT NOT BE THE BEST-LOOKING GIRLS IN HERE, BUT I DON'T MIND FUCKING WITH THE LIGHTS OUT. WHAT DO YOU SAY?
WHAT?

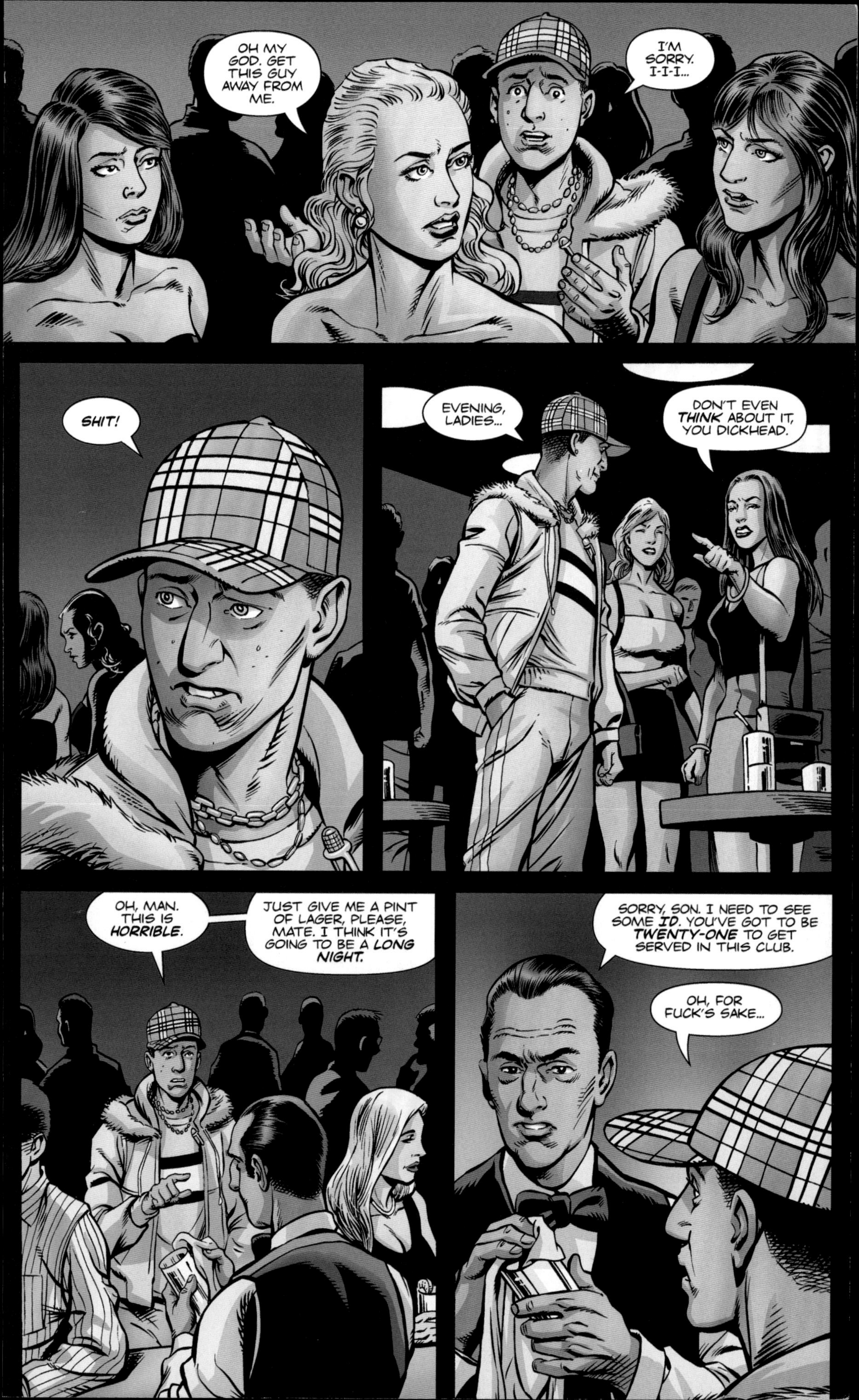
OH MY GOD. GET THIS GUY AWAY FROM ME.
I'M SORRY. I-I-I...
SHIT!
EVENING, LADIES...
DON'T EVEN THINK ABOUT IT, YOU DICKHEAD.
OH, MAN. THIS IS HORRIBLE.
JUST GIVE ME A PINT OF LAGER, PLEASE, MATE. I THINK IT'S GOING TO BE A LONG NIGHT.
SORRY, SON. I NEED TO SEE SOME ID. YOU'VE GOT TO BE TWENTY-ONE TO GET SERVED IN THIS CLUB.
OH, FOR FUCK'S SAKE...

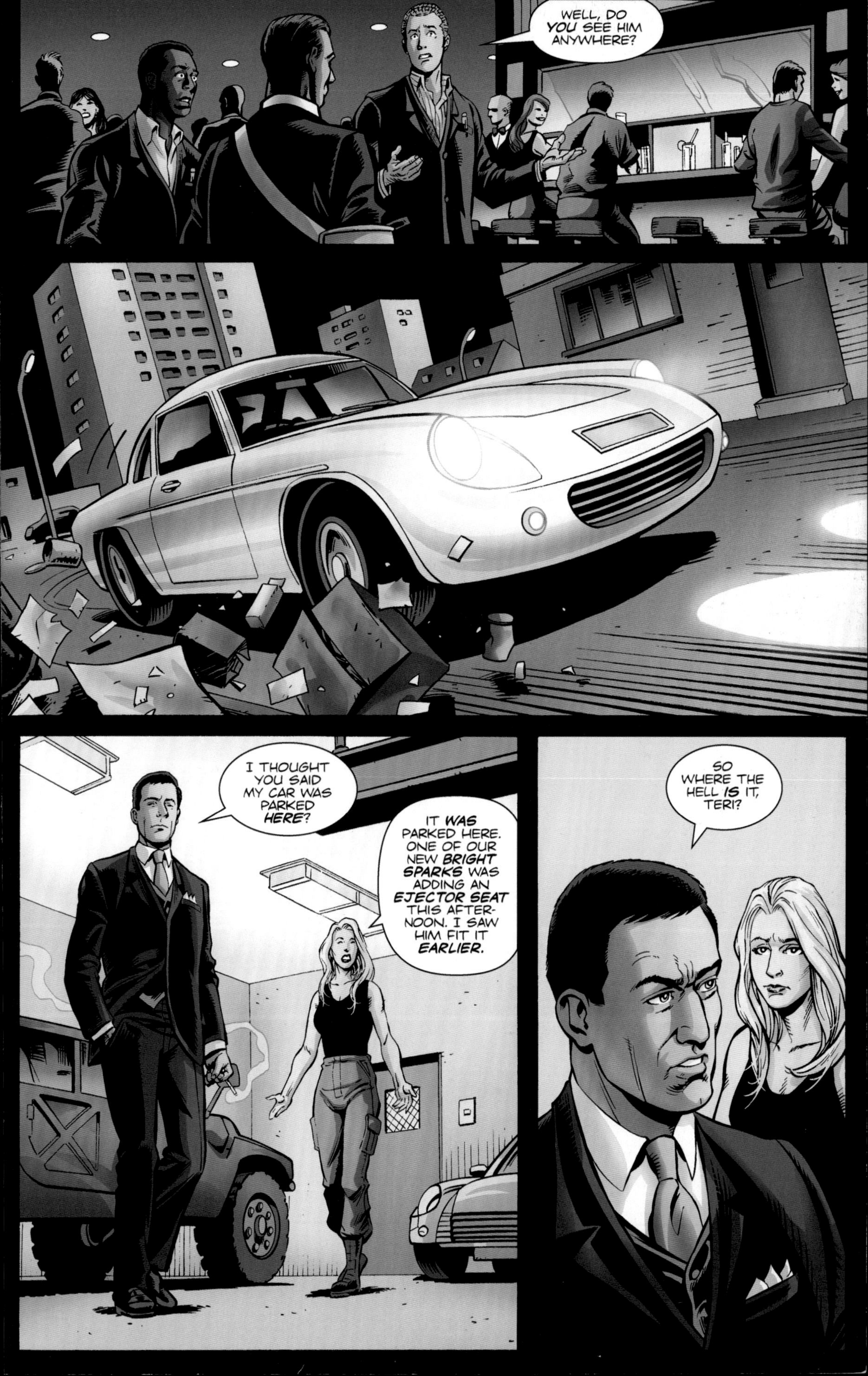
WELL, DO YOU SEE HIM ANYWHERE?
I THOUGHT YOU SAID MY CAR WAS PARKED HERE?
IT WAS PARKED HERE. ONE OF OUR NEW BRIGHT SPARKS WAS ADDING AN EJECTOR SEAT THIS AFTER-NOON. I SAW HIM FIT IT EARLIER.
SO WHERE THE HELL IS IT, TERI?

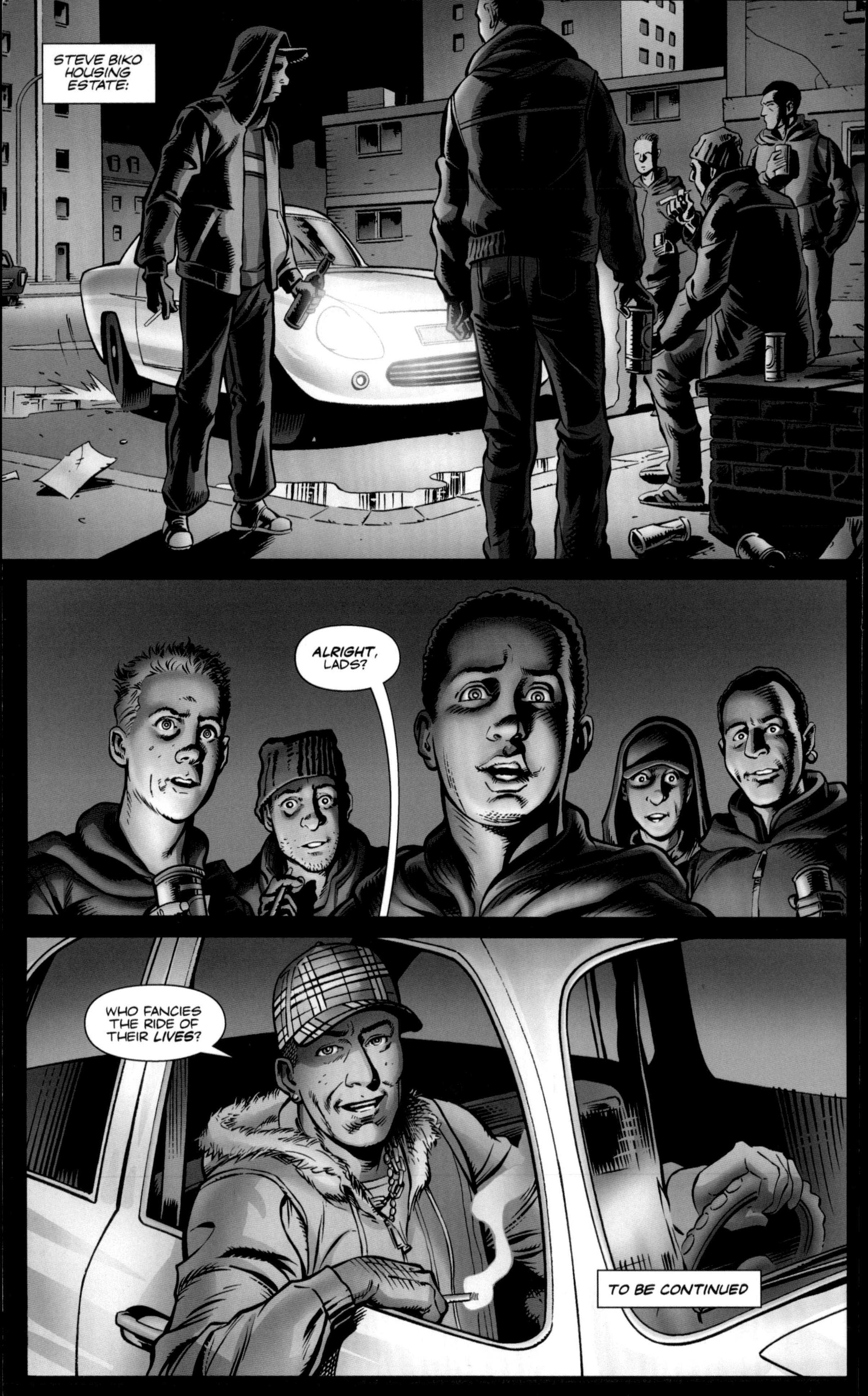
STEVE BIKO HOUSING ESTATE:
ALRIGHT, LADS?
WHO FANCIES THE RIDE OF THEIR *LIVES*?
TO BE CONTINUED

FOUR

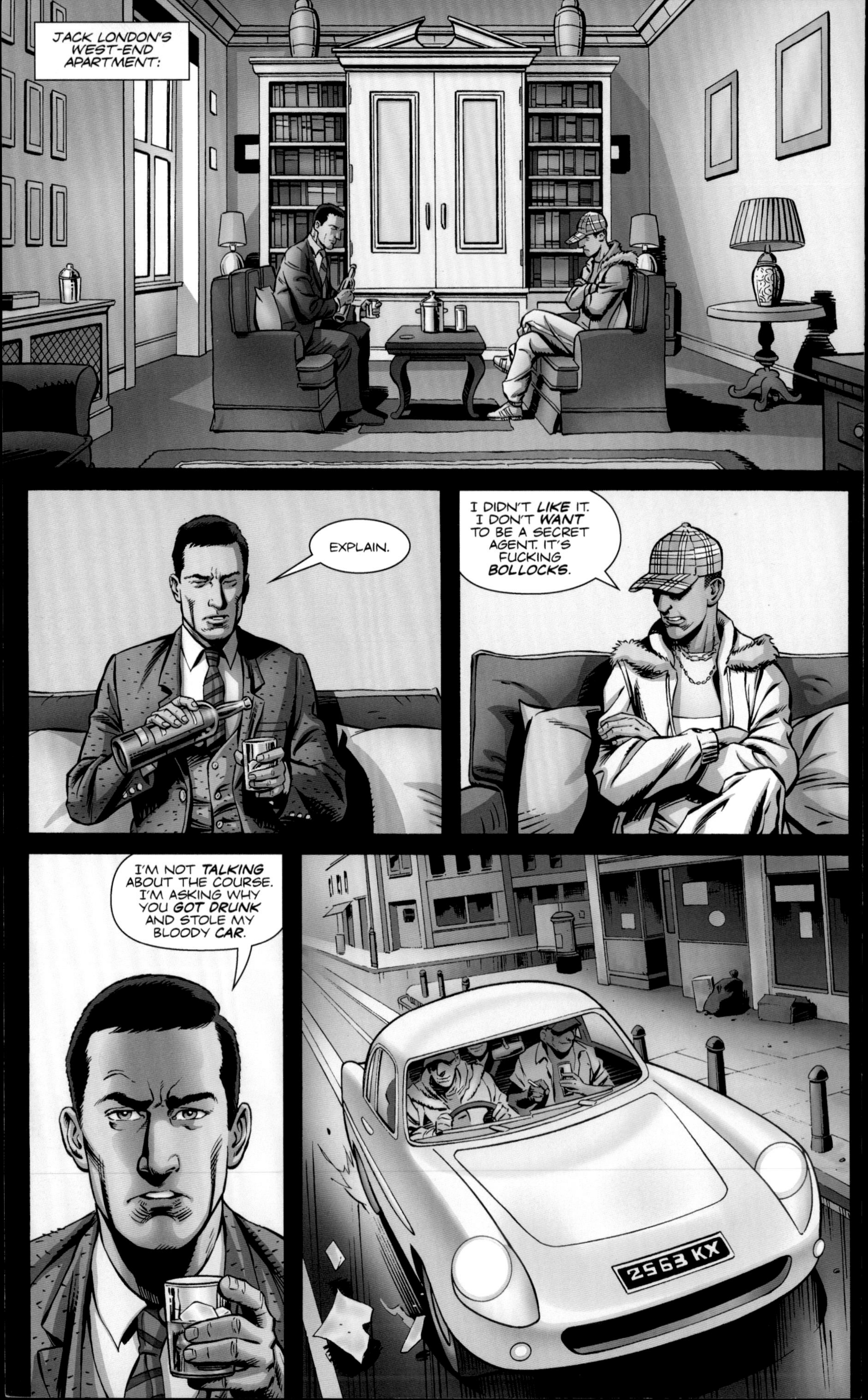
JACK LONDON'S WEST-END APARTMENT:
EXPLAIN.
I DIDN'T LIKE IT. I DON'T WANT TO BE A SECRET AGENT. IT'S FUCKING BOLLOCKS.
I'M NOT TALKING ABOUT THE COURSE. I'M ASKING WHY YOU GOT DRUNK AND STOLE MY BLOODY CAR.
2563 KX

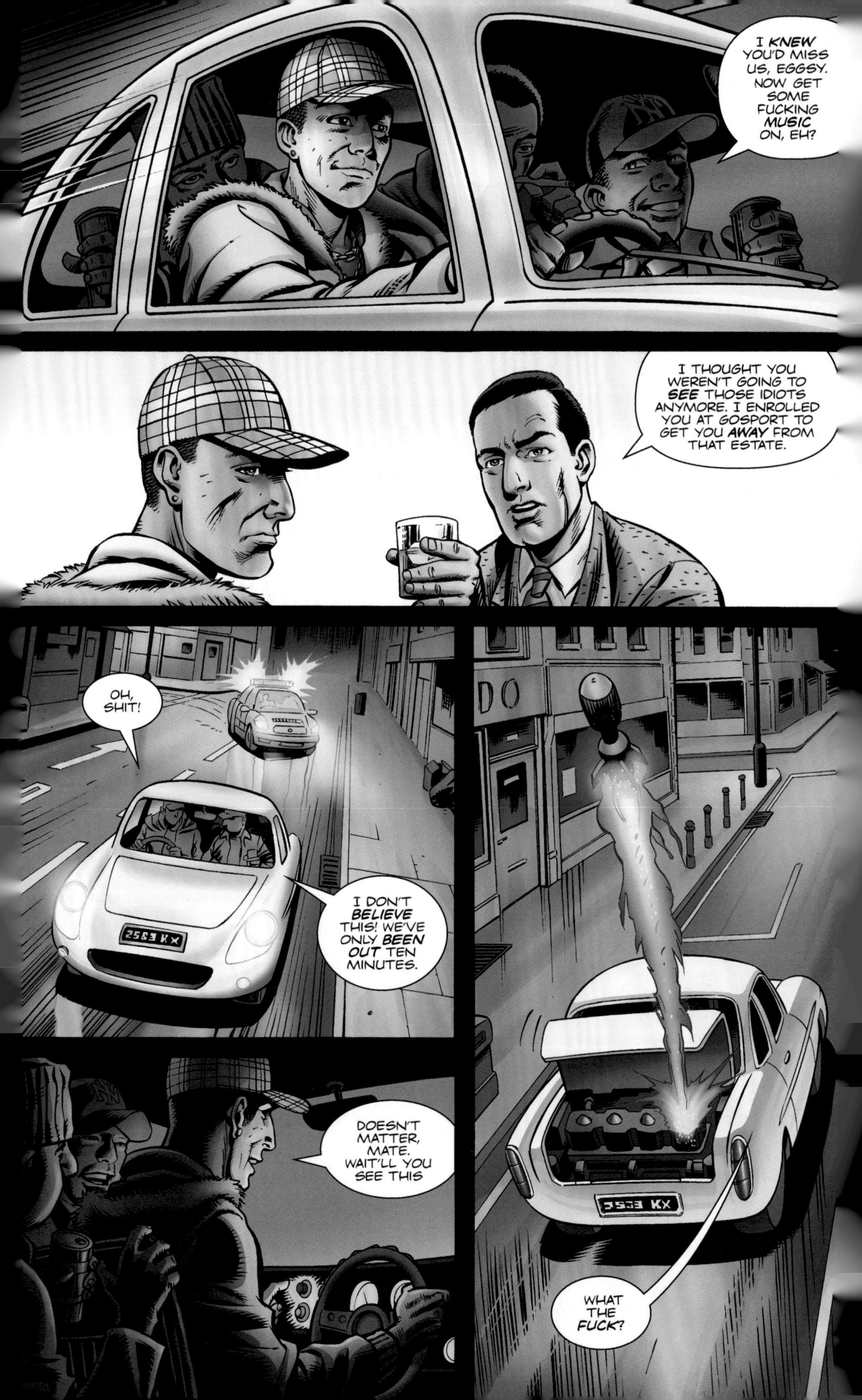
I KNEW YOU'D MISS US, EGGSY. NOW GET SOME FUCKING MUSIC ON, EH?
I THOUGHT YOU WEREN'T GOING TO SEE THOSE IDIOTS ANYMORE. I ENROLLED YOU AT GOSPORT TO GET YOU AWAY FROM THAT ESTATE.
OH, SHIT!
I DON'T BELIEVE THIS! WE'VE ONLY BEEN OUT TEN MINUTES.
DOESN'T MATTER, MATE. WAIT'LL YOU SEE THIS
WHAT THE FUCK?

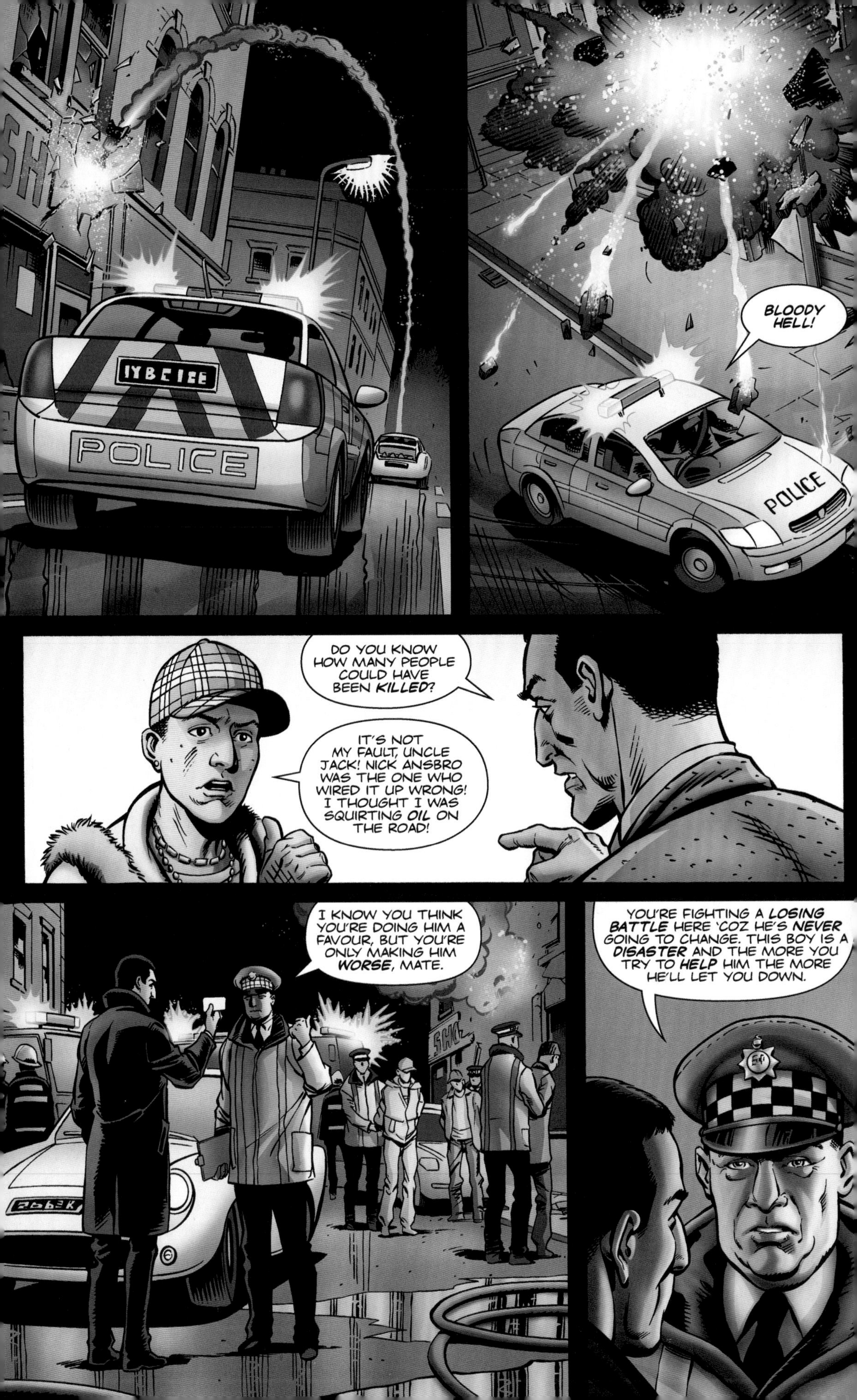

IYBCICE
POLICE
BLOODY HELL!
POLICE
DO YOU KNOW HOW MANY PEOPLE COULD HAVE BEEN **KILLED**?
IT'S NOT MY FAULT, UNCLE JACK! NICK ANSBRO WAS THE ONE WHO WIRED IT UP WRONG! I THOUGHT I WAS SQUIRTING **OIL** ON THE ROAD!
I KNOW YOU THINK YOU'RE DOING HIM A FAVOUR, BUT YOU'RE ONLY MAKING HIM **WORSE**, MATE.
YOU'RE FIGHTING A **LOSING BATTLE** HERE 'COZ HE'S **NEVER** GOING TO CHANGE. THIS BOY IS A **DISASTER** AND THE MORE YOU TRY TO **HELP** HIM THE MORE HE'LL LET YOU DOWN.

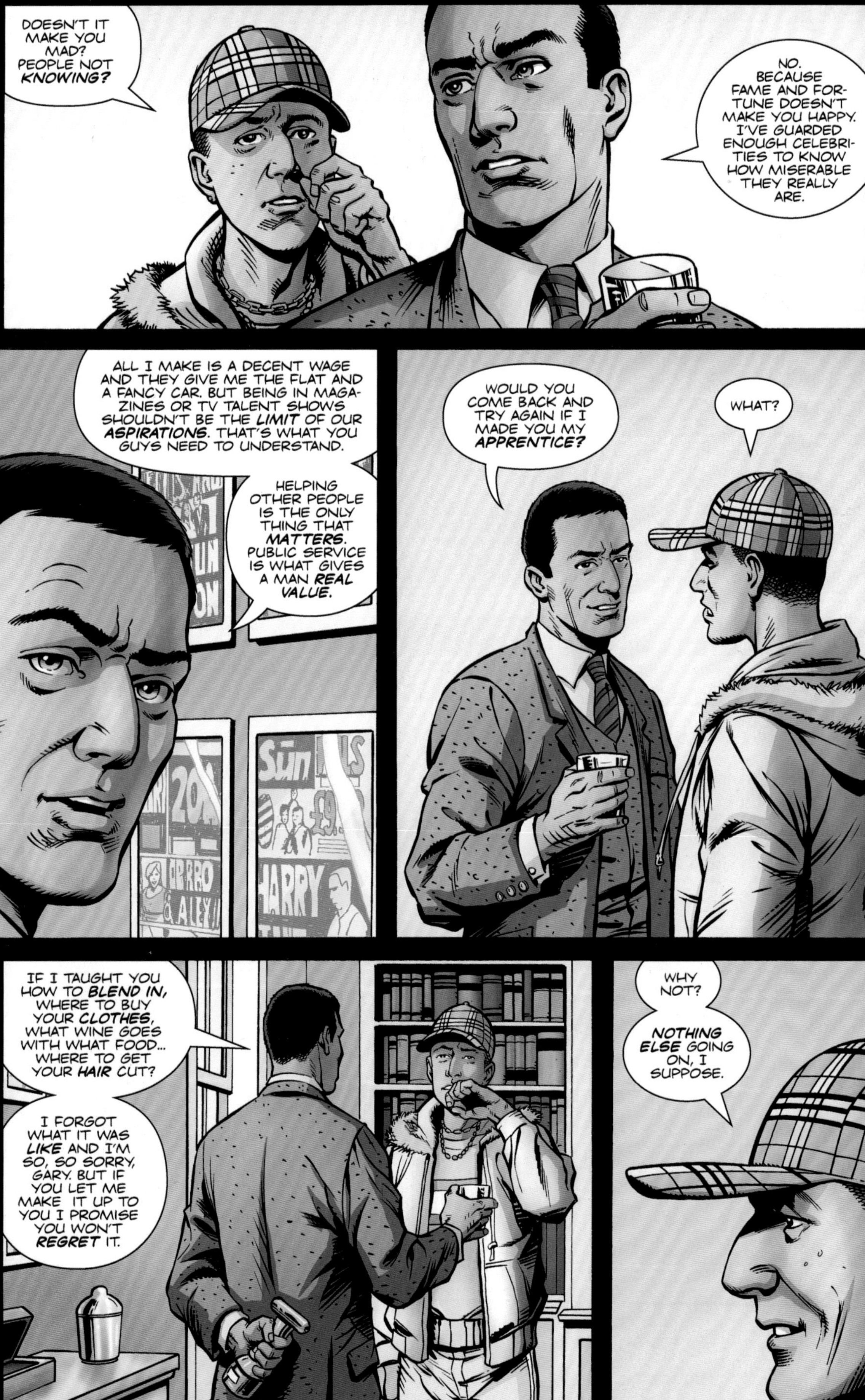

DOESN'T IT MAKE YOU MAD? PEOPLE NOT KNOWING?
NO. BECAUSE FAME AND FORTUNE DOESN'T MAKE YOU HAPPY. I'VE GUARDED ENOUGH CELEBRITIES TO KNOW HOW MISERABLE THEY REALLY ARE.
ALL I MAKE IS A DECENT WAGE AND THEY GIVE ME THE FLAT AND A FANCY CAR. BUT BEING IN MAGAZINES OR TV TALENT SHOWS SHOULDN'T BE THE LIMIT OF OUR ASPIRATIONS. THAT'S WHAT YOU GUYS NEED TO UNDERSTAND.
HELPING OTHER PEOPLE IS THE ONLY THING THAT MATTERS. PUBLIC SERVICE IS WHAT GIVES A MAN REAL VALUE.
WOULD YOU COME BACK AND TRY AGAIN IF I MADE YOU MY APPRENTICE?
WHAT?
IF I TAUGHT YOU HOW TO BLEND IN, WHERE TO BUY YOUR CLOTHES, WHAT WINE GOES WITH WHAT FOOD... WHERE TO GET YOUR HAIR CUT?
I FORGOT WHAT IT WAS LIKE AND I'M SO, SO SORRY, GARY. BUT IF YOU LET ME MAKE IT UP TO YOU I PROMISE YOU WON'T REGRET IT.
WHY NOT?
NOTHING ELSE GOING ON, I SUPPOSE.

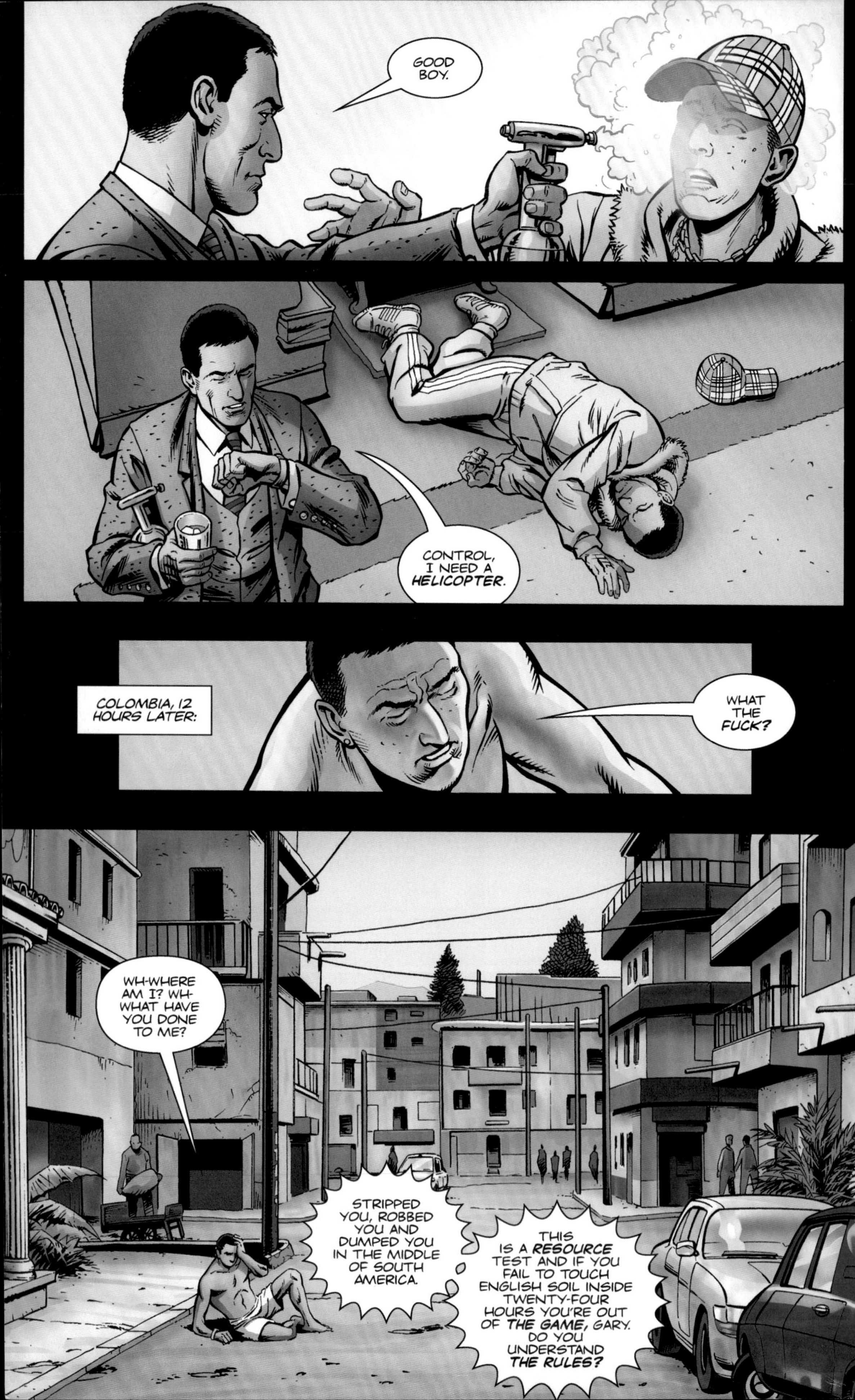
GOOD BOY.
CONTROL, I NEED A HELICOPTER.
COLOMBIA, 12 HOURS LATER:
WHAT THE FUCK?
WH-WHERE AM I? WH-WHAT HAVE YOU DONE TO ME?
STRIPPED YOU, ROBBED YOU AND DUMPED YOU IN THE MIDDLE OF SOUTH AMERICA.
THIS IS A RESOURCE TEST AND IF YOU FAIL TO TOUCH ENGLISH SOIL INSIDE TWENTY-FOUR HOURS YOU'RE OUT OF THE GAME, GARY. DO YOU UNDERSTAND THE RULES?

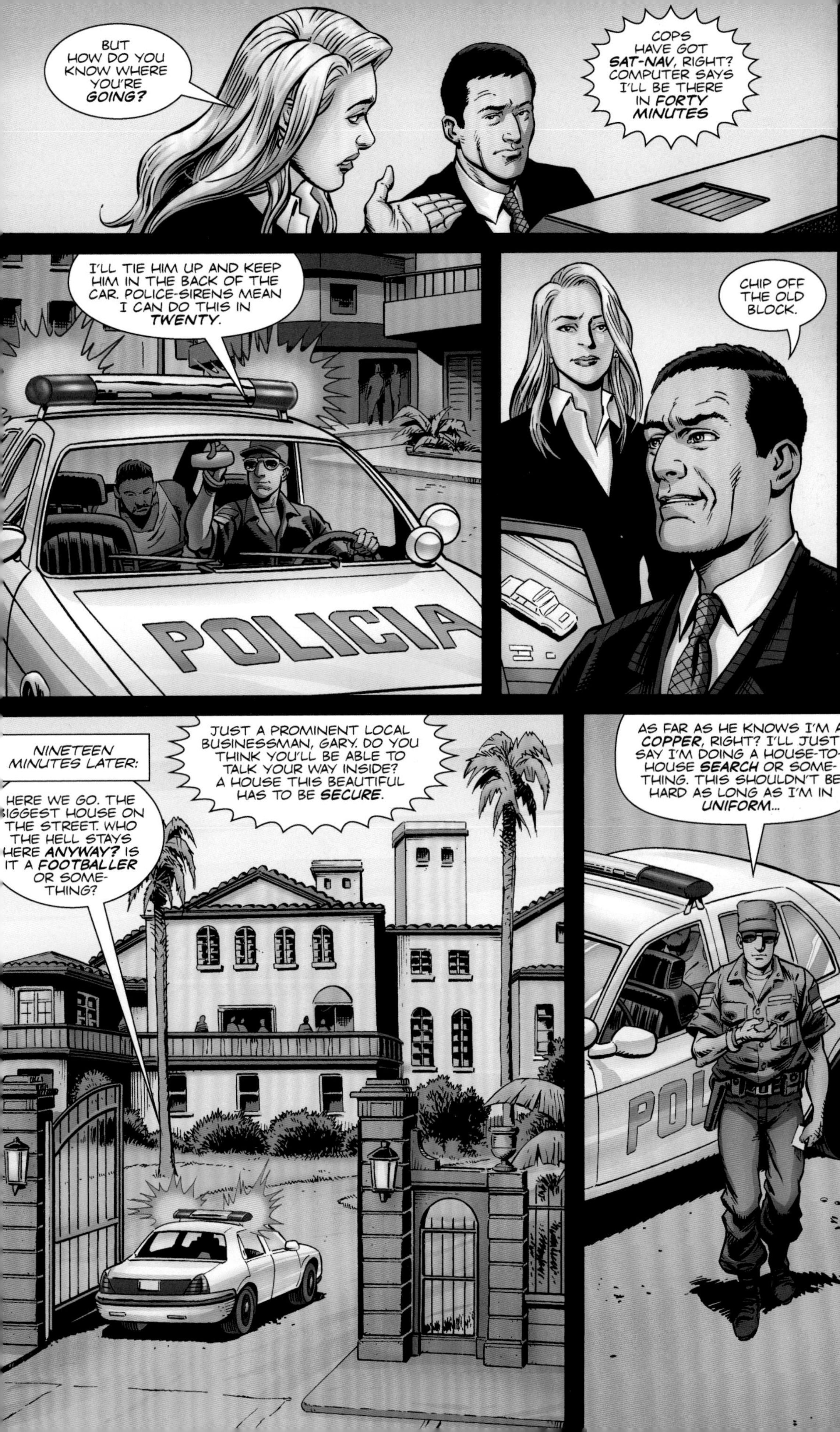

BUT HOW DO YOU KNOW WHERE YOU'RE ***GOING?***
COPS HAVE GOT **SAT-NAV**, RIGHT? COMPUTER SAYS I'LL BE THERE IN ***FORTY MINUTES***
I'LL TIE HIM UP AND KEEP HIM IN THE BACK OF THE CAR. POLICE-SIRENS MEAN I CAN DO THIS IN ***TWENTY***.
POLICIA
CHIP OFF THE OLD BLOCK.
NINETEEN MINUTES LATER:
HERE WE GO. THE BIGGEST HOUSE ON THE STREET. WHO THE HELL STAYS HERE ***ANYWAY?*** IS IT A ***FOOTBALLER*** OR SOMETHING?
JUST A PROMINENT LOCAL BUSINESSMAN, GARY. DO YOU THINK YOU'LL BE ABLE TO TALK YOUR WAY INSIDE? A HOUSE THIS BEAUTIFUL HAS TO BE ***SECURE***.
AS FAR AS HE KNOWS I'M A ***COPPER***, RIGHT? I'LL JUST SAY I'M DOING A HOUSE-TO-HOUSE ***SEARCH*** OR SOMETHING. THIS SHOULDN'T BE HARD AS LONG AS I'M IN ***UNIFORM***...

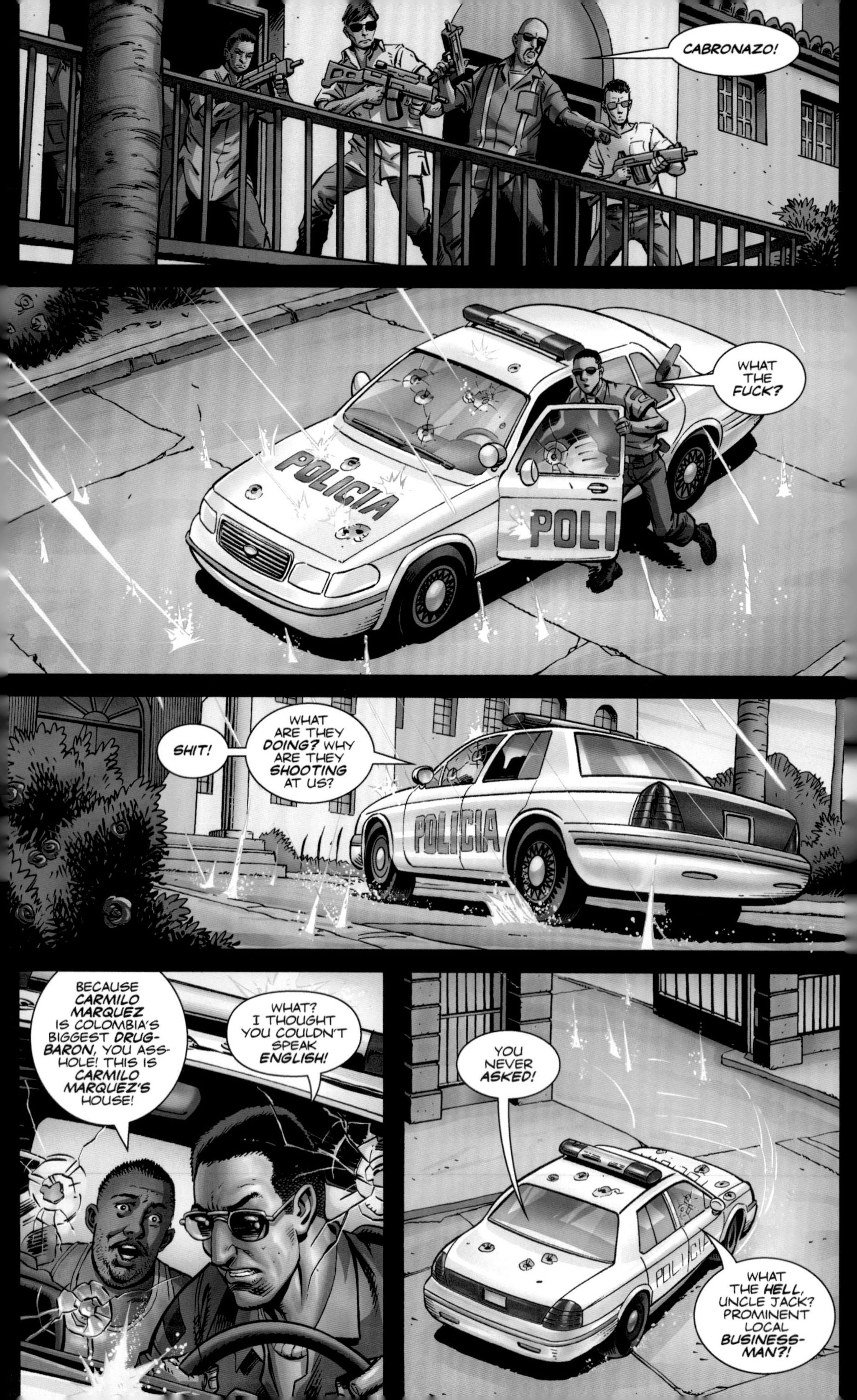
CABRONAZO!
WHAT THE FUCK?
POLICIA
POLI
SHIT!
WHAT ARE THEY DOING? WHY ARE THEY SHOOTING AT US?
POLICIA
BECAUSE CARMILO MARQUEZ IS COLOMBIA'S BIGGEST DRUG-BARON, YOU ASS-HOLE! THIS IS CARMILO MARQUEZ'S HOUSE!
WHAT? I THOUGHT YOU COULDN'T SPEAK ENGLISH!
YOU NEVER ASKED!
WHAT THE HELL, UNCLE JACK? PROMINENT LOCAL BUSINESS-MAN?!

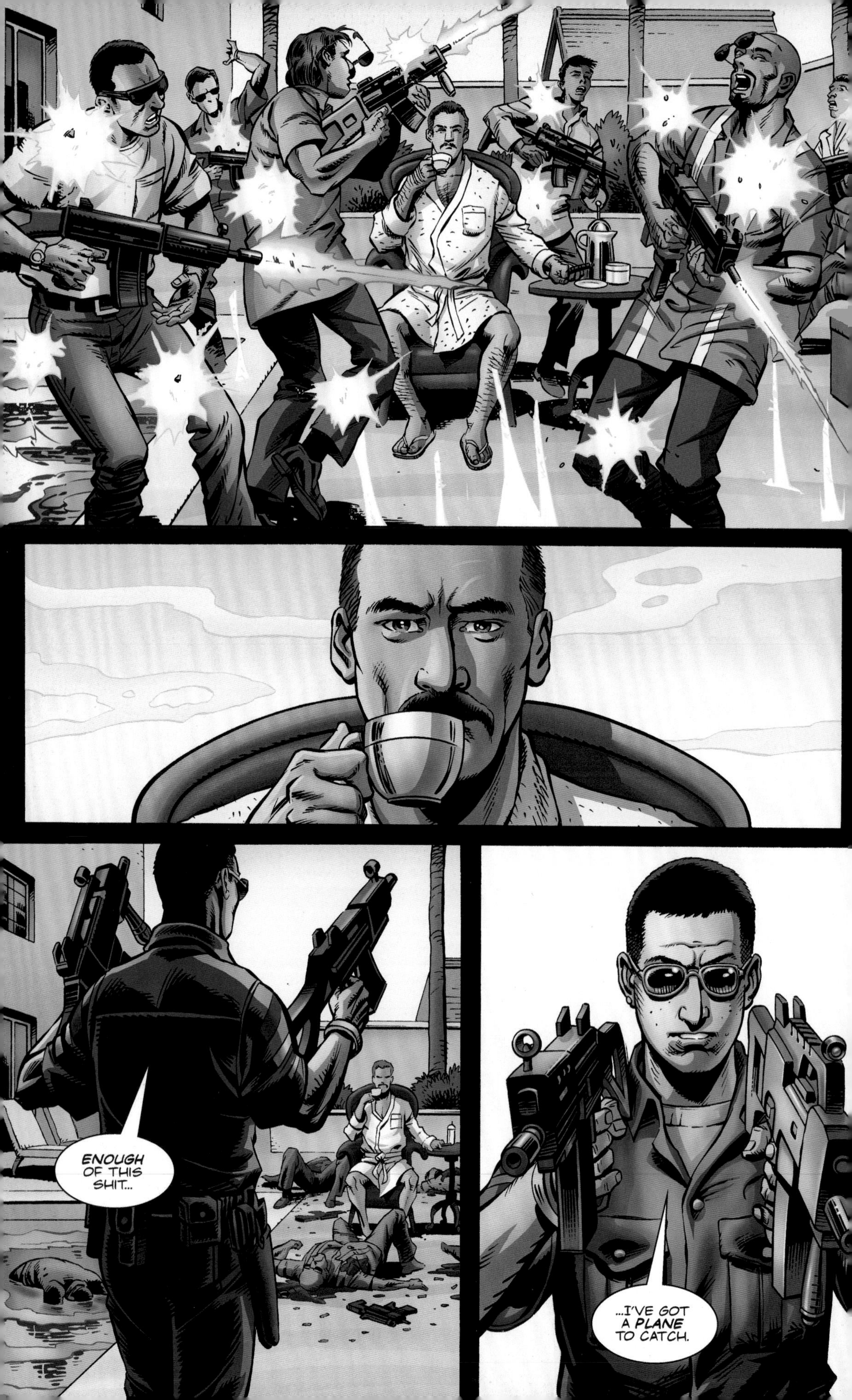
ENOUGH OF THIS SHIT...
...I'VE GOT A PLANE TO CATCH.

I RESPECT YOUR *FAITH* IN THIS GUY, BUT HE ISN'T GOING TO MAKE IT, JACK. I CHECKED THE PASSENGER LIST AND THERE'S NO GARY UNWIN.

SO MAYBE HE'S USING AN *ALIAS*.

WE CHECKED THE SECURITY TAPES AT THE AIRPORT TOO AND HE IS *NOT* ON THIS OR ANY OTHER FLIGHTS COMING IN.

I APPRECIATE YOU'RE TRYING TO HELP HIM HERE AND THE DEPARTMENT HAS BENT OVER BACKWARDS TO ACCOMMODATE...

...BUT HOW MANY LAST CHANCES SHOULD THIS GUY *HAVE*? WHEN DO WE ADMIT THAT HE MIGHT NOT BE *GOOD ENOUGH*?

HE'LL *BE* HERE, TERI. STOP *GRUMBLING*.

IT'S EIGHTY-FIVE HUNDRED KILOMETERS AND HE MISSED HIS *FLIGHT*. HOW THE HELL'S HE GOING TO BE HERE *NOW*?

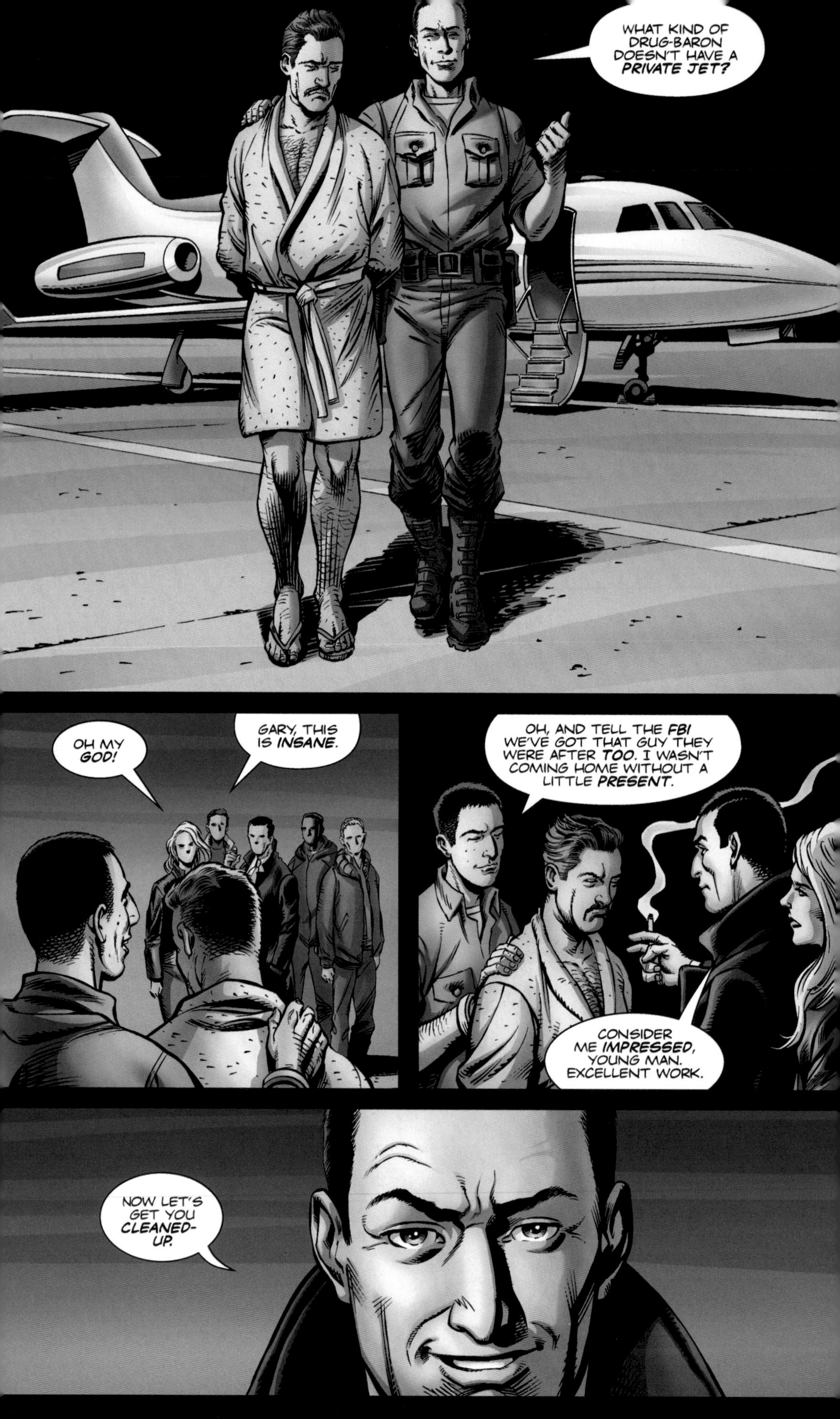
WHAT KIND OF DRUG-BARON DOESN'T HAVE A PRIVATE JET?
OH MY GOD!
GARY, THIS IS INSANE.
OH, AND TELL THE FBI WE'VE GOT THAT GUY THEY WERE AFTER TOO. I WASN'T COMING HOME WITHOUT A LITTLE PRESENT.
CONSIDER ME IMPRESSED, YOUNG MAN. EXCELLENT WORK.
NOW LET'S GET YOU CLEANED-UP.

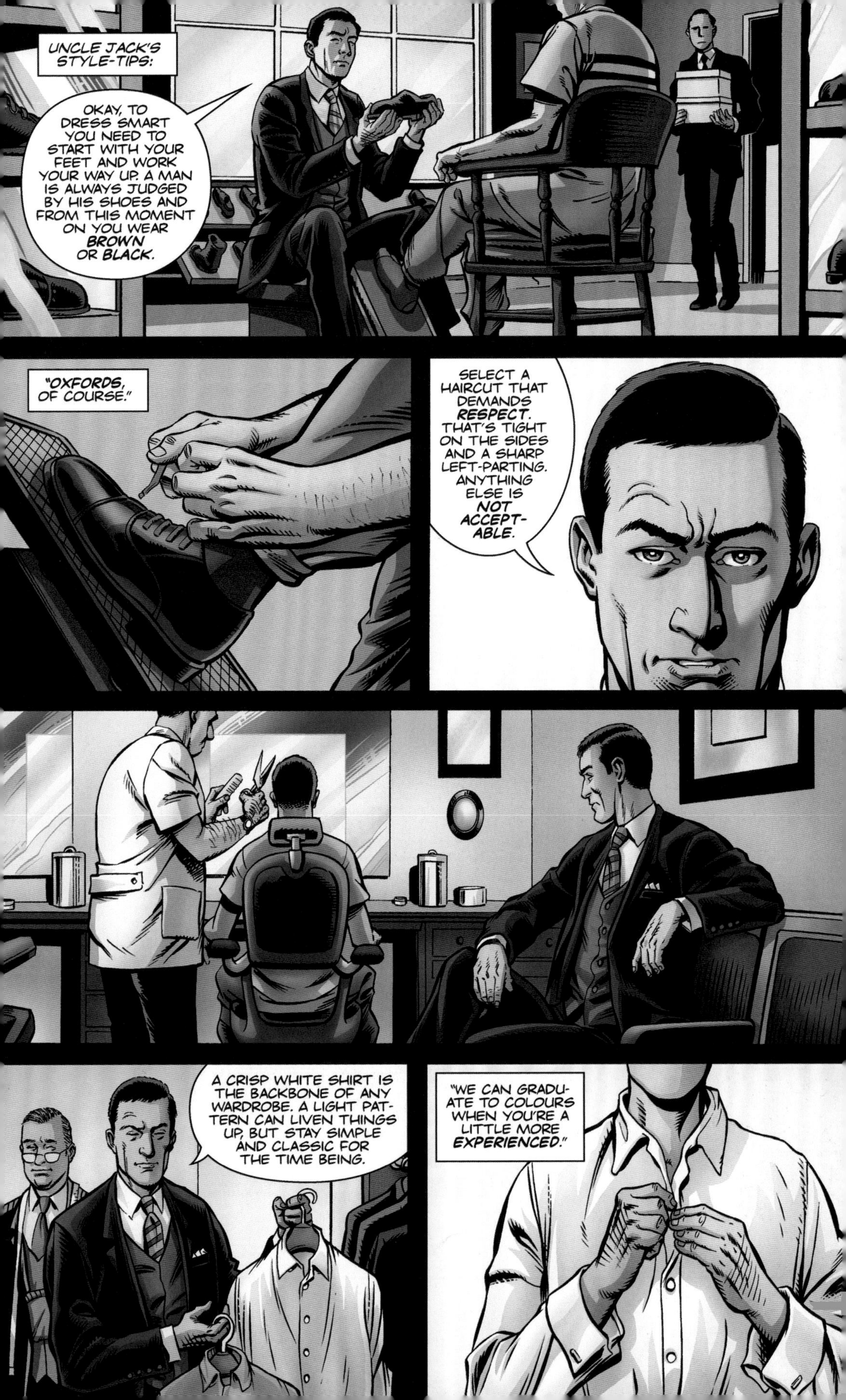
UNCLE JACK'S STYLE-TIPS:
OKAY, TO DRESS SMART YOU NEED TO START WITH YOUR FEET AND WORK YOUR WAY UP. A MAN IS ALWAYS JUDGED BY HIS SHOES AND FROM THIS MOMENT ON YOU WEAR BROWN OR BLACK.
"OXFORDS, OF COURSE."
SELECT A HAIRCUT THAT DEMANDS RESPECT. THAT'S TIGHT ON THE SIDES AND A SHARP LEFT-PARTING. ANYTHING ELSE IS NOT ACCEPT-ABLE.
A CRISP WHITE SHIRT IS THE BACKBONE OF ANY WARDROBE. A LIGHT PAT-TERN CAN LIVEN THINGS UP, BUT STAY SIMPLE AND CLASSIC FOR THE TIME BEING.
"WE CAN GRADU-ATE TO COLOURS WHEN YOU'RE A LITTLE MORE EXPERIENCED."

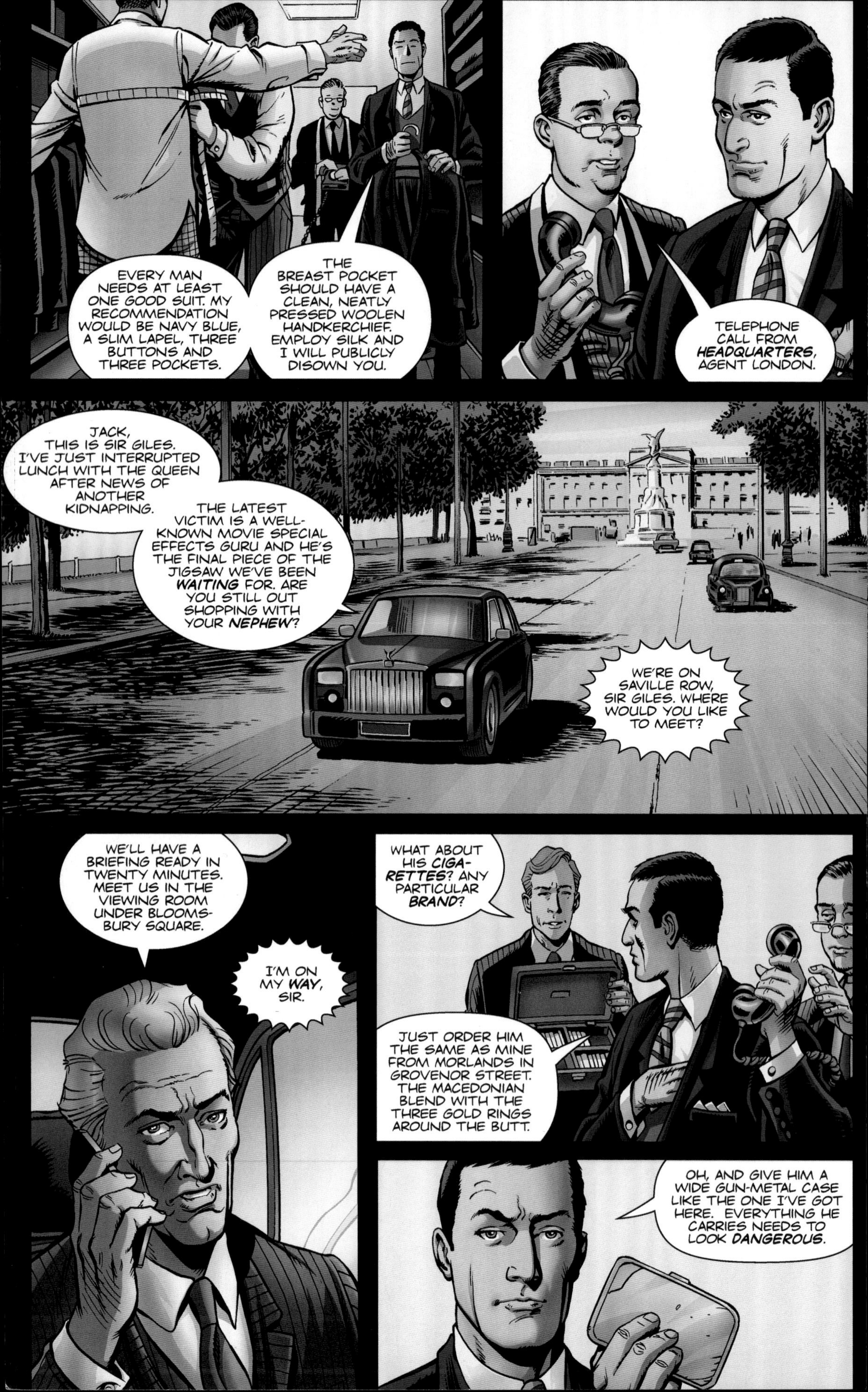
EVERY MAN NEEDS AT LEAST ONE GOOD SUIT. MY RECOMMENDATION WOULD BE NAVY BLUE, A SLIM LAPEL, THREE BUTTONS AND THREE POCKETS.
THE BREAST POCKET SHOULD HAVE A CLEAN, NEATLY PRESSED WOOLEN HANDKERCHIEF. EMPLOY SILK AND I WILL PUBLICLY DISOWN YOU.
TELEPHONE CALL FROM HEADQUARTERS, AGENT LONDON.
JACK, THIS IS SIR GILES. I'VE JUST INTERRUPTED LUNCH WITH THE QUEEN AFTER NEWS OF ANOTHER KIDNAPPING.
THE LATEST VICTIM IS A WELL-KNOWN MOVIE SPECIAL EFFECTS GURU AND HE'S THE FINAL PIECE OF THE JIGSAW WE'VE BEEN WAITING FOR. ARE YOU STILL OUT SHOPPING WITH YOUR NEPHEW?
WE'RE ON SAVILLE ROW, SIR GILES. WHERE WOULD YOU LIKE TO MEET?
WE'LL HAVE A BRIEFING READY IN TWENTY MINUTES. MEET US IN THE VIEWING ROOM UNDER BLOOMSBURY SQUARE.
I'M ON MY WAY, SIR.
WHAT ABOUT HIS CIGARETTES? ANY PARTICULAR BRAND?
JUST ORDER HIM THE SAME AS MINE FROM MORLANDS IN GROVENOR STREET. THE MACEDONIAN BLEND WITH THE THREE GOLD RINGS AROUND THE BUTT.
OH, AND GIVE HIM A WIDE GUN-METAL CASE LIKE THE ONE I'VE GOT HERE. EVERYTHING HE CARRIES NEEDS TO LOOK DANGEROUS.

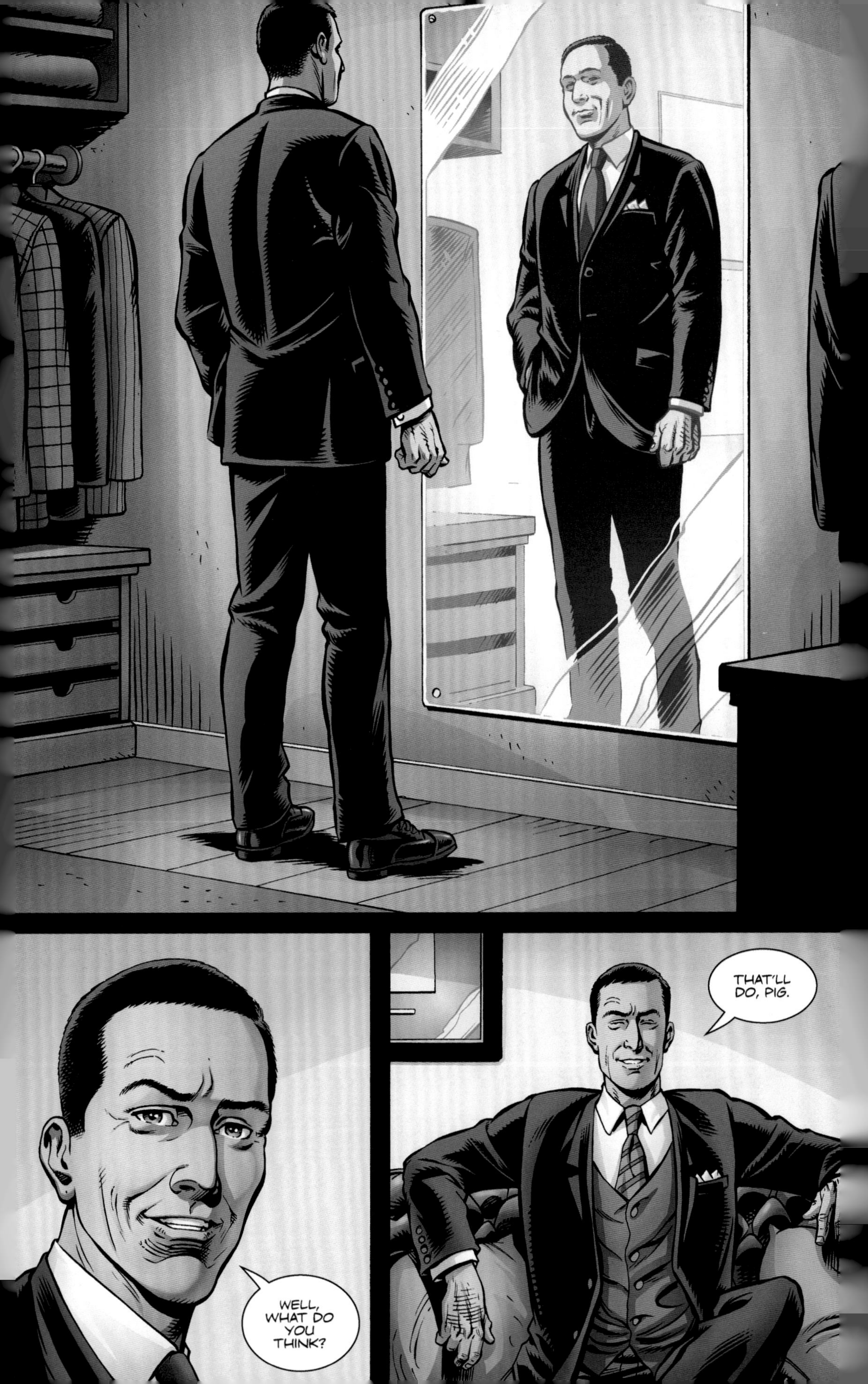
WELL, WHAT DO YOU THINK?
THAT'LL DO, PIG.

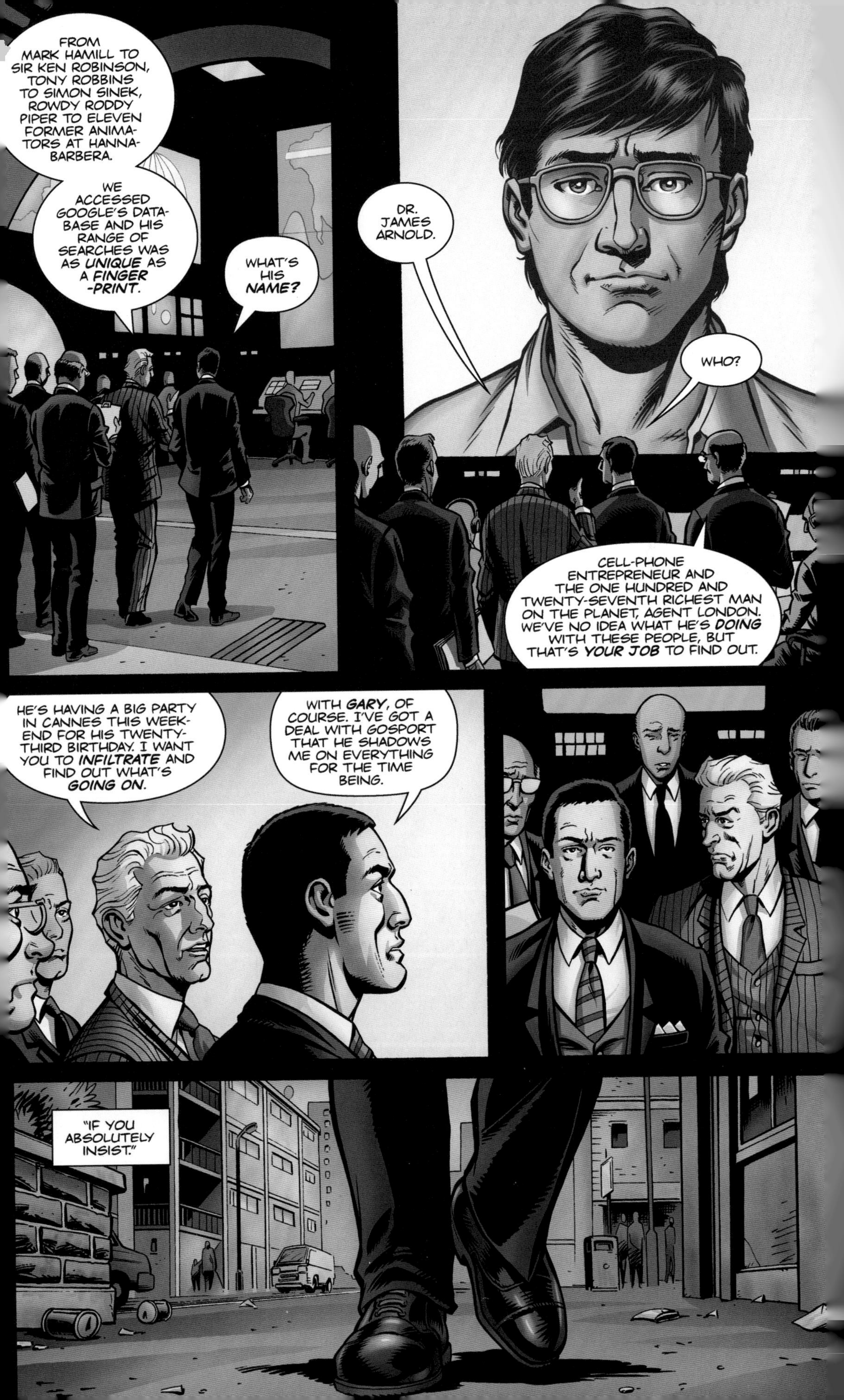
FROM MARK HAMILL TO SIR KEN ROBINSON, TONY ROBBINS TO SIMON SINEK, ROWDY RODDY PIPER TO ELEVEN FORMER ANIMATORS AT HANNA-BARBERA.
WE ACCESSED GOOGLE'S DATABASE AND HIS RANGE OF SEARCHES WAS AS UNIQUE AS A FINGERPRINT.
WHAT'S HIS NAME?
DR. JAMES ARNOLD.
WHO?
CELL-PHONE ENTREPRENEUR AND THE ONE HUNDRED AND TWENTY-SEVENTH RICHEST MAN ON THE PLANET, AGENT LONDON. WE'VE NO IDEA WHAT HE'S DOING WITH THESE PEOPLE, BUT THAT'S YOUR JOB TO FIND OUT.
HE'S HAVING A BIG PARTY IN CANNES THIS WEEKEND FOR HIS TWENTY-THIRD BIRTHDAY. I WANT YOU TO INFILTRATE AND FIND OUT WHAT'S GOING ON.
WITH GARY, OF COURSE. I'VE GOT A DEAL WITH GOSPORT THAT HE SHADOWS ME ON EVERYTHING FOR THE TIME BEING.
"IF YOU ABSOLUTELY INSIST."

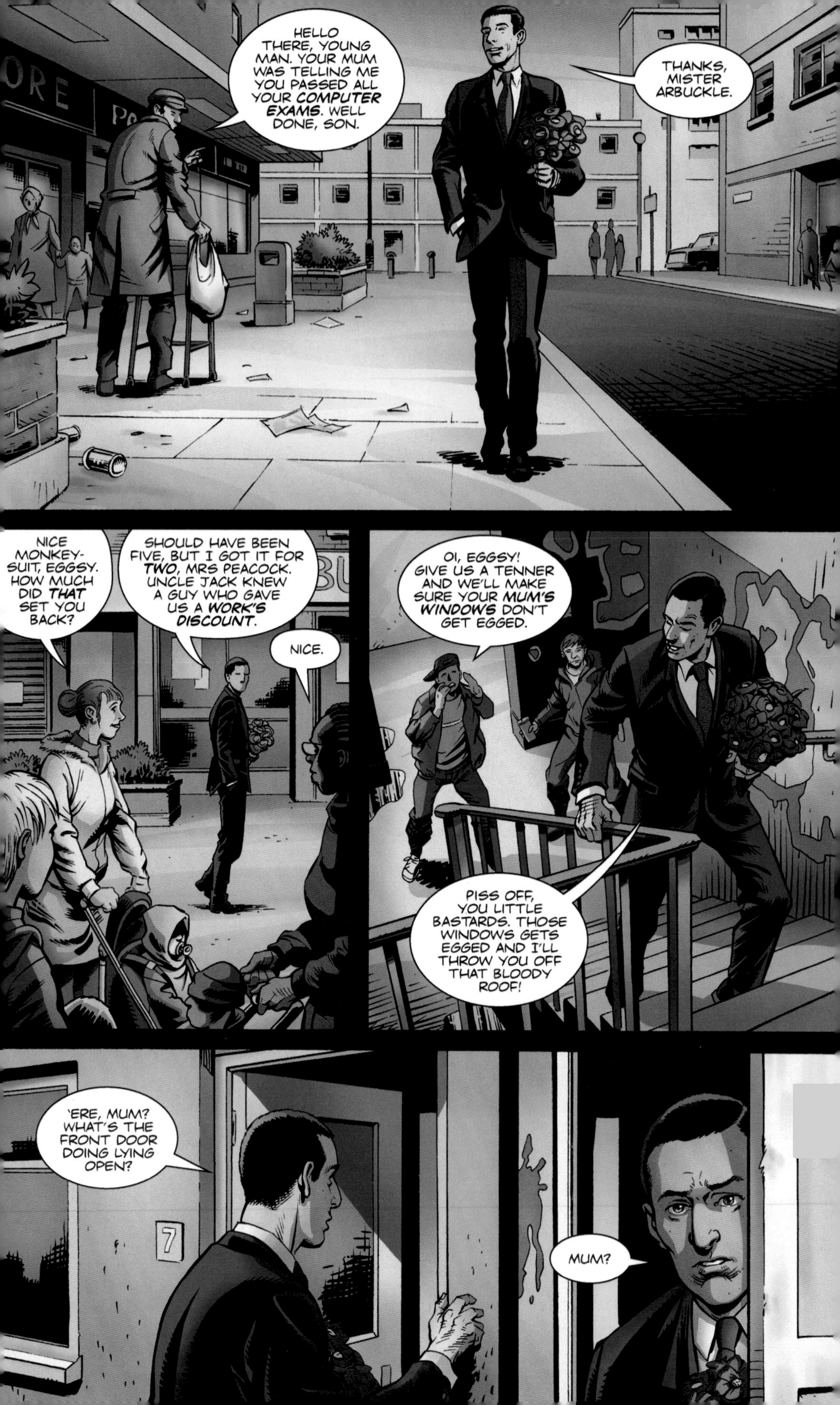
HELLO THERE, YOUNG MAN. YOUR MUM WAS TELLING ME YOU PASSED ALL YOUR **COMPUTER EXAMS**. WELL DONE, SON.
THANKS, MISTER ARBUCKLE.
NICE MONKEY-SUIT, EGGSY. HOW MUCH DID **THAT** SET YOU BACK?
SHOULD HAVE BEEN FIVE, BUT I GOT IT FOR **TWO**, MRS PEACOCK. UNCLE JACK KNEW A GUY WHO GAVE US A **WORK'S DISCOUNT**.
NICE.
OI, EGGSY! GIVE US A TENNER AND WE'LL MAKE SURE YOUR **MUM'S WINDOWS** DON'T GET EGGED.
PISS OFF, YOU LITTLE BASTARDS. THOSE WINDOWS GETS EGGED AND I'LL THROW YOU OFF THAT BLOODY ROOF!
'ERE, MUM? WHAT'S THE FRONT DOOR DOING LYING OPEN?
7
MUM?

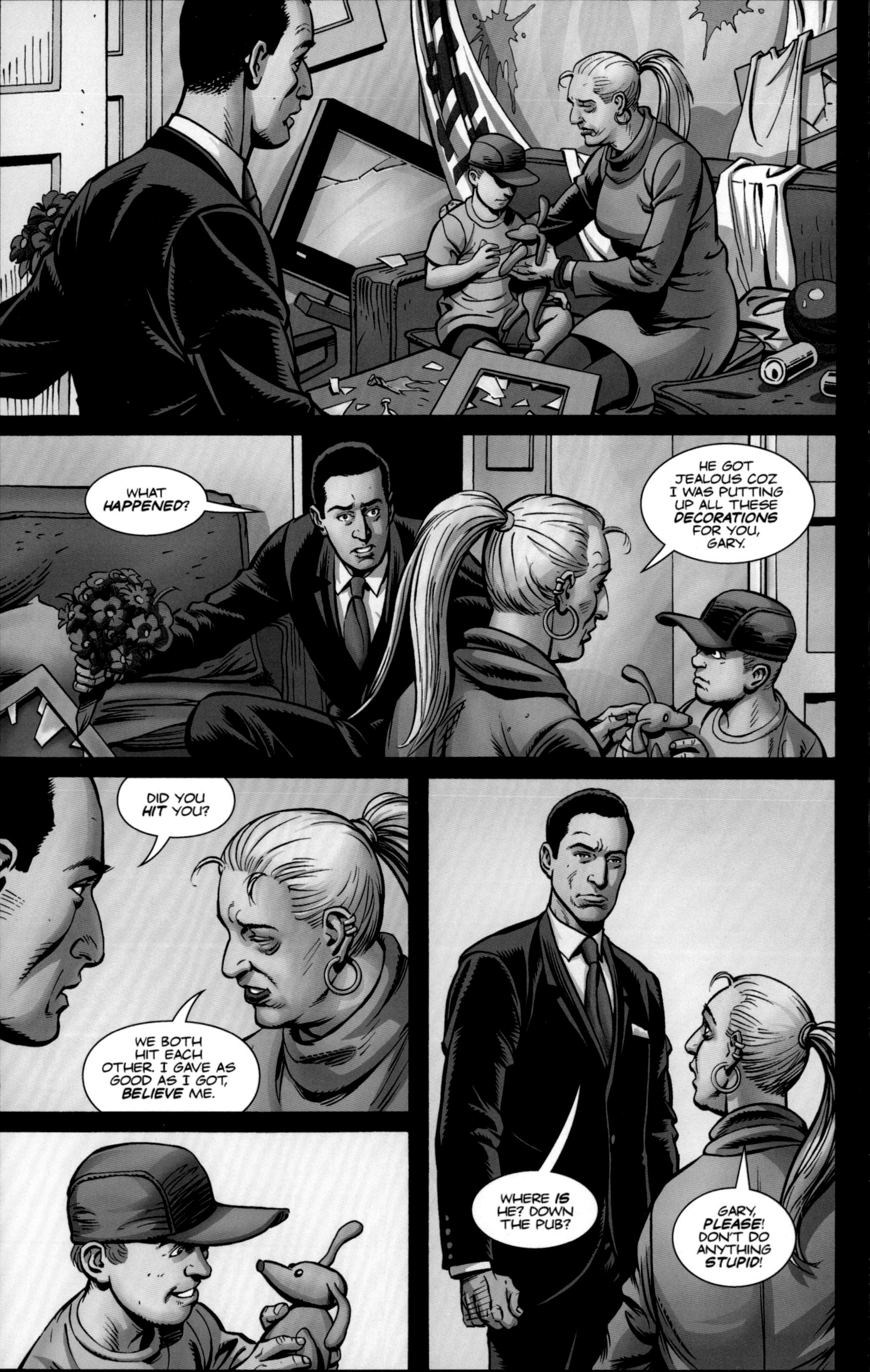
WHAT HAPPENED?
HE GOT JEALOUS COZ I WAS PUTTING UP ALL THESE DECORATIONS FOR YOU, GARY.
DID YOU HIT YOU?
WE BOTH HIT EACH OTHER. I GAVE AS GOOD AS I GOT, BELIEVE ME.
WHERE IS HE? DOWN THE PUB?
GARY, PLEASE! DON'T DO ANYTHING STUPID!

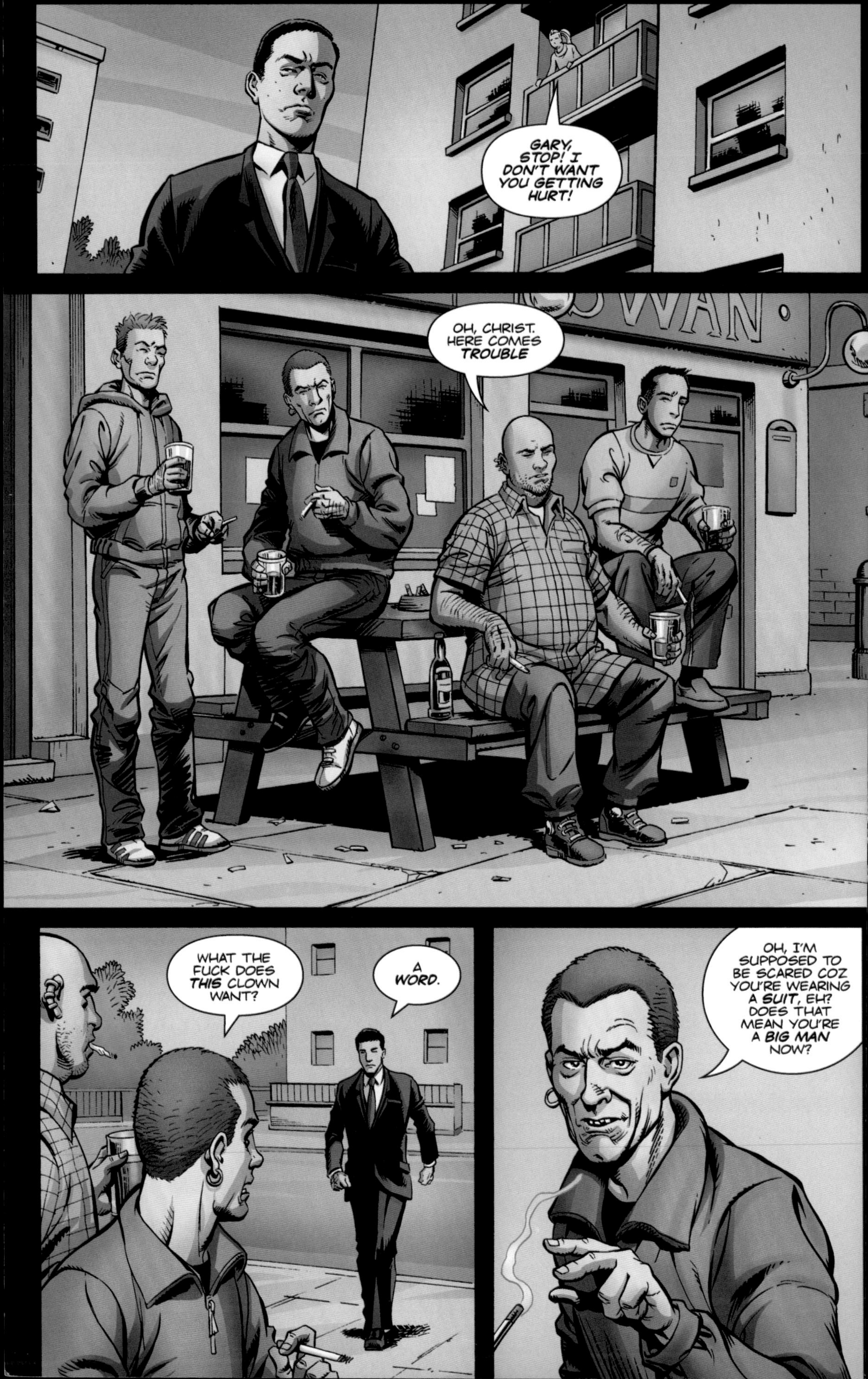
GARY, STOP! I DON'T WANT YOU GETTING HURT!
WAN
OH, CHRIST. HERE COMES TROUBLE
WHAT THE FUCK DOES THIS CLOWN WANT?
A WORD.
OH, I'M SUPPOSED TO BE SCARED COZ YOU'RE WEARING A SUIT, EH? DOES THAT MEAN YOU'RE A BIG MAN NOW?

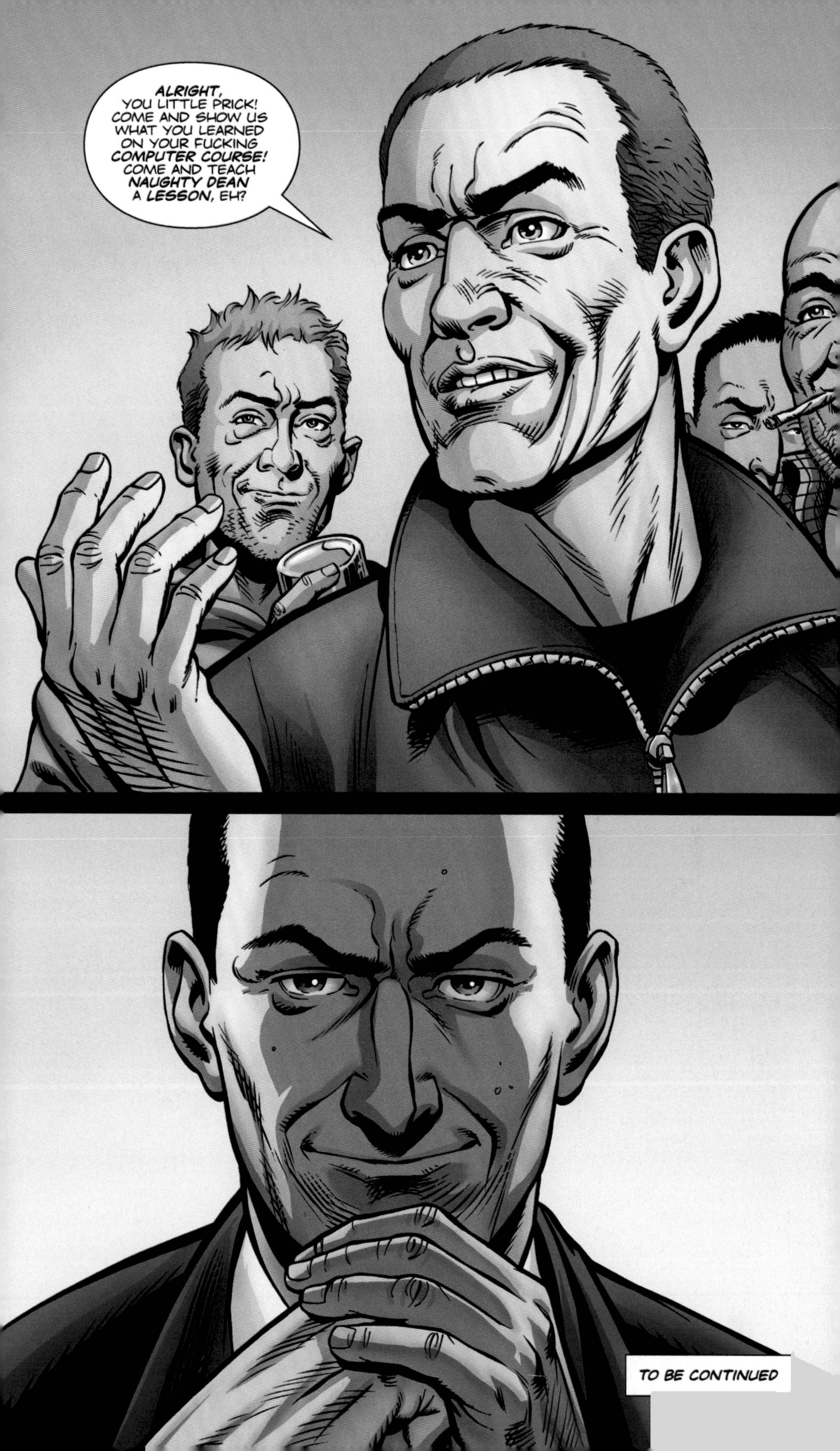
ALRIGHT, YOU LITTLE PRICK! COME AND SHOW US WHAT YOU LEARNED ON YOUR FUCKING COMPUTER COURSE! COME AND TEACH NAUGHTY DEAN A LESSON, EH?
TO BE CONTINUED

FIVE

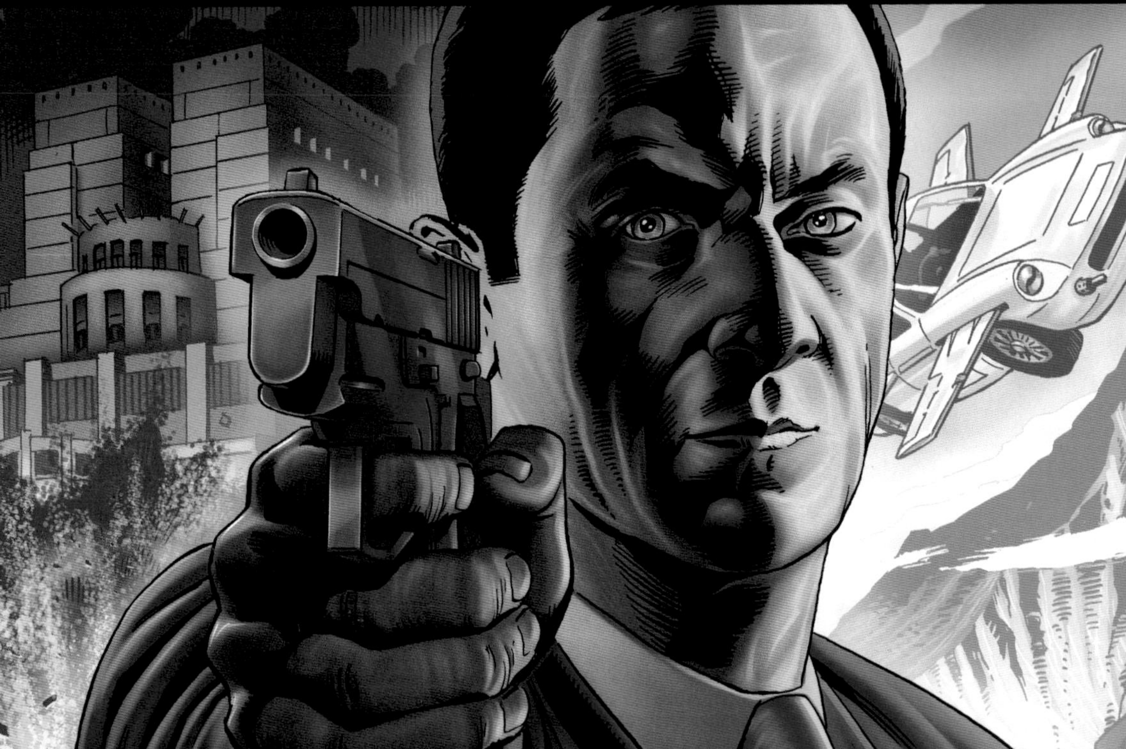

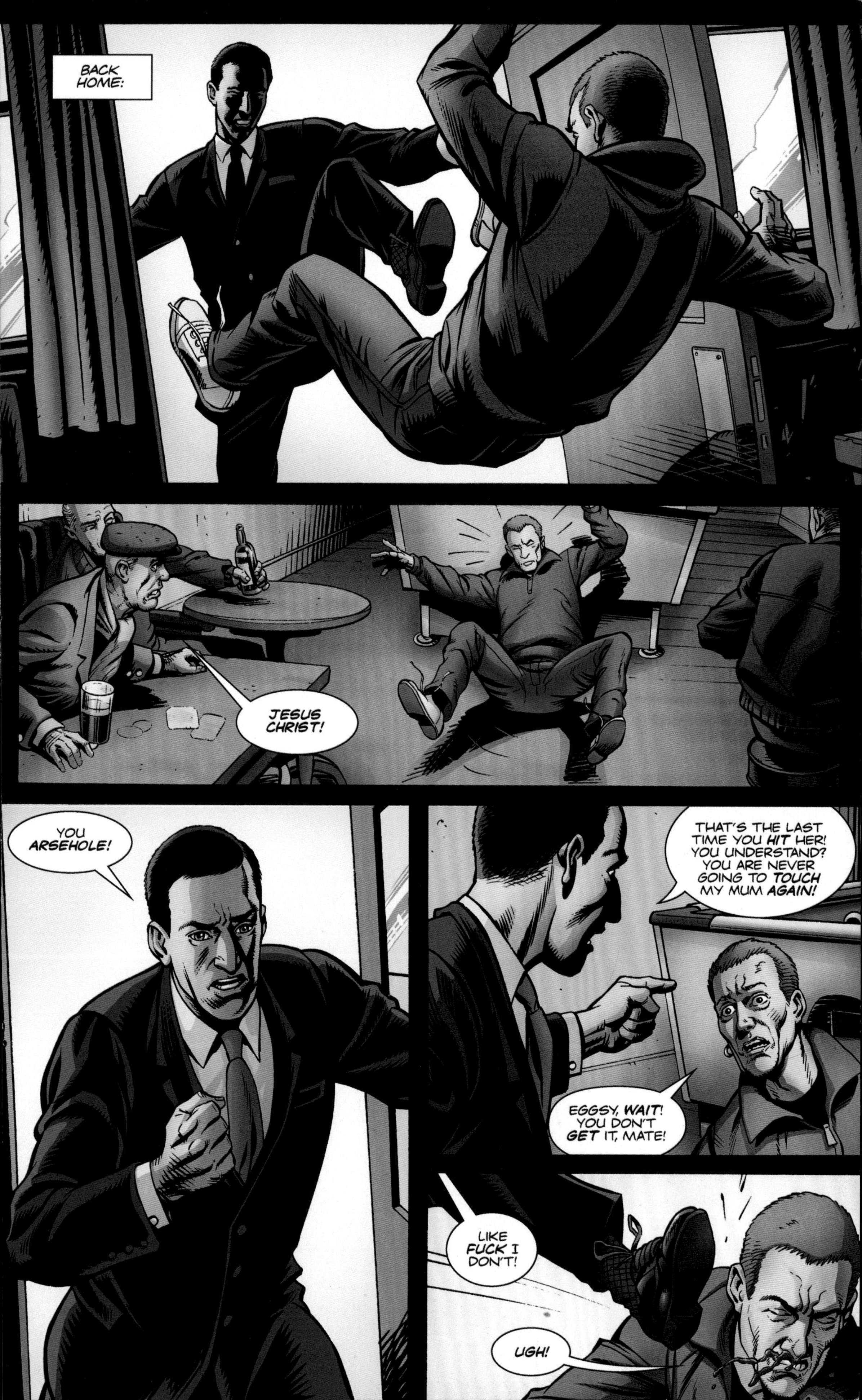
BACK HOME:
JESUS CHRIST!
YOU ARSEHOLE!
THAT'S THE LAST TIME YOU HIT HER! YOU UNDERSTAND? YOU ARE NEVER GOING TO TOUCH MY MUM AGAIN!
EGGSY, WAIT! YOU DON'T GET IT, MATE!
LIKE FUCK I DON'T!
UGH!

MAN, DID I REALLY USED TO BE **SCARED** OF YOU IDIOTS?

WHAT THE **HELL?**

OW!

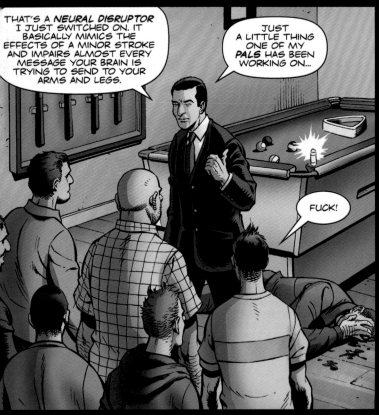

THAT'S A **NEURAL DISRUPTOR** I JUST SWITCHED ON. IT BASICALLY MIMICS THE EFFECTS OF A MINOR STROKE AND IMPAIRS ALMOST EVERY MESSAGE YOUR BRAIN IS TRYING TO SEND TO YOUR ARMS AND LEGS.

JUST A LITTLE THING ONE OF MY **PALS** HAS BEEN WORKING ON...

FUCK!

THE EFFECTS ARE **TEMPORARY,** YOU'LL BE HAPPY TO HEAR, BUT FOR THE NEXT THREE MINUTES YOU'VE PRETTY MUCH BEEN IM-MOBILIZED.

WH-WHAT?

THREE MINUTES BEING ALL I'M GOING TO **NEED...**

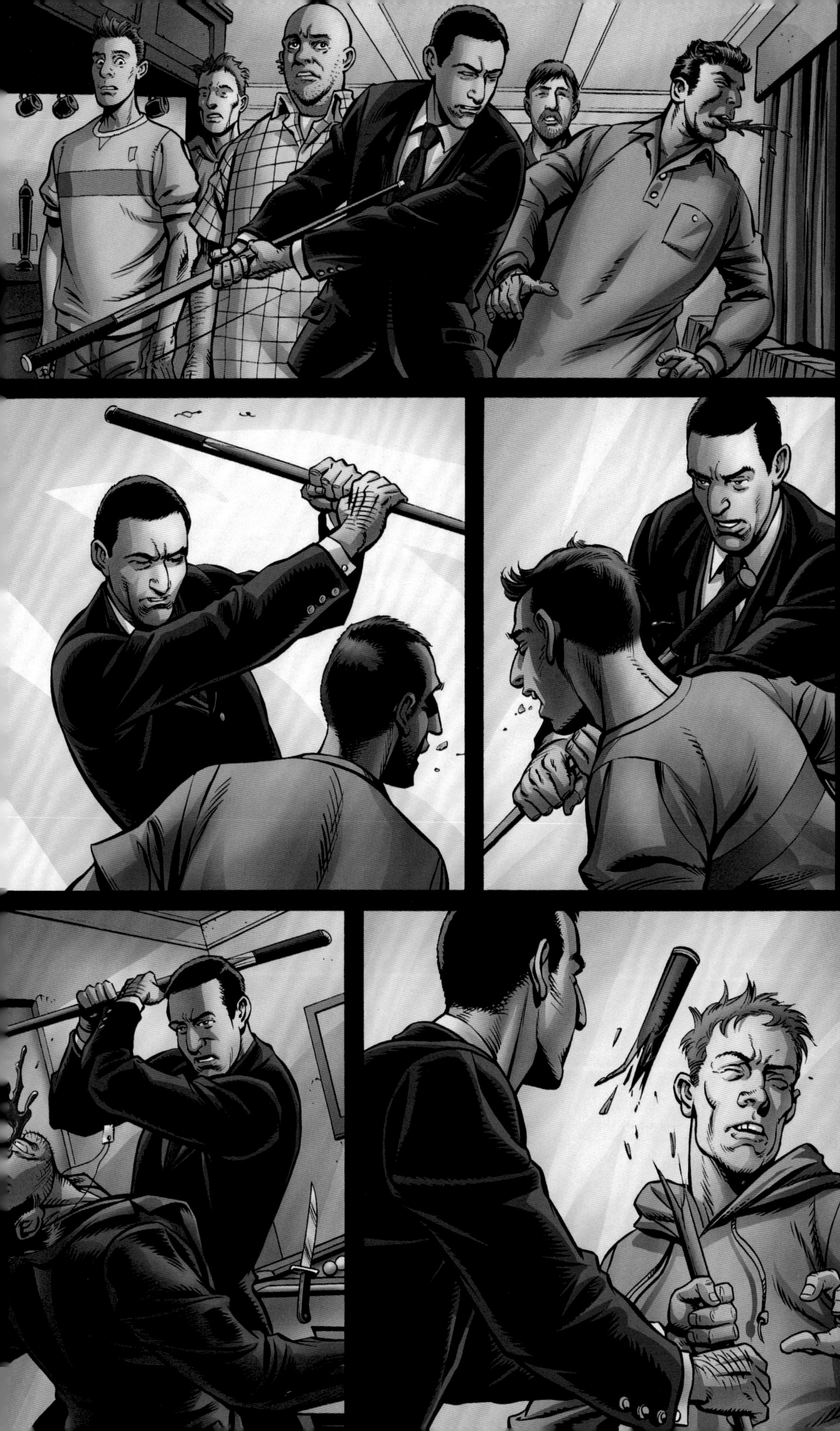

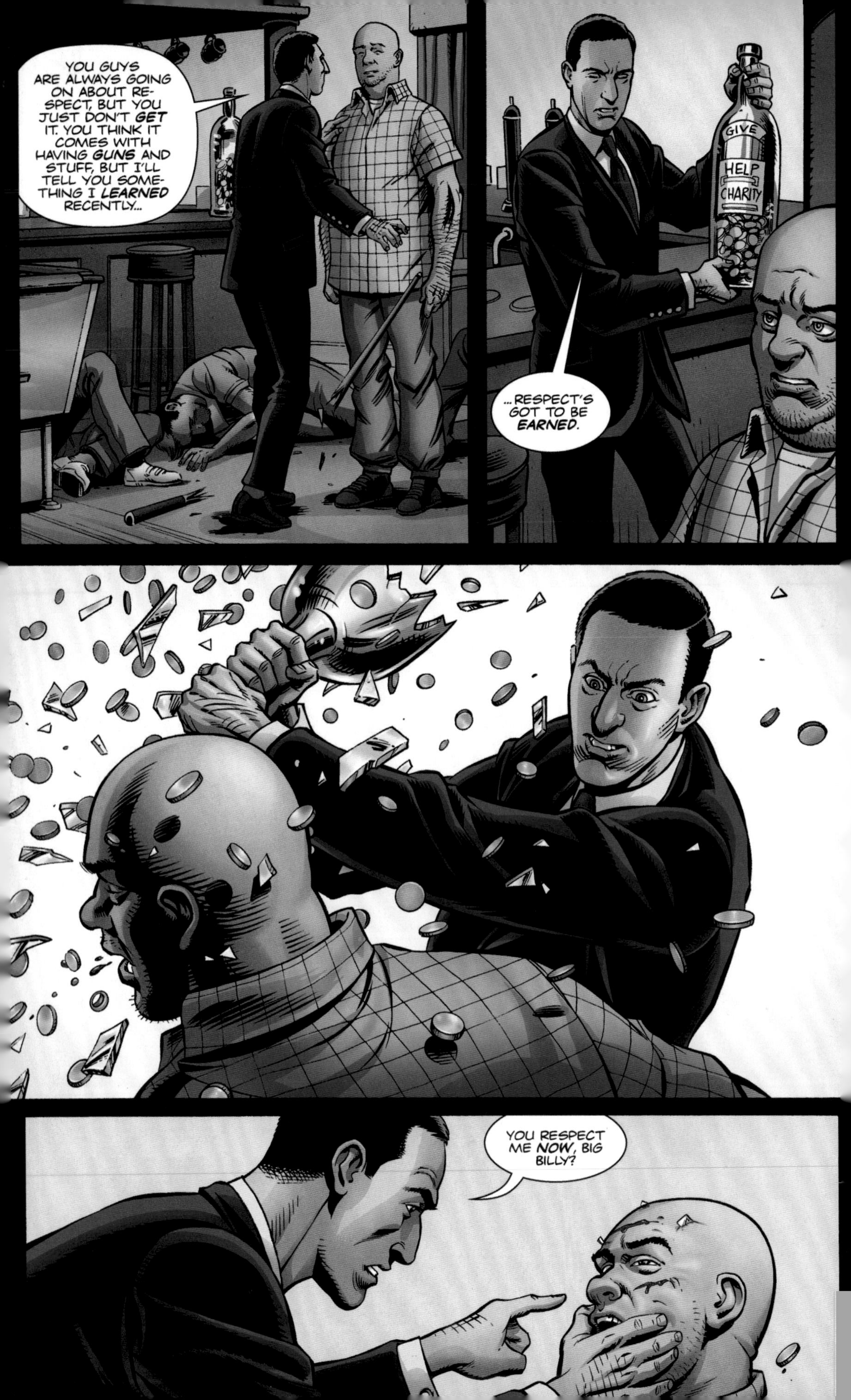
YOU GUYS ARE ALWAYS GOING ON ABOUT RE-SPECT, BUT YOU JUST DON'T GET IT. YOU THINK IT COMES WITH HAVING GUNS AND STUFF, BUT I'LL TELL YOU SOME-THING I LEARNED RECENTLY...
GIVE
HELP
CHARITY
...RESPECT'S GOT TO BE EARNED.
YOU RESPECT ME NOW, BIG BILLY?

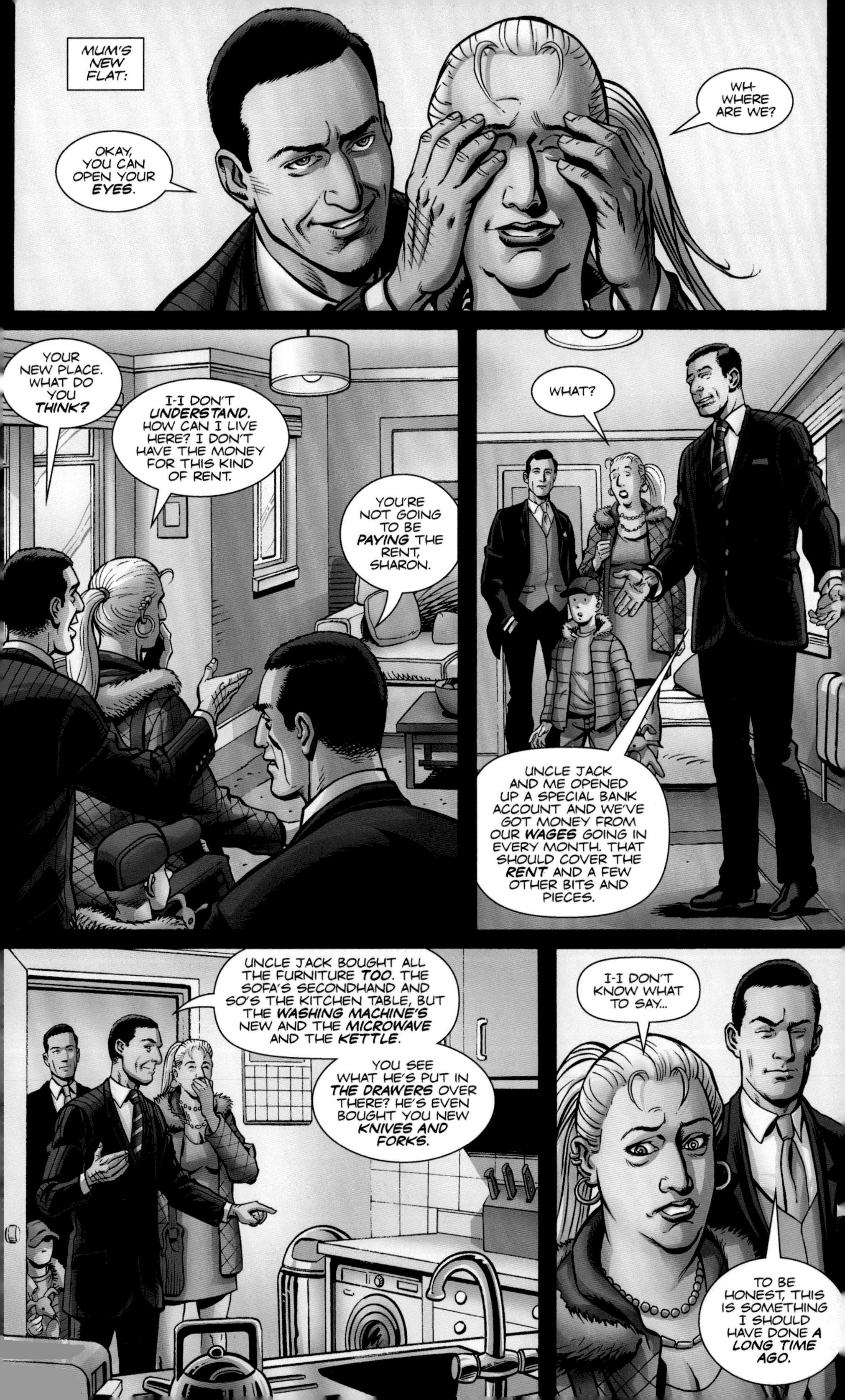
MUM'S NEW FLAT:
OKAY, YOU CAN OPEN YOUR EYES.
WH- WHERE ARE WE?
YOUR NEW PLACE. WHAT DO YOU THINK?
I-I DON'T UNDERSTAND. HOW CAN I LIVE HERE? I DON'T HAVE THE MONEY FOR THIS KIND OF RENT.
YOU'RE NOT GOING TO BE PAYING THE RENT, SHARON.
WHAT?
UNCLE JACK AND ME OPENED UP A SPECIAL BANK ACCOUNT AND WE'VE GOT MONEY FROM OUR WAGES GOING IN EVERY MONTH. THAT SHOULD COVER THE RENT AND A FEW OTHER BITS AND PIECES.
UNCLE JACK BOUGHT ALL THE FURNITURE TOO. THE SOFA'S SECONDHAND AND SO'S THE KITCHEN TABLE, BUT THE WASHING MACHINE'S NEW AND THE MICROWAVE AND THE KETTLE.
YOU SEE WHAT HE'S PUT IN THE DRAWERS OVER THERE? HE'S EVEN BOUGHT YOU NEW KNIVES AND FORKS.
I-I DON'T KNOW WHAT TO SAY...
TO BE HONEST, THIS IS SOMETHING I SHOULD HAVE DONE A LONG TIME AGO.

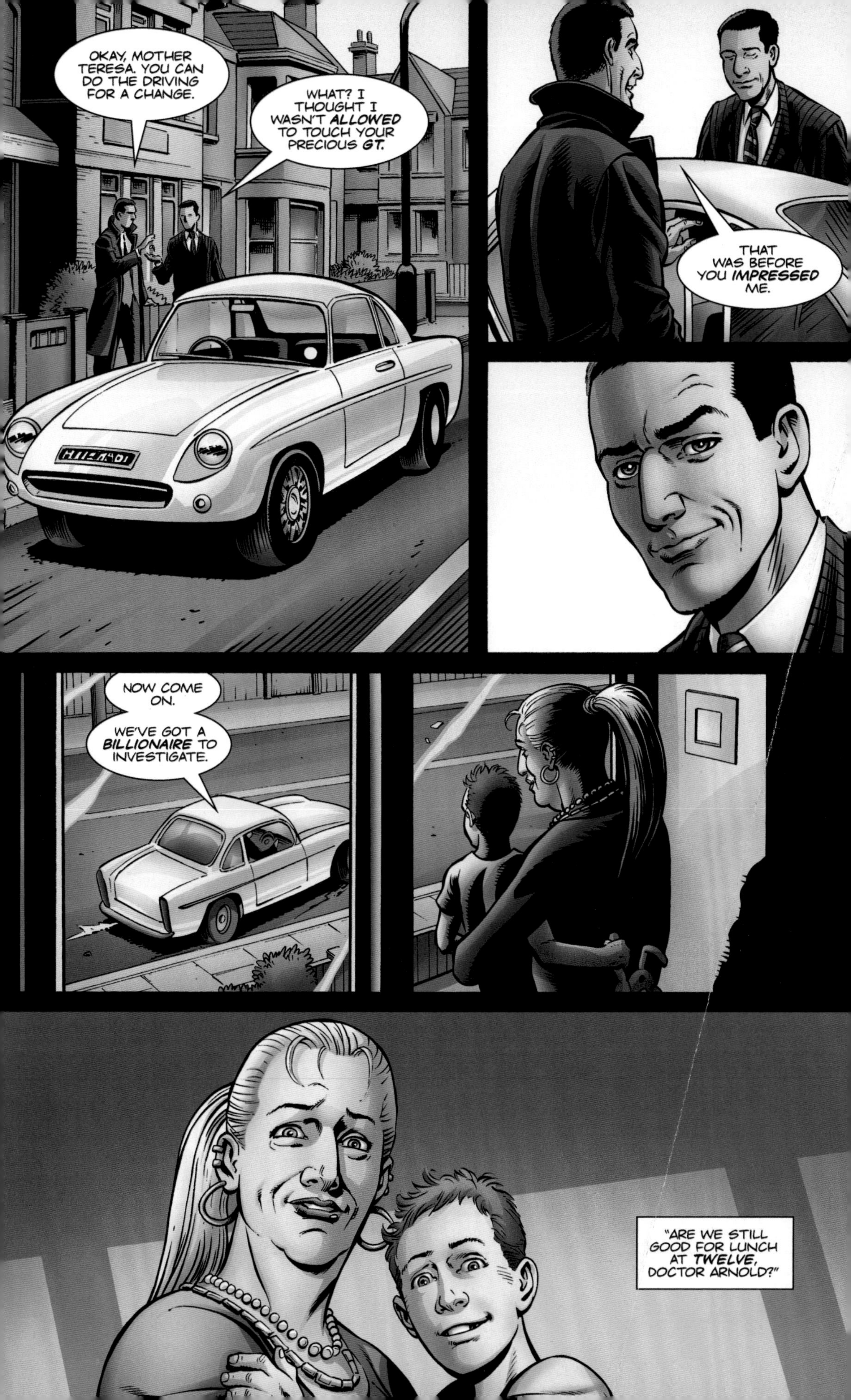
OKAY, MOTHER TERESA. YOU CAN DO THE DRIVING FOR A CHANGE.
WHAT? I THOUGHT I WASN'T ALLOWED TO TOUCH YOUR PRECIOUS GT.
THAT WAS BEFORE YOU IMPRESSED ME.
NOW COME ON.
WE'VE GOT A BILLIONAIRE TO INVESTIGATE.
"ARE WE STILL GOOD FOR LUNCH AT TWELVE, DOCTOR ARNOLD?"

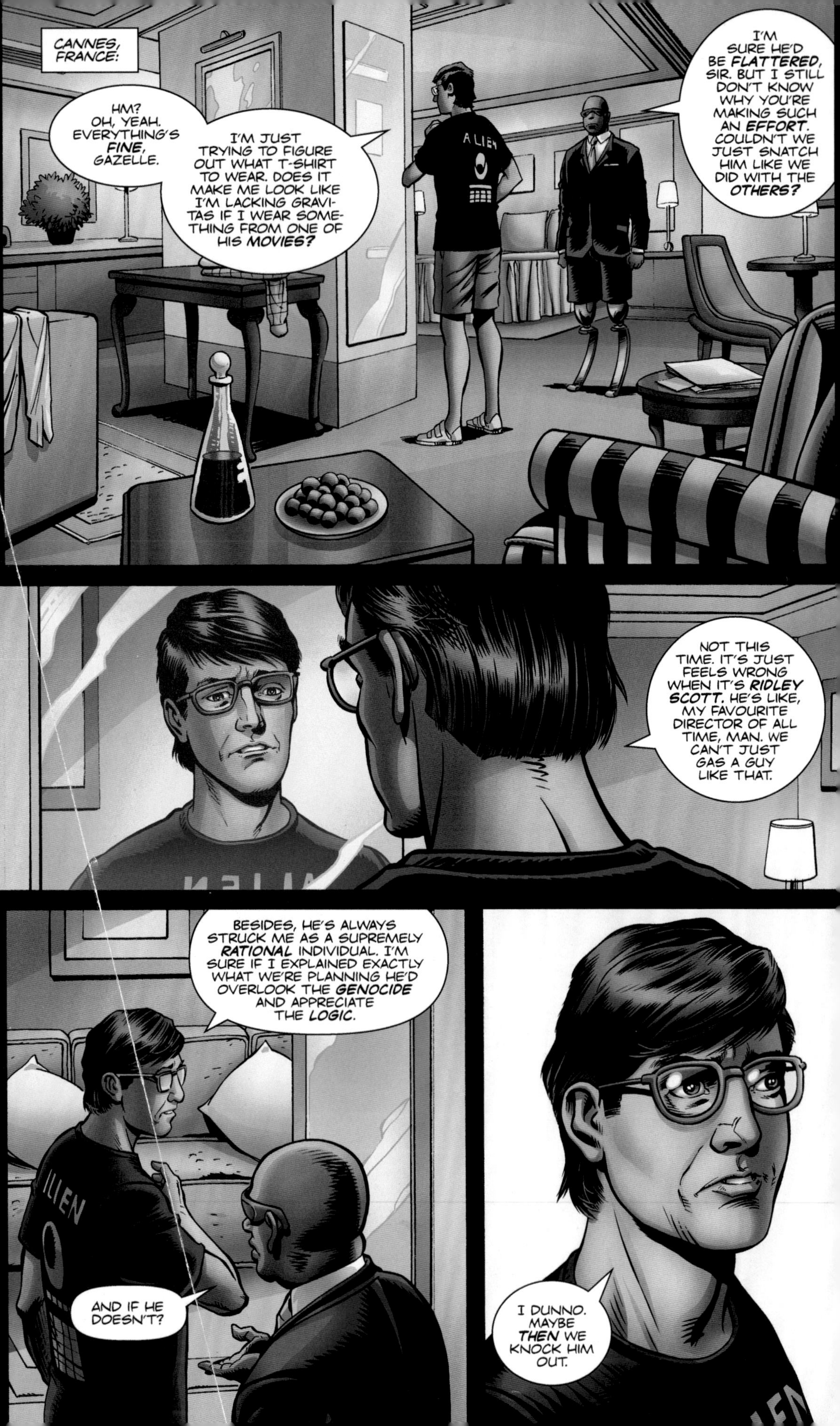
CANNES, FRANCE:
HM? OH, YEAH. EVERYTHING'S **FINE**, GAZELLE.
I'M JUST TRYING TO FIGURE OUT WHAT T-SHIRT TO WEAR. DOES IT MAKE ME LOOK LIKE I'M LACKING GRAVITAS IF I WEAR SOMETHING FROM ONE OF HIS **MOVIES?**
ALIEN
I'M SURE HE'D BE **FLATTERED**, SIR. BUT I STILL DON'T KNOW WHY YOU'RE MAKING SUCH AN **EFFORT**. COULDN'T WE JUST SNATCH HIM LIKE WE DID WITH THE **OTHERS?**
NOT THIS TIME. IT'S JUST FEELS WRONG WHEN IT'S **RIDLEY SCOTT.** HE'S LIKE, MY FAVOURITE DIRECTOR OF ALL TIME, MAN. WE CAN'T JUST GAS A GUY LIKE THAT.
BESIDES, HE'S ALWAYS STRUCK ME AS A SUPREMELY **RATIONAL** INDIVIDUAL. I'M SURE IF I EXPLAINED EXACTLY WHAT WE'RE PLANNING HE'D OVERLOOK THE **GENOCIDE** AND APPRECIATE THE **LOGIC**.
ALIEN
AND IF HE DOESN'T?
I DUNNO. MAYBE **THEN** WE KNOCK HIM OUT.

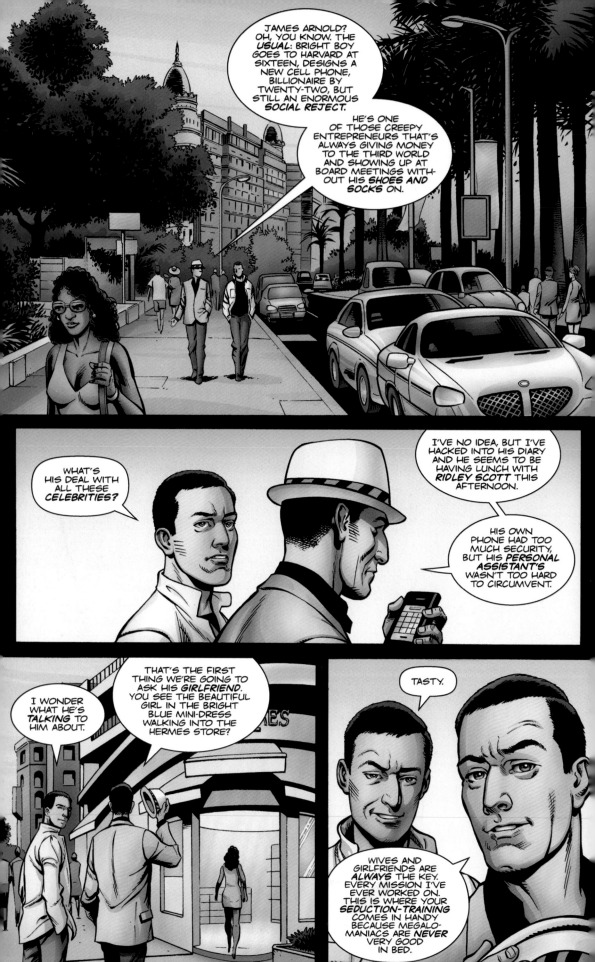

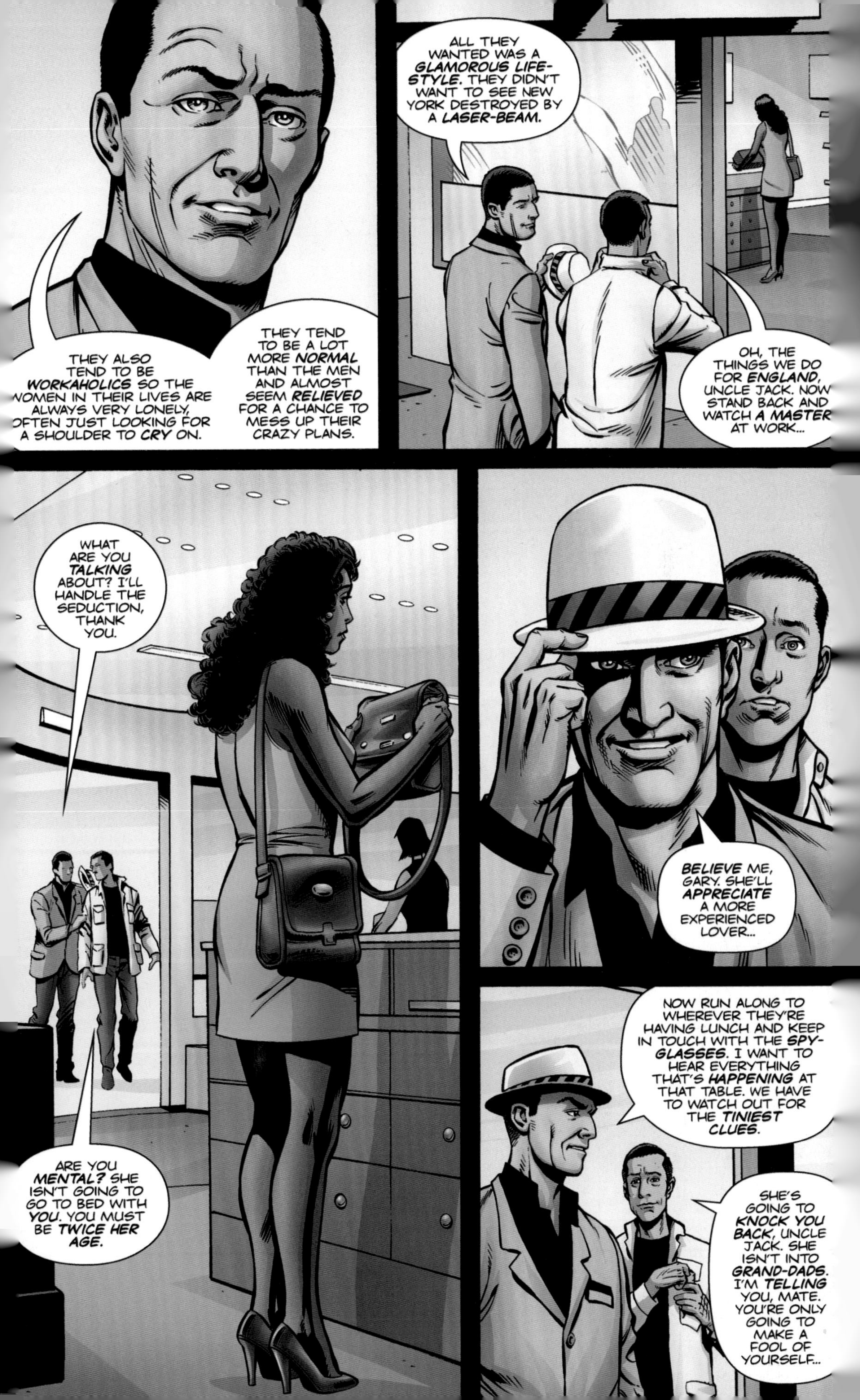
THEY ALSO TEND TO BE WORKAHOLICS SO THE WOMEN IN THEIR LIVES ARE ALWAYS VERY LONELY, OFTEN JUST LOOKING FOR A SHOULDER TO CRY ON.
THEY TEND TO BE A LOT MORE NORMAL THAN THE MEN AND ALMOST SEEM RELIEVED FOR A CHANCE TO MESS UP THEIR CRAZY PLANS.
ALL THEY WANTED WAS A GLAMOROUS LIFE-STYLE. THEY DIDN'T WANT TO SEE NEW YORK DESTROYED BY A LASER-BEAM.
OH, THE THINGS WE DO FOR ENGLAND, UNCLE JACK. NOW STAND BACK AND WATCH A MASTER AT WORK...
WHAT ARE YOU TALKING ABOUT? I'LL HANDLE THE SEDUCTION, THANK YOU.
ARE YOU MENTAL? SHE ISN'T GOING TO GO TO BED WITH YOU. YOU MUST BE TWICE HER AGE.
BELIEVE ME, GARY. SHE'LL APPRECIATE A MORE EXPERIENCED LOVER...
NOW RUN ALONG TO WHEREVER THEY'RE HAVING LUNCH AND KEEP IN TOUCH WITH THE SPY-GLASSES. I WANT TO HEAR EVERYTHING THAT'S HAPPENING AT THAT TABLE. WE HAVE TO WATCH OUT FOR THE TINIEST CLUES.
SHE'S GOING TO KNOCK YOU BACK, UNCLE JACK. SHE ISN'T INTO GRAND-DADS. I'M TELLING YOU, MATE. YOU'RE ONLY GOING TO MAKE A FOOL OF YOURSELF...

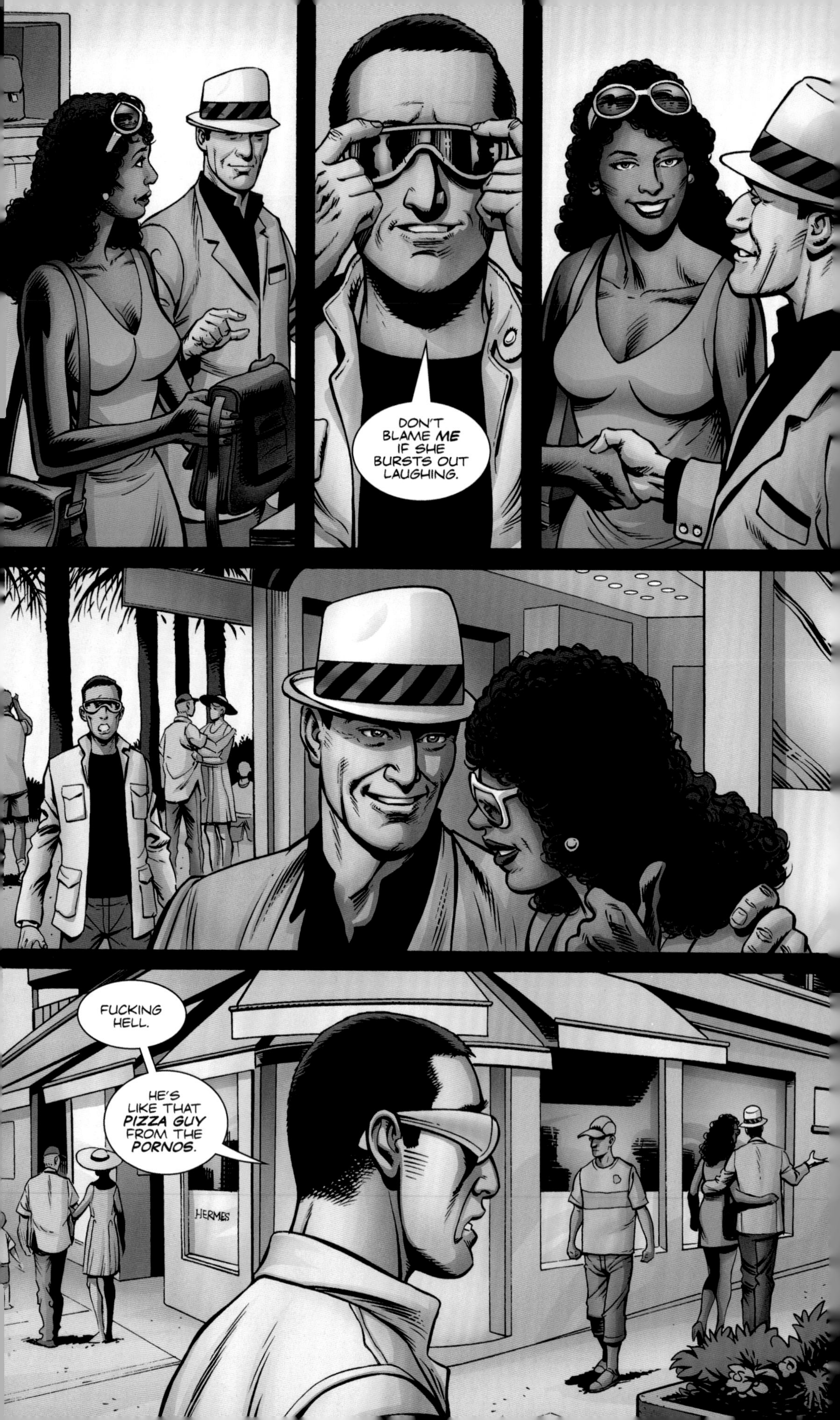
DON'T BLAME ME IF SHE BURSTS OUT LAUGHING.
FUCKING HELL.
HE'S LIKE THAT PIZZA GUY FROM THE PORNOS.
HERMES

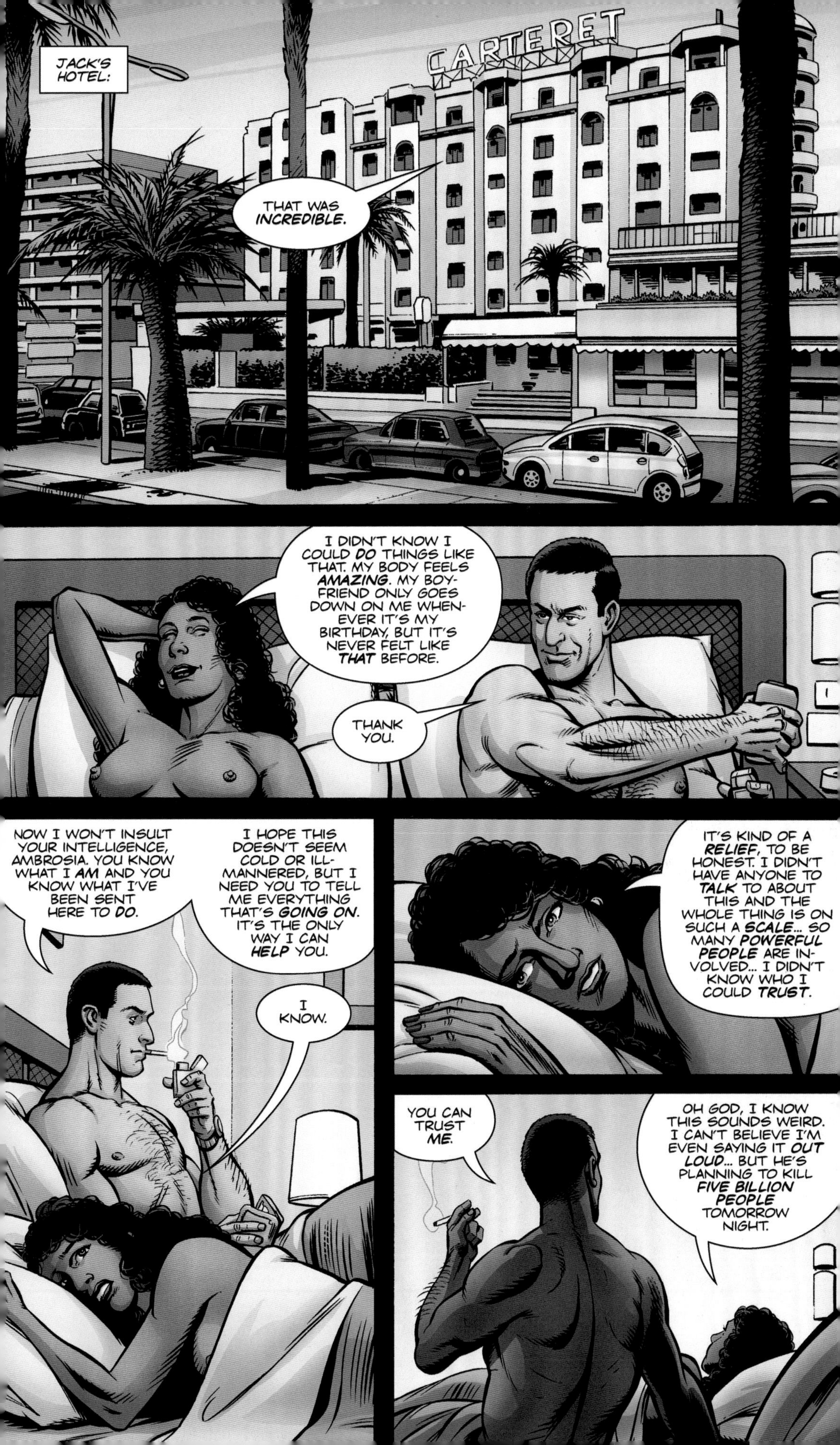
JACK'S HOTEL:
CARTERET
THAT WAS INCREDIBLE.
I DIDN'T KNOW I COULD DO THINGS LIKE THAT. MY BODY FEELS AMAZING. MY BOY-FRIEND ONLY GOES DOWN ON ME WHEN-EVER IT'S MY BIRTHDAY, BUT IT'S NEVER FELT LIKE THAT BEFORE.
THANK YOU.
NOW I WON'T INSULT YOUR INTELLIGENCE, AMBROSIA. YOU KNOW WHAT I AM AND YOU KNOW WHAT I'VE BEEN SENT HERE TO DO.
I HOPE THIS DOESN'T SEEM COLD OR ILL-MANNERED, BUT I NEED YOU TO TELL ME EVERYTHING THAT'S GOING ON. IT'S THE ONLY WAY I CAN HELP YOU.
I KNOW.
IT'S KIND OF A RELIEF, TO BE HONEST. I DIDN'T HAVE ANYONE TO TALK TO ABOUT THIS AND THE WHOLE THING IS ON SUCH A SCALE... SO MANY POWERFUL PEOPLE ARE IN-VOLVED... I DIDN'T KNOW WHO I COULD TRUST.
YOU CAN TRUST ME.
OH GOD, I KNOW THIS SOUNDS WEIRD. I CAN'T BELIEVE I'M EVEN SAYING IT OUT LOUD... BUT HE'S PLANNING TO KILL FIVE BILLION PEOPLE TOMORROW NIGHT.

HE ESTIMATES THAT FIVE BILLION OF US WILL HAVE KILLED EACH OTHER INSIDE NINETEEN MINUTES WITH ZERO DAMAGE TO THE *ENVIRONMENT*.

HE'S TAKING US BACK TO WHERE WE WERE IN *EIGHTEEN HUNDRED* AND GIVING US A SECOND CHANCE TO KEEP THINGS UNDER CONTROL AGAIN.

BY ACTIVATING THE R-COMPLEX IN THE PRIMITIVE BASE OF OUR BRAINS HE CAN MAKE US ANGRY AND TERRITORIAL LIKE THAT WEDDING PARTY IN HAWAII.

THAT WAS JUST A TEST TO SEE IF IT *WORKED*, BUT TOMORROW NIGHT IT ALL GOES *GLOBAL*.

JUST BY FLICKING A SWITCH. CLEVER.

SO WHERE DOES MARK HAMILL FIT INTO ALL THIS? WHY HAS ARNOLD BEEN KIDNAPPING ALL THESE ACTORS AND DIRECTORS?

BECAUSE HE WANTS TO MAKE SURE THEY *SURVIVE*. HE *LOVES* THOSE GUYS. HE'S BEEN GATHERING THEM UP AND KEEPING THEM SAFE IN HIS MOUNTAIN BASE. THEY'LL ALL BE RELEASED AS SOON AS IT'S *OVER*.

OF COURSE HE DOES. HE'S A TWENTY-SOME-THING *NERD*. WHY DID NOBODY PUT TWO AND TWO *TOGETHER*?

WHO ELSE WOULD YOU WANT TO SURVIVE THE APOCALYPSE?

THANK YOU, AMBROSIA. YOU'VE BEEN VERY HELPFUL. REST ASSURED, THIS IS ALL GOING TO BE FINE. I'VE DONE THIS JOB FOR ALMOST *THIRTY YEARS* NOW. THIS WILL ALL BE SORTED IN A COUPLE OF HOURS.

YOU MUST THINK I'M A PRETTY *DESPICABLE PERSON* BEING INVOLVED IN ALL THIS SHIT?

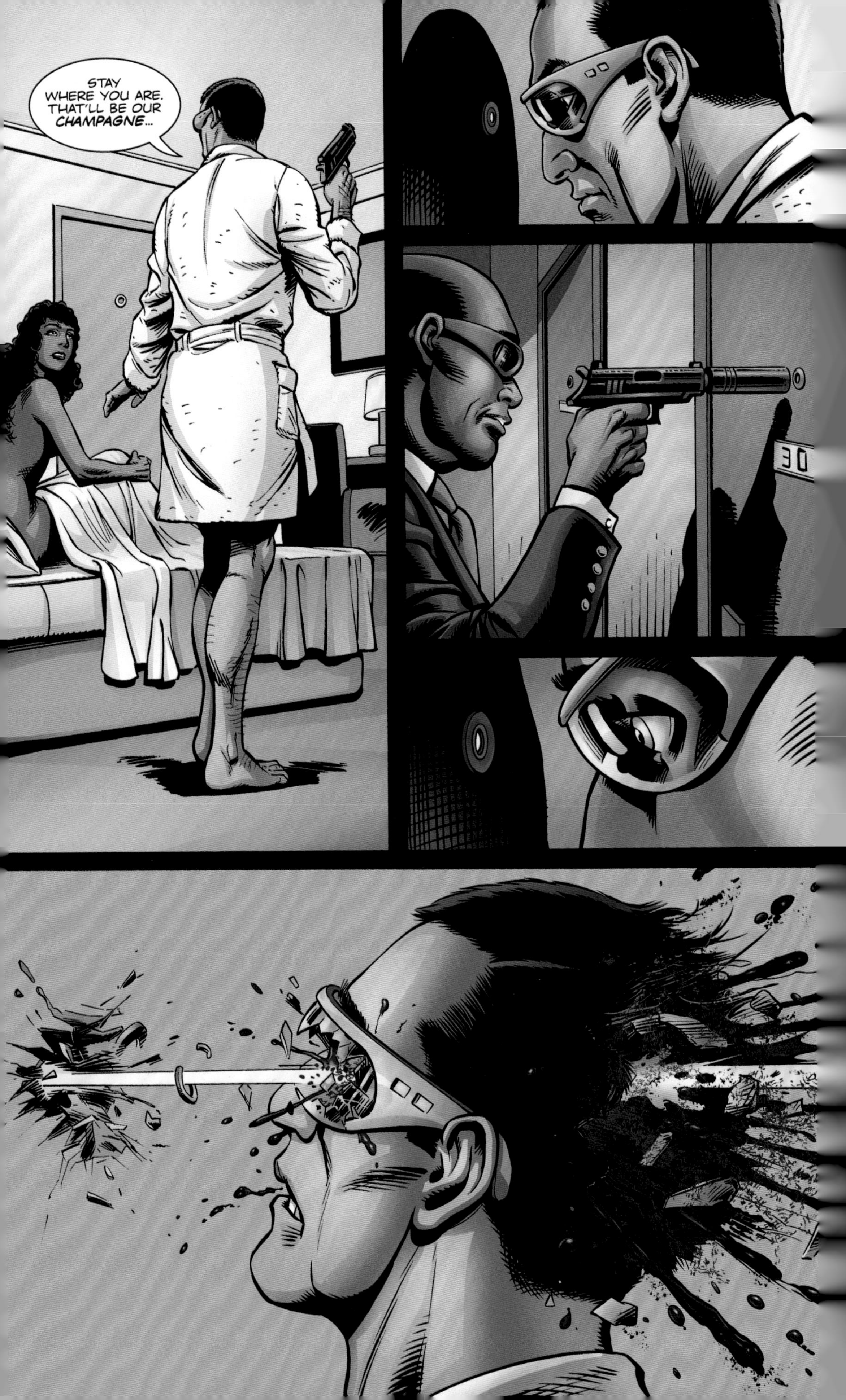
STAY WHERE YOU ARE. THAT'LL BE OUR *CHAMPAGNE*...

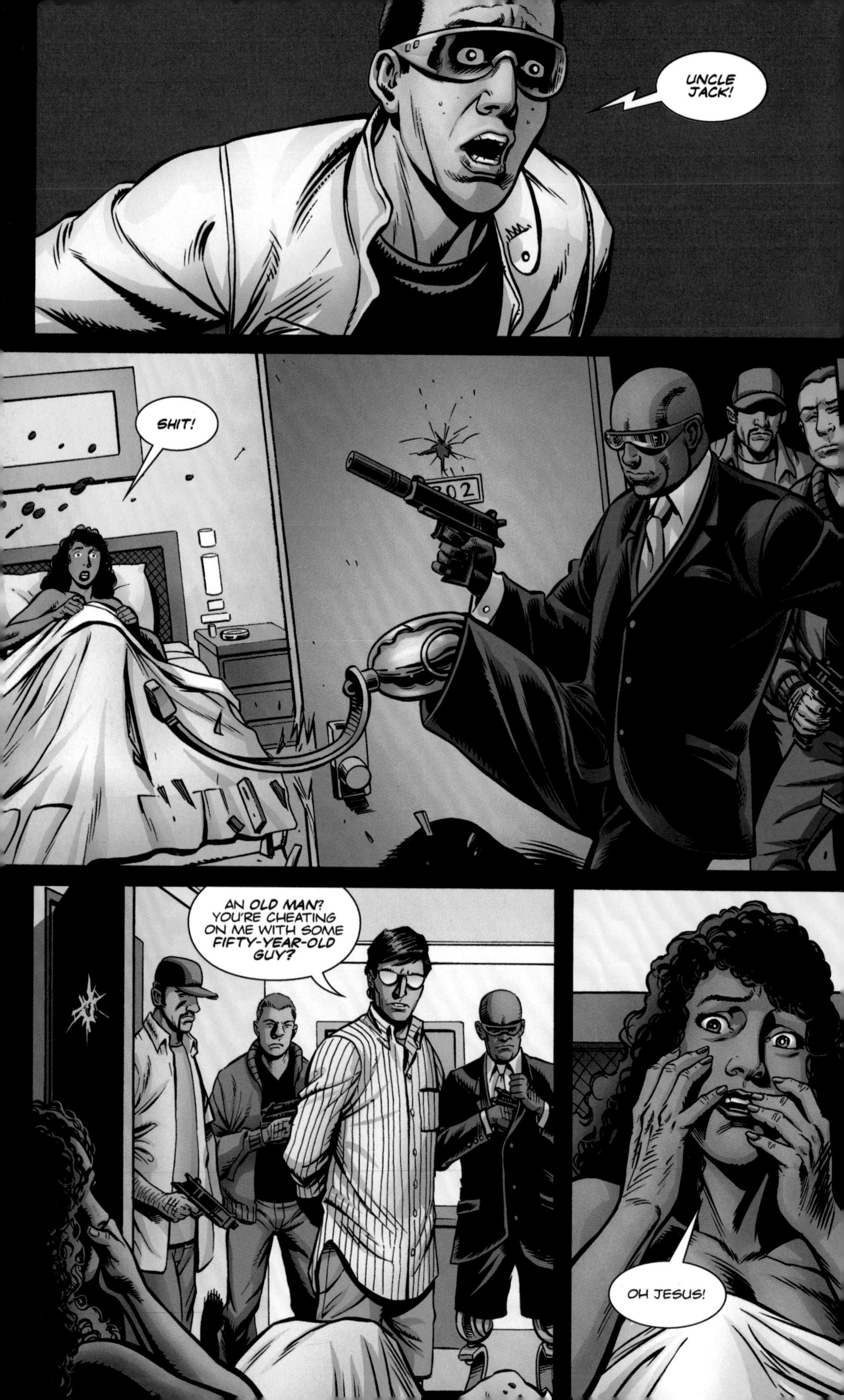
UNCLE JACK!
SHIT!
302
AN OLD MAN? YOU'RE CHEATING ON ME WITH SOME FIFTY-YEAR-OLD GUY?
OH JESUS!

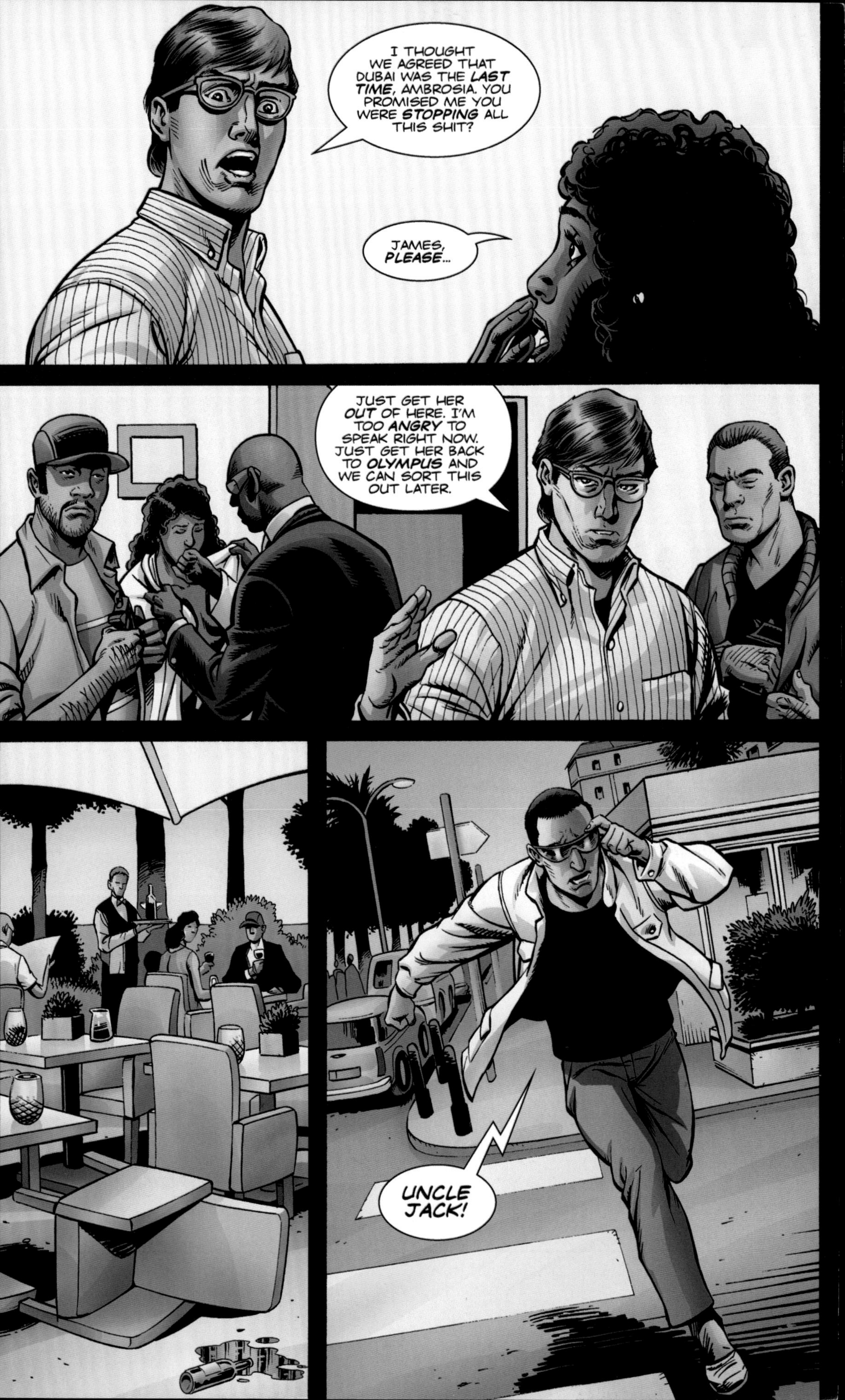

I THOUGHT WE AGREED THAT DUBAI WAS THE LAST TIME, AMBROSIA. YOU PROMISED ME YOU WERE STOPPING ALL THIS SHIT?
JAMES, PLEASE...
JUST GET HER OUT OF HERE. I'M TOO ANGRY TO SPEAK RIGHT NOW. JUST GET HER BACK TO OLYMPUS AND WE CAN SORT THIS OUT LATER.
UNCLE JACK!

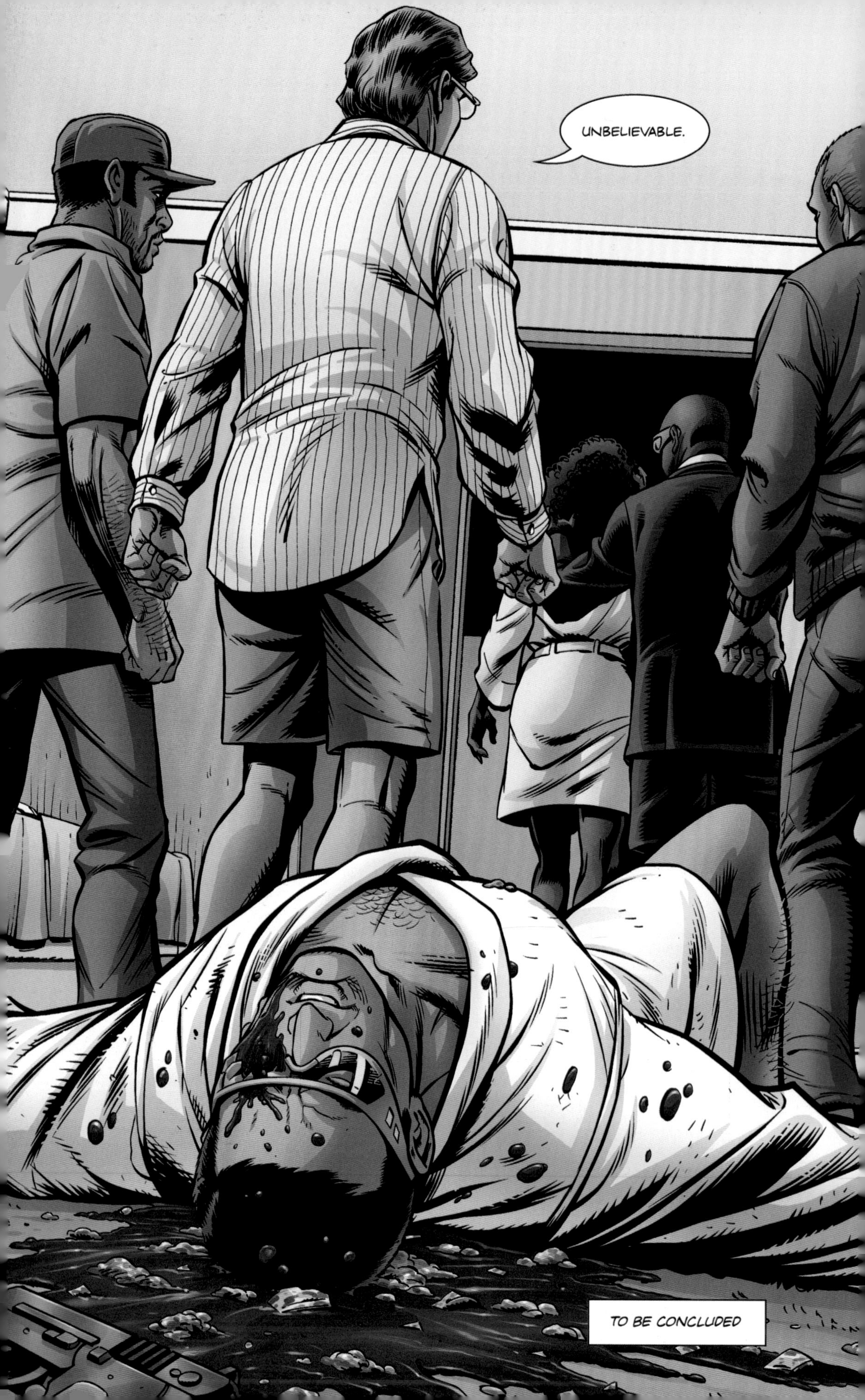
UNBELIEVABLE.
TO BE CONCLUDED

SIX

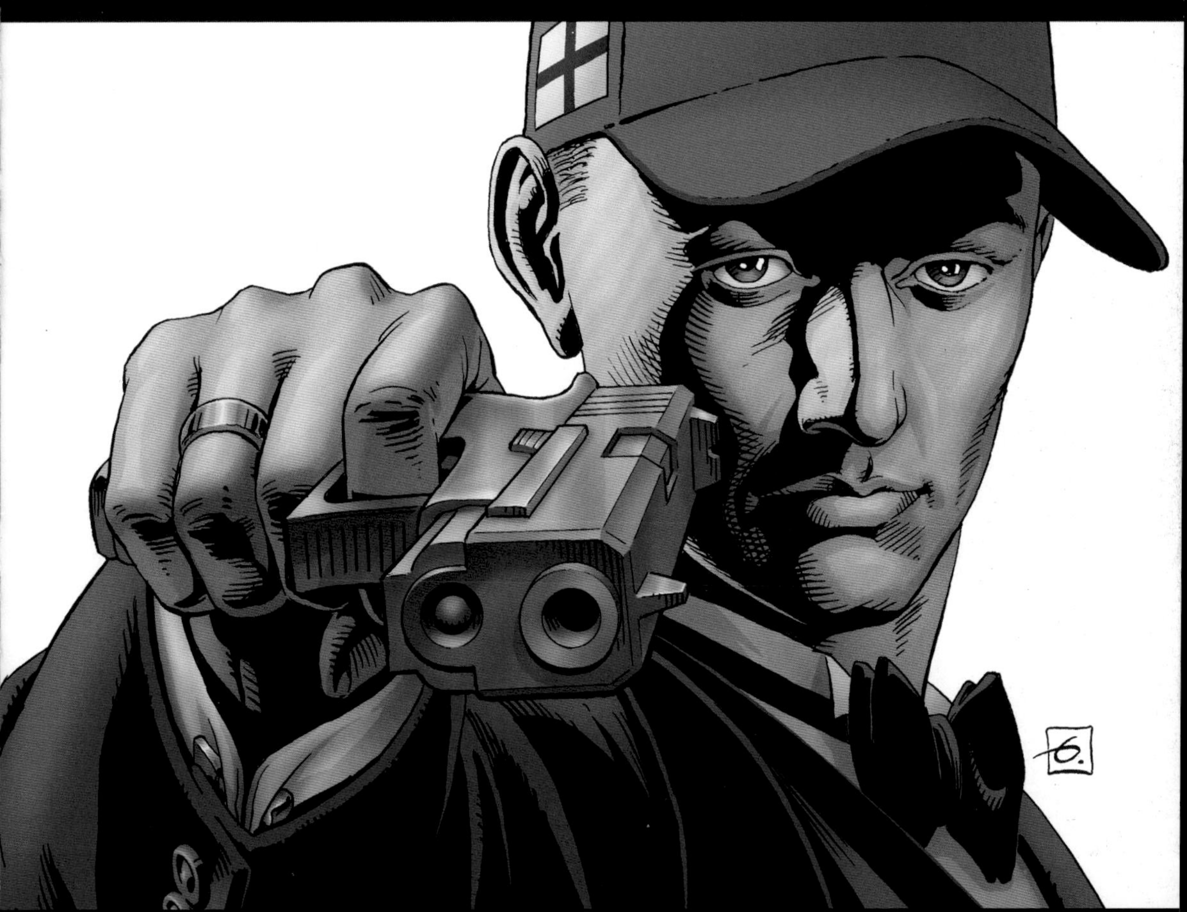

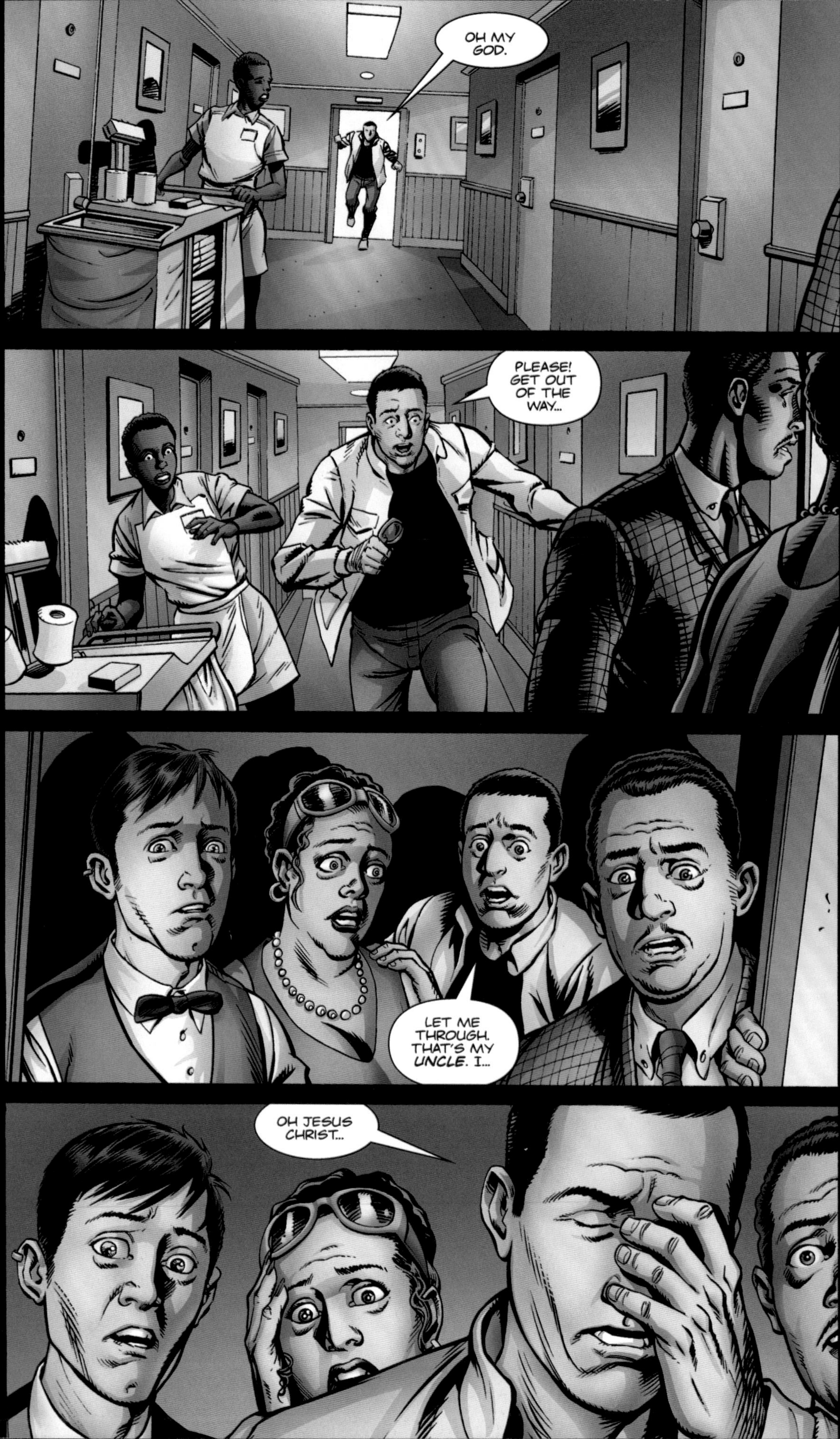
OH MY GOD.
PLEASE! GET OUT OF THE WAY...
LET ME THROUGH. THAT'S MY *UNCLE*. I...
OH JESUS CHRIST...

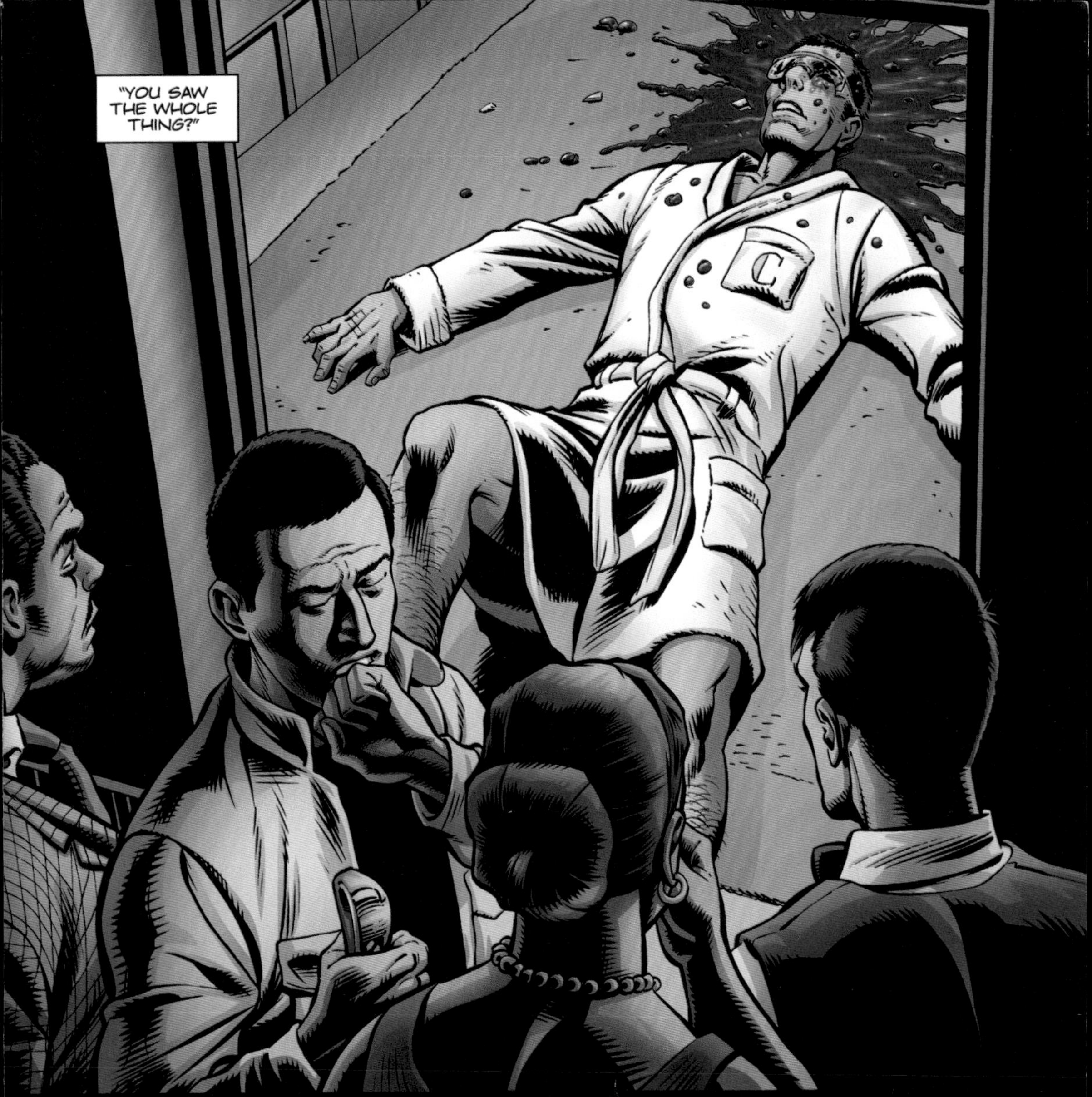
"YOU SAW THE WHOLE THING?"

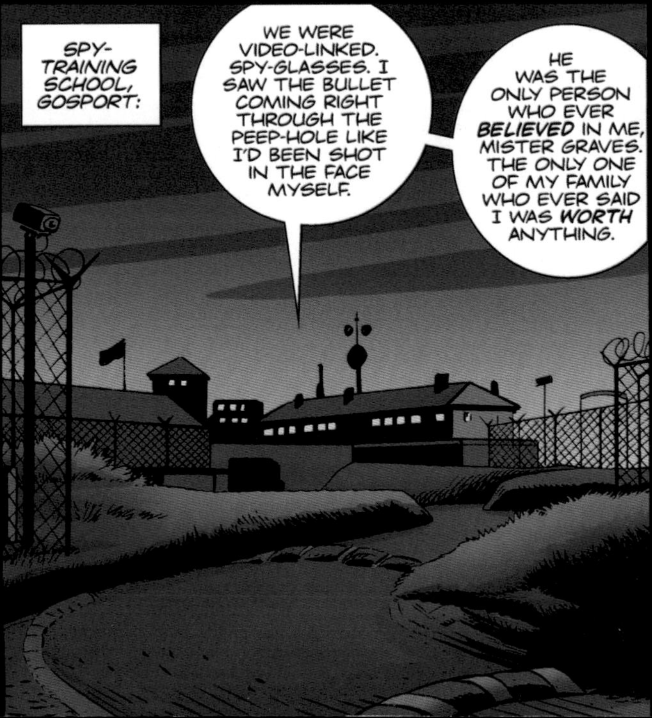
SPY-TRAINING SCHOOL, GOSPORT:
WE WERE VIDEO-LINKED. SPY-GLASSES. I SAW THE BULLET COMING RIGHT THROUGH THE PEEP-HOLE LIKE I'D BEEN SHOT IN THE FACE MYSELF.
HE WAS THE ONLY PERSON WHO EVER BELIEVED IN ME, MISTER GRAVES. THE ONLY ONE OF MY FAMILY WHO EVER SAID I WAS WORTH ANYTHING.

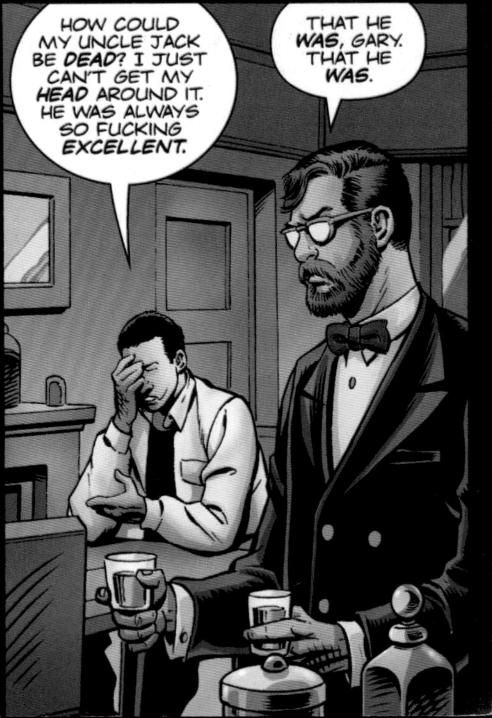
HOW COULD MY UNCLE JACK BE DEAD? I JUST CAN'T GET MY HEAD AROUND IT. HE WAS ALWAYS SO FUCKING EXCELLENT.
THAT HE WAS, GARY. THAT HE WAS.

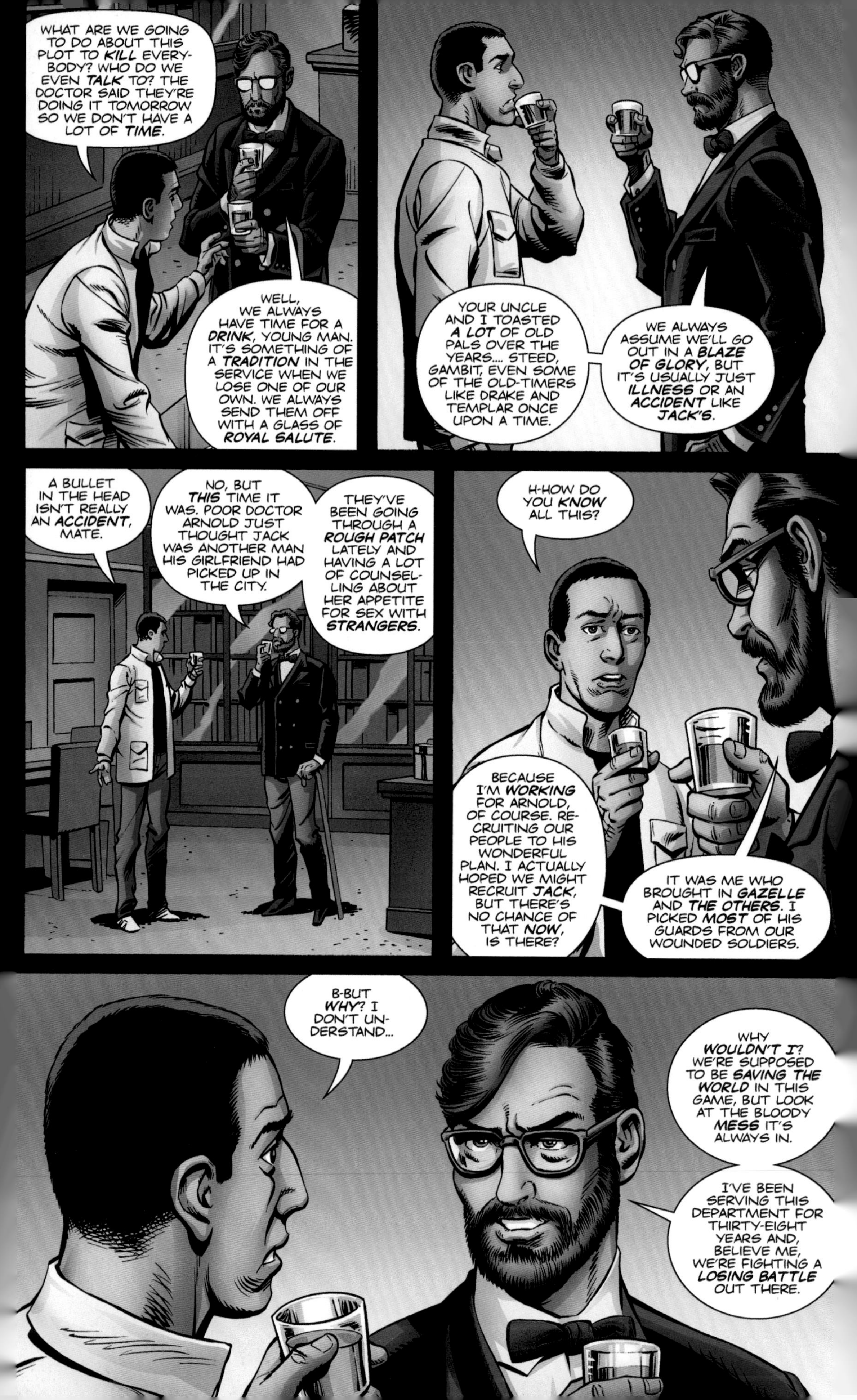

WHAT ARE WE GOING TO DO ABOUT THIS PLOT TO KILL EVERYBODY? WHO DO WE EVEN TALK TO? THE DOCTOR SAID THEY'RE DOING IT TOMORROW SO WE DON'T HAVE A LOT OF TIME.
WELL, WE ALWAYS HAVE TIME FOR A DRINK, YOUNG MAN. IT'S SOMETHING OF A TRADITION IN THE SERVICE WHEN WE LOSE ONE OF OUR OWN. WE ALWAYS SEND THEM OFF WITH A GLASS OF ROYAL SALUTE.
YOUR UNCLE AND I TOASTED A LOT OF OLD PALS OVER THE YEARS.... STEED, GAMBIT, EVEN SOME OF THE OLD-TIMERS LIKE DRAKE AND TEMPLAR ONCE UPON A TIME.
WE ALWAYS ASSUME WE'LL GO OUT IN A BLAZE OF GLORY, BUT IT'S USUALLY JUST ILLNESS OR AN ACCIDENT LIKE JACK'S.
A BULLET IN THE HEAD ISN'T REALLY AN ACCIDENT, MATE.
NO, BUT THIS TIME IT WAS. POOR DOCTOR ARNOLD JUST THOUGHT JACK WAS ANOTHER MAN HIS GIRLFRIEND HAD PICKED UP IN THE CITY.
THEY'VE BEEN GOING THROUGH A ROUGH PATCH LATELY AND HAVING A LOT OF COUNSELLING ABOUT HER APPETITE FOR SEX WITH STRANGERS.
H-HOW DO YOU KNOW ALL THIS?
BECAUSE I'M WORKING FOR ARNOLD, OF COURSE. RECRUITING OUR PEOPLE TO HIS WONDERFUL PLAN. I ACTUALLY HOPED WE MIGHT RECRUIT JACK, BUT THERE'S NO CHANCE OF THAT NOW, IS THERE?
IT WAS ME WHO BROUGHT IN GAZELLE AND THE OTHERS. I PICKED MOST OF HIS GUARDS FROM OUR WOUNDED SOLDIERS.
B-BUT WHY? I DON'T UNDERSTAND...
WHY WOULDN'T I? WE'RE SUPPOSED TO BE SAVING THE WORLD IN THIS GAME, BUT LOOK AT THE BLOODY MESS IT'S ALWAYS IN.
I'VE BEEN SERVING THIS DEPARTMENT FOR THIRTY-EIGHT YEARS AND, BELIEVE ME, WE'RE FIGHTING A LOSING BATTLE OUT THERE.

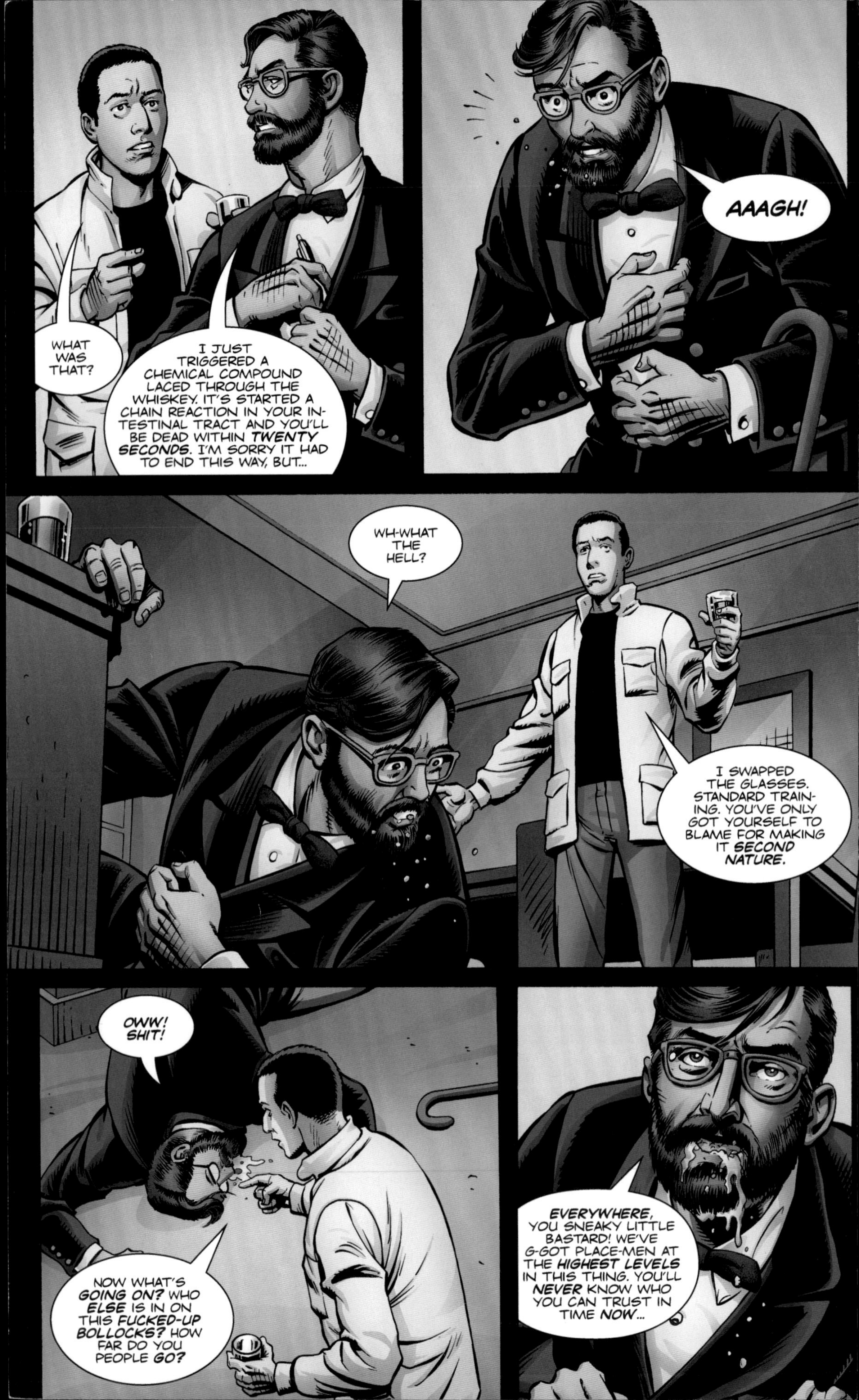
WHAT WAS THAT?
I JUST TRIGGERED A CHEMICAL COMPOUND LACED THROUGH THE WHISKEY. IT'S STARTED A CHAIN REACTION IN YOUR INTESTINAL TRACT AND YOU'LL BE DEAD WITHIN TWENTY SECONDS. I'M SORRY IT HAD TO END THIS WAY, BUT...
AAAGH!
WH-WHAT THE HELL?
I SWAPPED THE GLASSES. STANDARD TRAINING. YOU'VE ONLY GOT YOURSELF TO BLAME FOR MAKING IT SECOND NATURE.
OWW! SHIT!
NOW WHAT'S GOING ON? WHO ELSE IS IN ON THIS FUCKED-UP BOLLOCKS? HOW FAR DO YOU PEOPLE GO?
EVERYWHERE, YOU SNEAKY LITTLE BASTARD! WE'VE G-GOT PLACE-MEN AT THE HIGHEST LEVELS IN THIS THING. YOU'LL NEVER KNOW WHO YOU CAN TRUST IN TIME NOW...

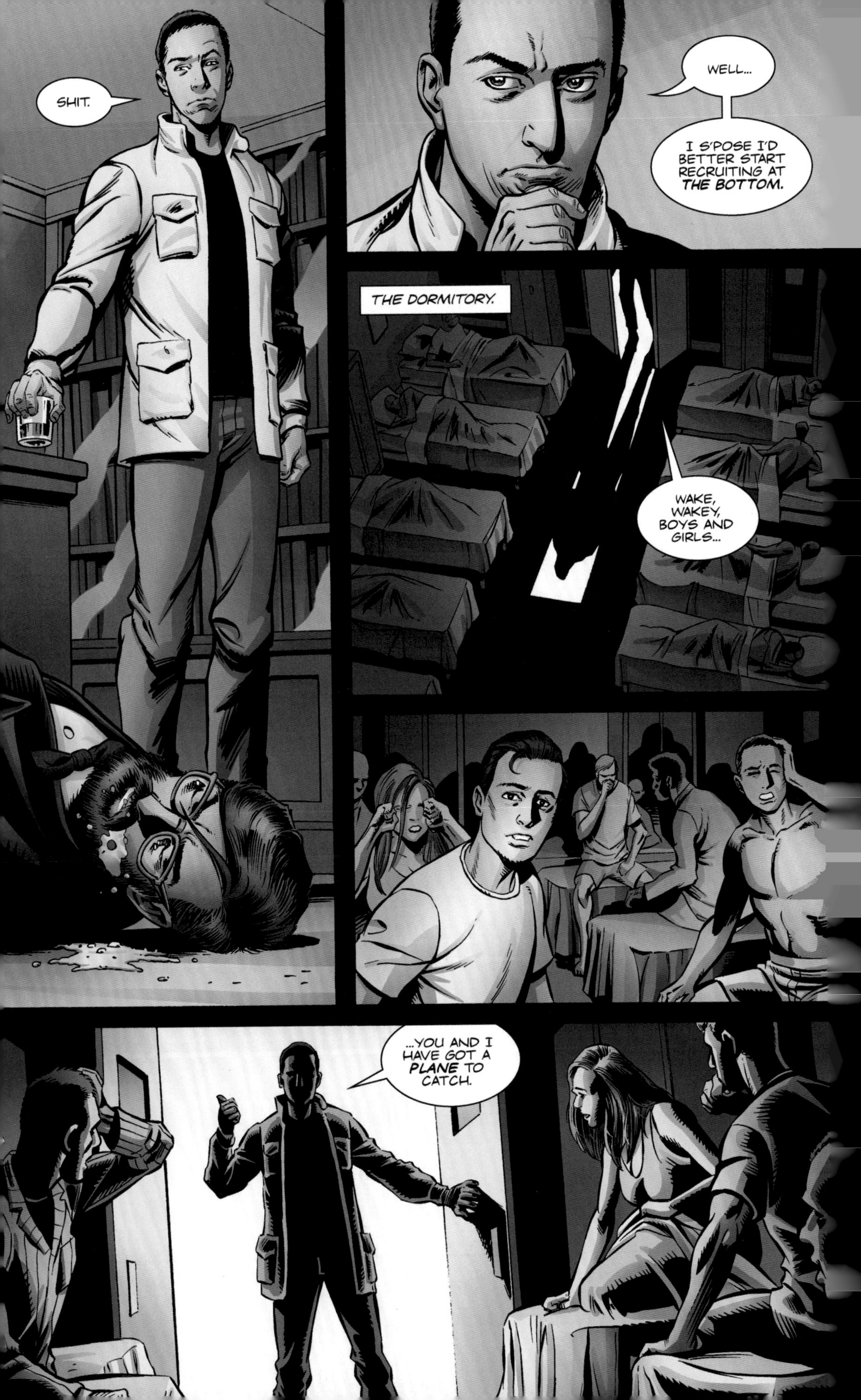
SHIT.
WELL...
I S'POSE I'D BETTER START RECRUITING AT THE BOTTOM.
THE DORMITORY.
WAKE, WAKEY, BOYS AND GIRLS...
...YOU AND I HAVE GOT A PLANE TO CATCH.

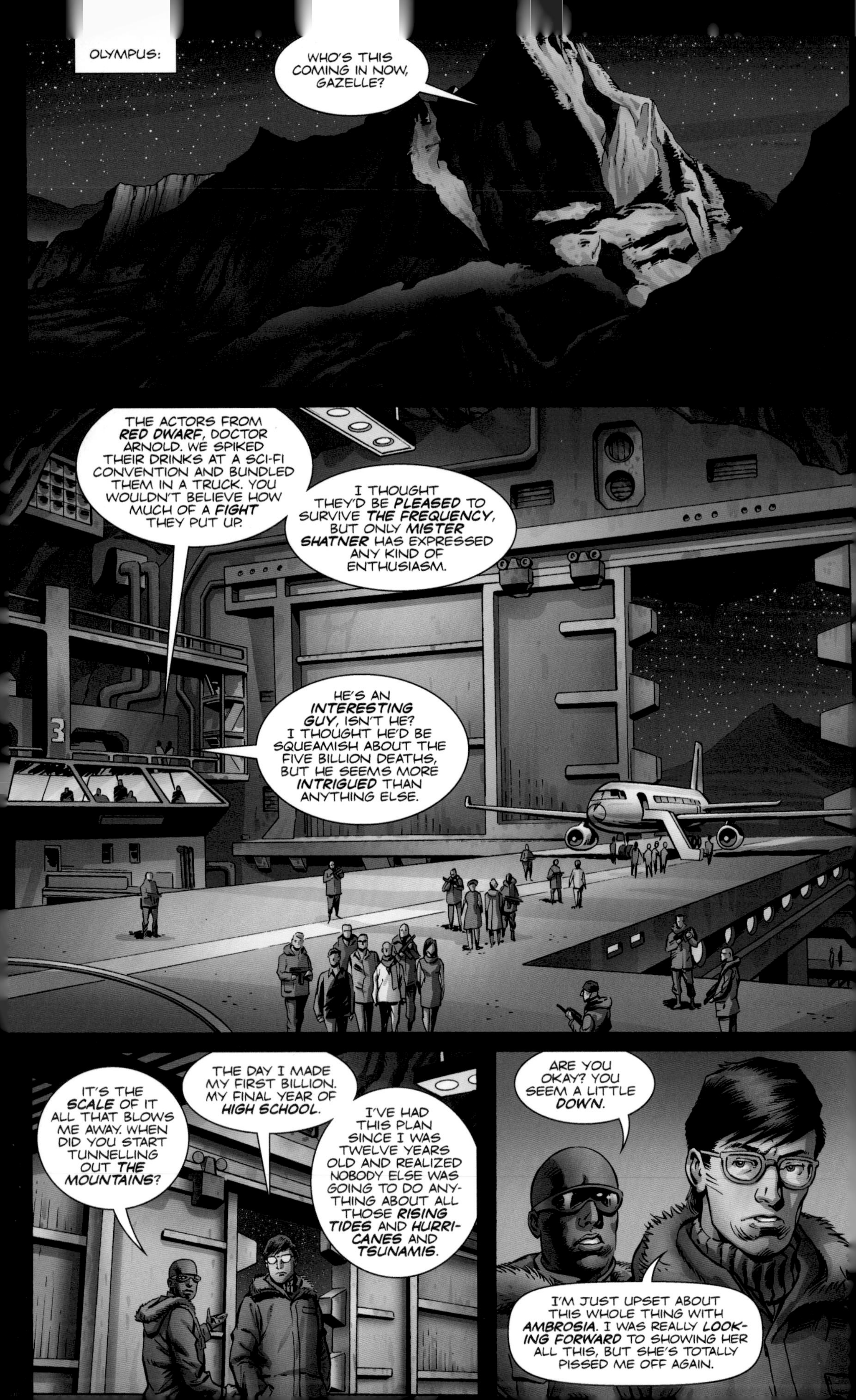
OLYMPUS:
WHO'S THIS COMING IN NOW, GAZELLE?
THE ACTORS FROM RED DWARF, DOCTOR ARNOLD. WE SPIKED THEIR DRINKS AT A SCI-FI CONVENTION AND BUNDLED THEM IN A TRUCK. YOU WOULDN'T BELIEVE HOW MUCH OF A FIGHT THEY PUT UP.
I THOUGHT THEY'D BE PLEASED TO SURVIVE THE FREQUENCY, BUT ONLY MISTER SHATNER HAS EXPRESSED ANY KIND OF ENTHUSIASM.
HE'S AN INTERESTING GUY, ISN'T HE? I THOUGHT HE'D BE SQUEAMISH ABOUT THE FIVE BILLION DEATHS, BUT HE SEEMS MORE INTRIGUED THAN ANYTHING ELSE.
3
IT'S THE SCALE OF IT ALL THAT BLOWS ME AWAY. WHEN DID YOU START TUNNELLING OUT THE MOUNTAINS?
THE DAY I MADE MY FIRST BILLION. MY FINAL YEAR OF HIGH SCHOOL.
I'VE HAD THIS PLAN SINCE I WAS TWELVE YEARS OLD AND REALIZED NOBODY ELSE WAS GOING TO DO ANYTHING ABOUT ALL THOSE RISING TIDES AND HURRICANES AND TSUNAMIS.
ARE YOU OKAY? YOU SEEM A LITTLE DOWN.
I'M JUST UPSET ABOUT THIS WHOLE THING WITH AMBROSIA. I WAS REALLY LOOKING FORWARD TO SHOWING HER ALL THIS, BUT SHE'S TOTALLY PISSED ME OFF AGAIN.

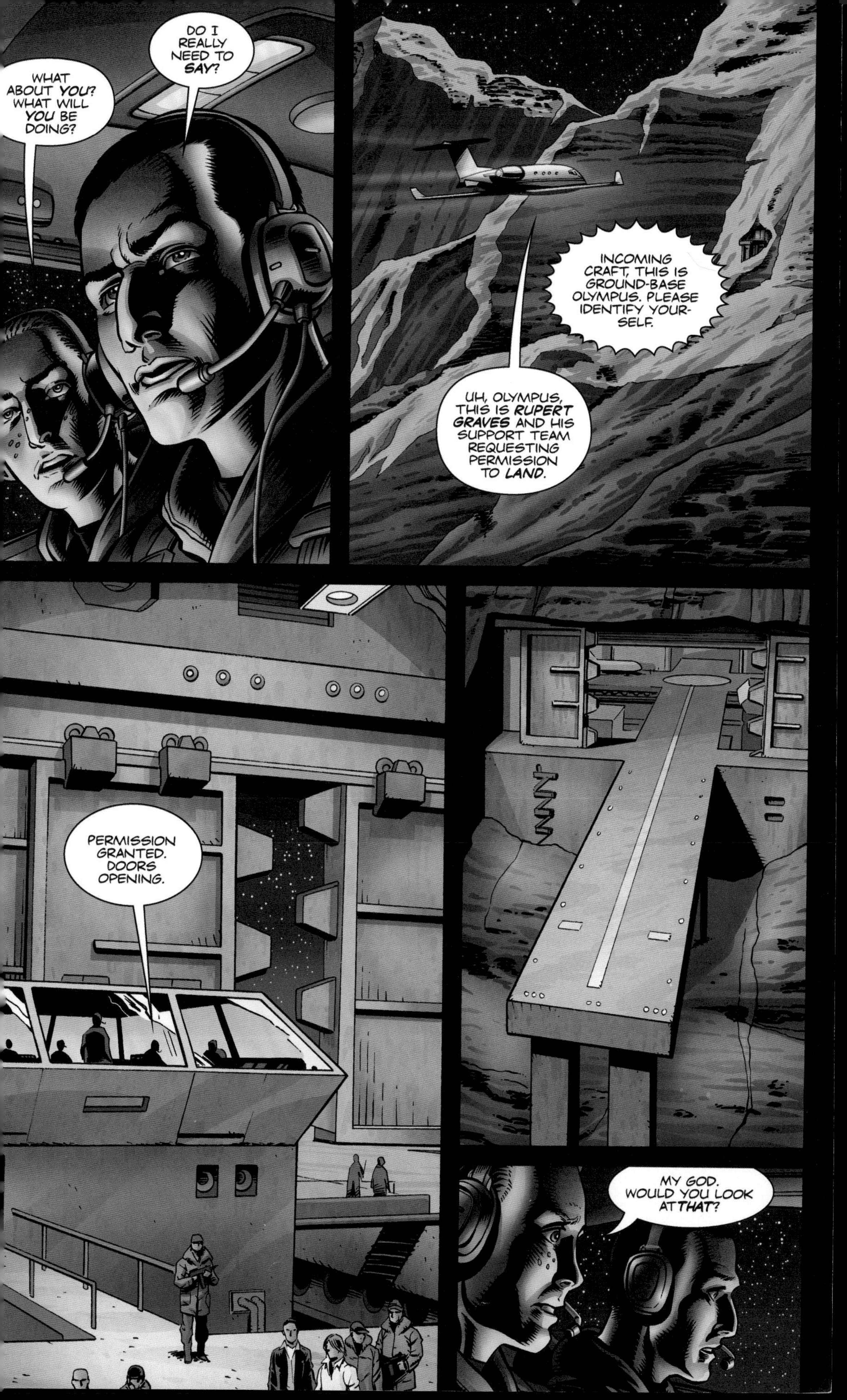
WHAT ABOUT YOU? WHAT WILL YOU BE DOING?
DO I REALLY NEED TO SAY?
INCOMING CRAFT, THIS IS GROUND-BASE OLYMPUS. PLEASE IDENTIFY YOURSELF.
UH, OLYMPUS, THIS IS RUPERT GRAVES AND HIS SUPPORT TEAM REQUESTING PERMISSION TO LAND.
PERMISSION GRANTED. DOORS OPENING.
MY GOD. WOULD YOU LOOK AT THAT?

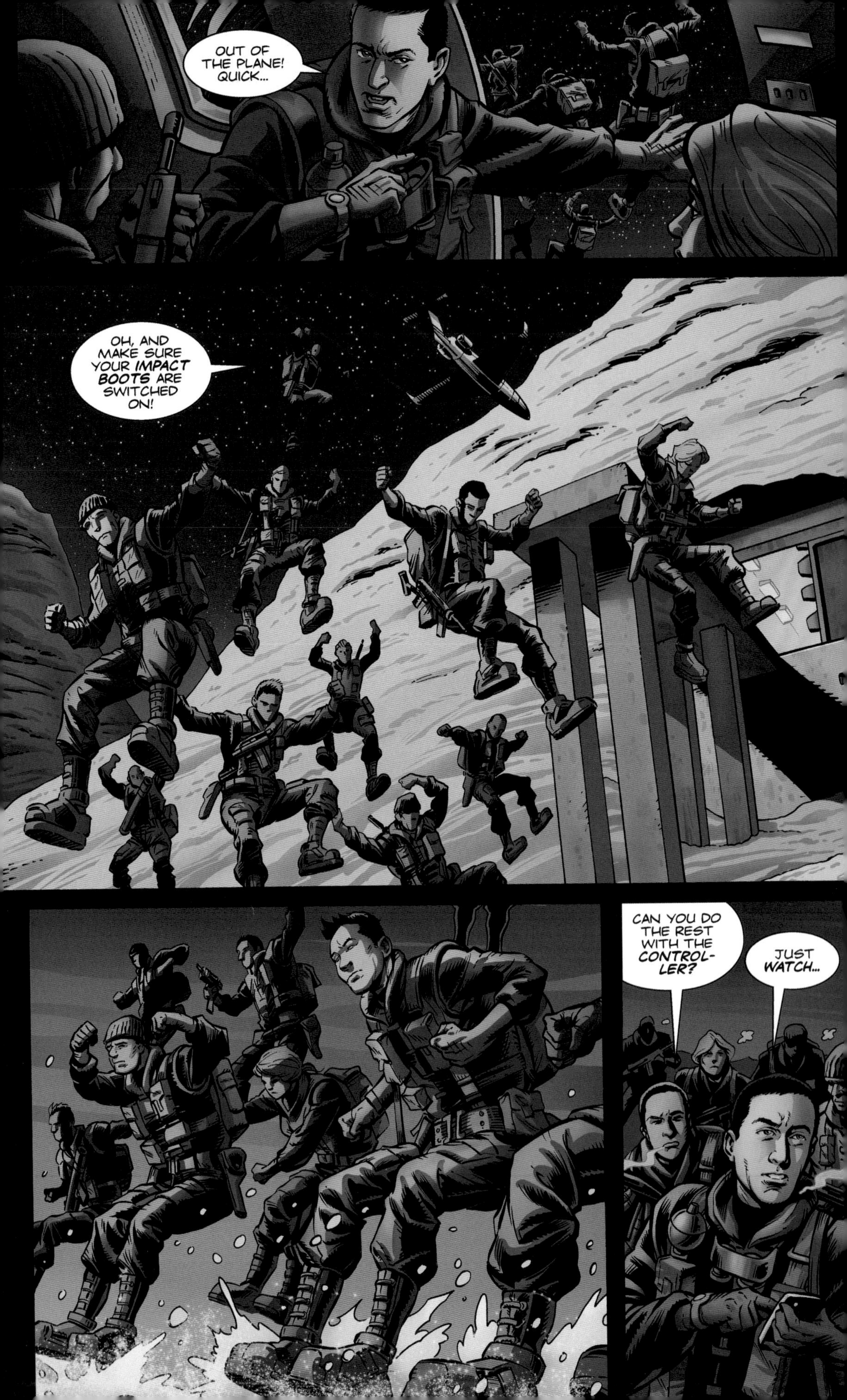
OUT OF THE PLANE! QUICK...
OH, AND MAKE SURE YOUR *IMPACT BOOTS* ARE SWITCHED ON!
CAN YOU DO THE REST WITH THE *CONTROL-LER?*
JUST *WATCH...*

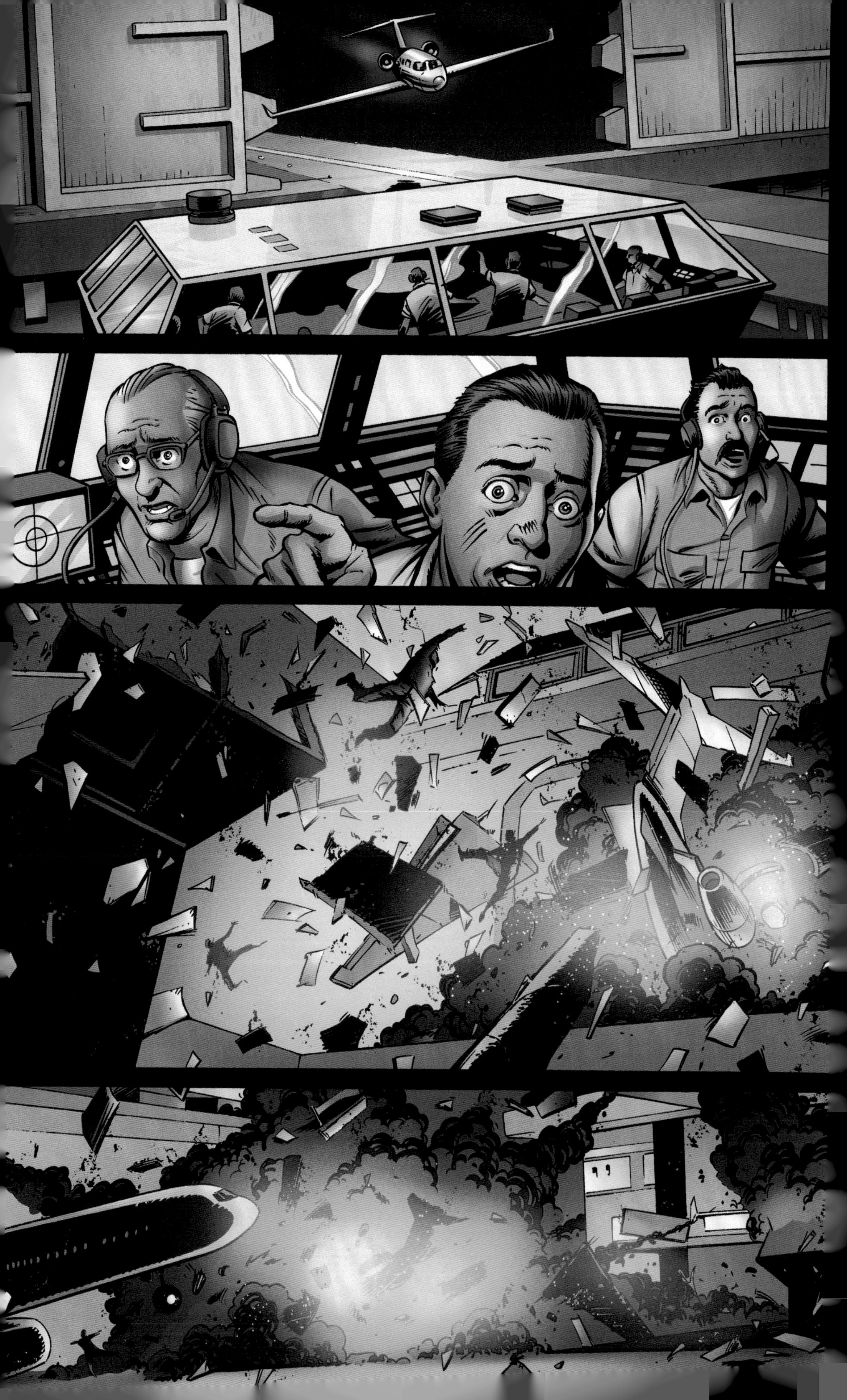

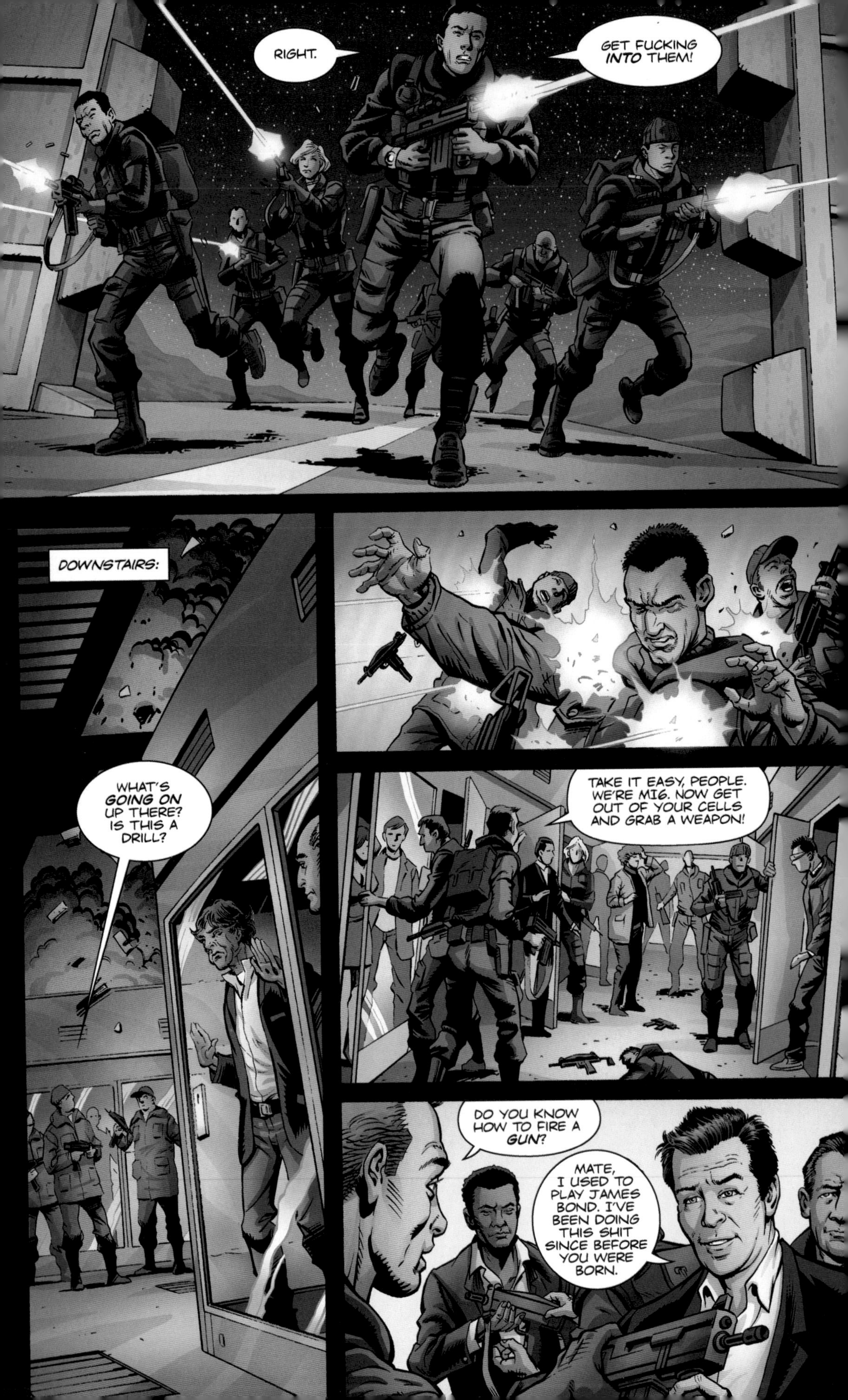
RIGHT.
GET FUCKING INTO THEM!
DOWNSTAIRS:
WHAT'S GOING ON UP THERE? IS THIS A DRILL?
TAKE IT EASY, PEOPLE. WE'RE MI6. NOW GET OUT OF YOUR CELLS AND GRAB A WEAPON!
DO YOU KNOW HOW TO FIRE A GUN?
MATE, I USED TO PLAY JAMES BOND. I'VE BEEN DOING THIS SHIT SINCE BEFORE YOU WERE BORN.

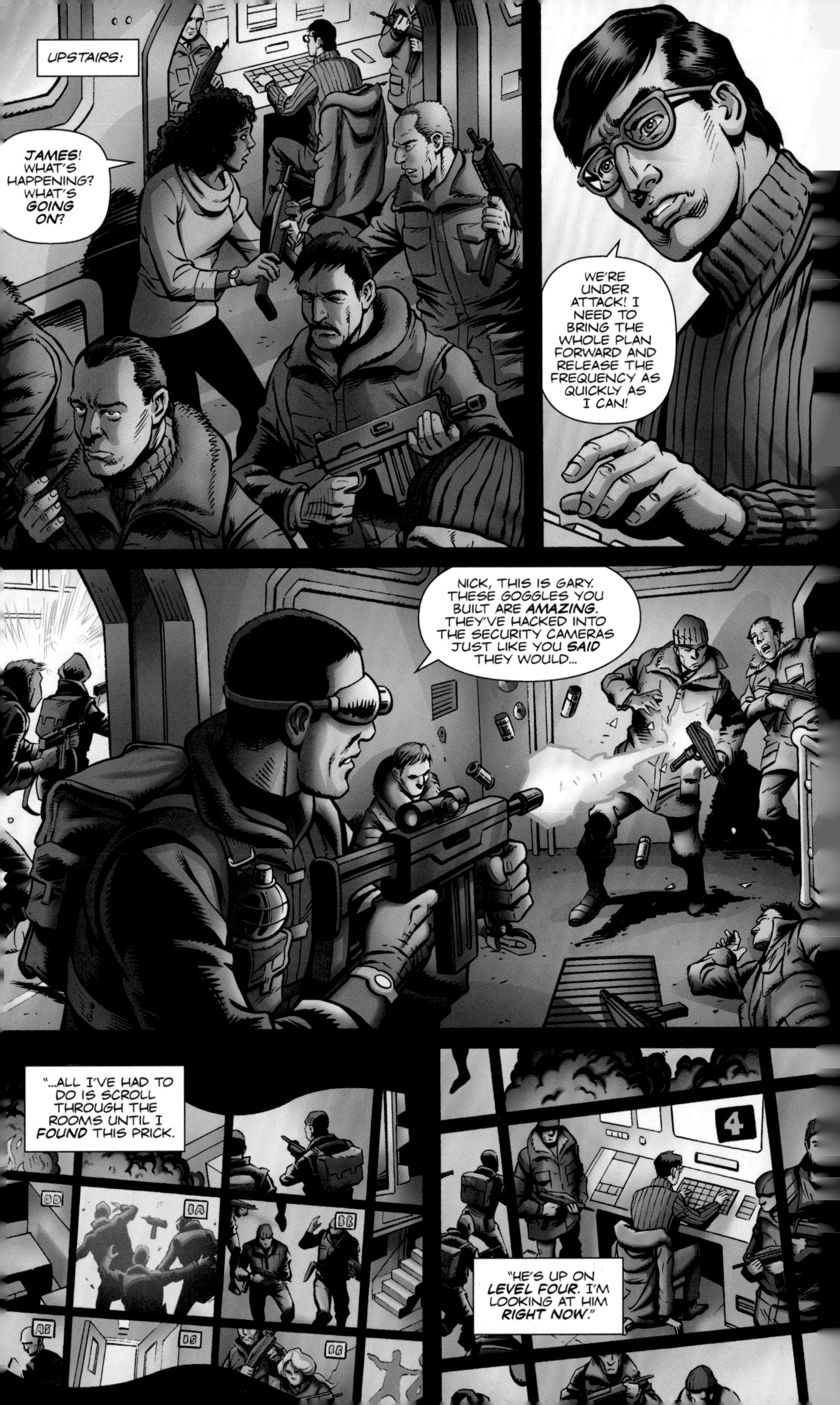
UPSTAIRS:
JAMES! WHAT'S HAPPENING? WHAT'S GOING ON?
WE'RE UNDER ATTACK! I NEED TO BRING THE WHOLE PLAN FORWARD AND RELEASE THE FREQUENCY AS QUICKLY AS I CAN!
NICK, THIS IS GARY. THESE GOGGLES YOU BUILT ARE AMAZING. THEY'VE HACKED INTO THE SECURITY CAMERAS JUST LIKE YOU SAID THEY WOULD...
"...ALL I'VE HAD TO DO IS SCROLL THROUGH THE ROOMS UNTIL I FOUND THIS PRICK.
4
"HE'S UP ON LEVEL FOUR. I'M LOOKING AT HIM RIGHT NOW."

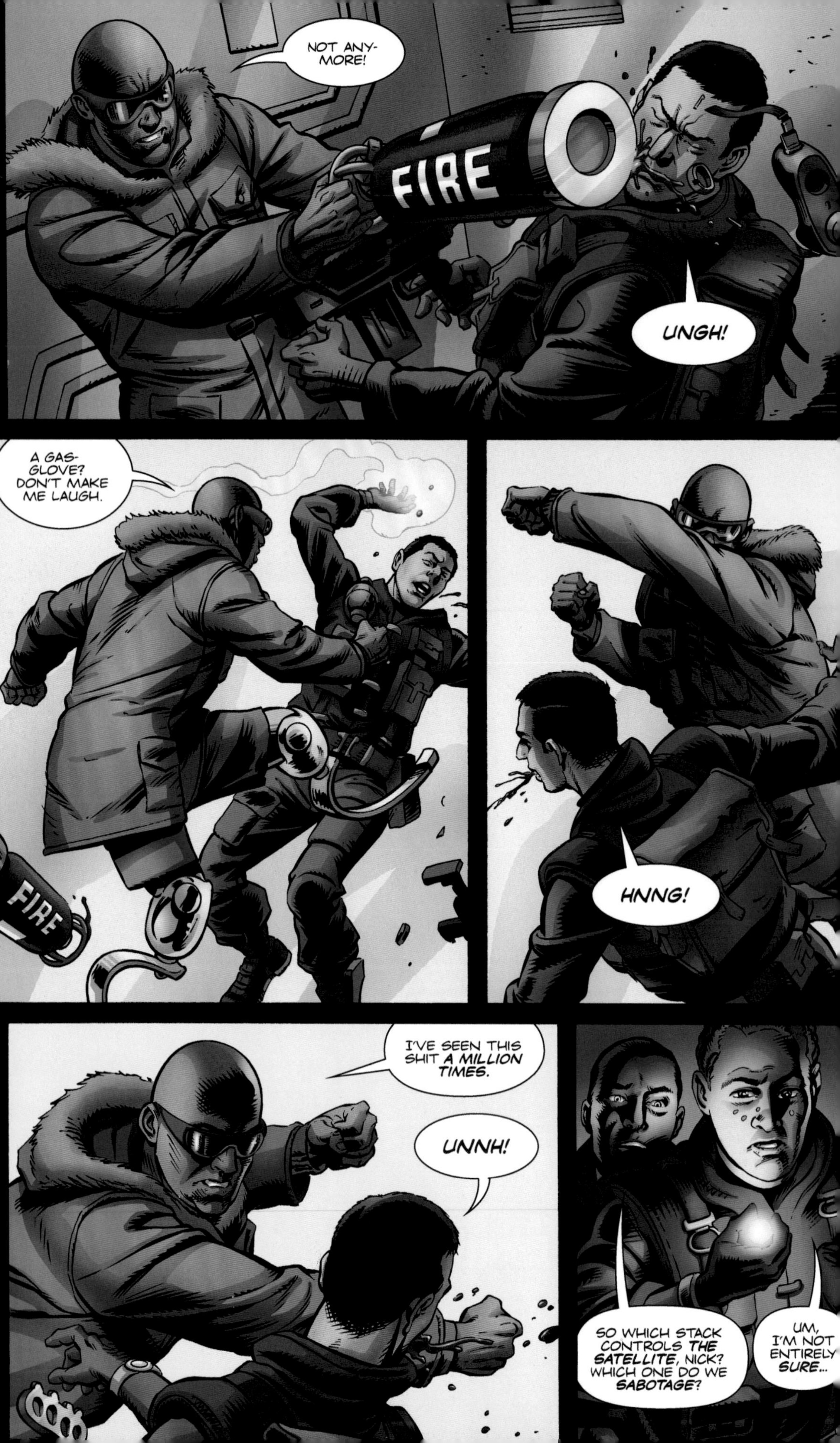
NOT ANY-
MORE!
FIRE
UNGH!
A GAS-
GLOVE?
DON'T MAKE
ME LAUGH.
FIRE
HNNG!
I'VE SEEN THIS
SHIT A MILLION
TIMES.
UNNH!
SO WHICH STACK
CONTROLS THE
SATELLITE, NICK?
WHICH ONE DO WE
SABOTAGE?
UM,
I'M NOT
ENTIRELY
SURE...

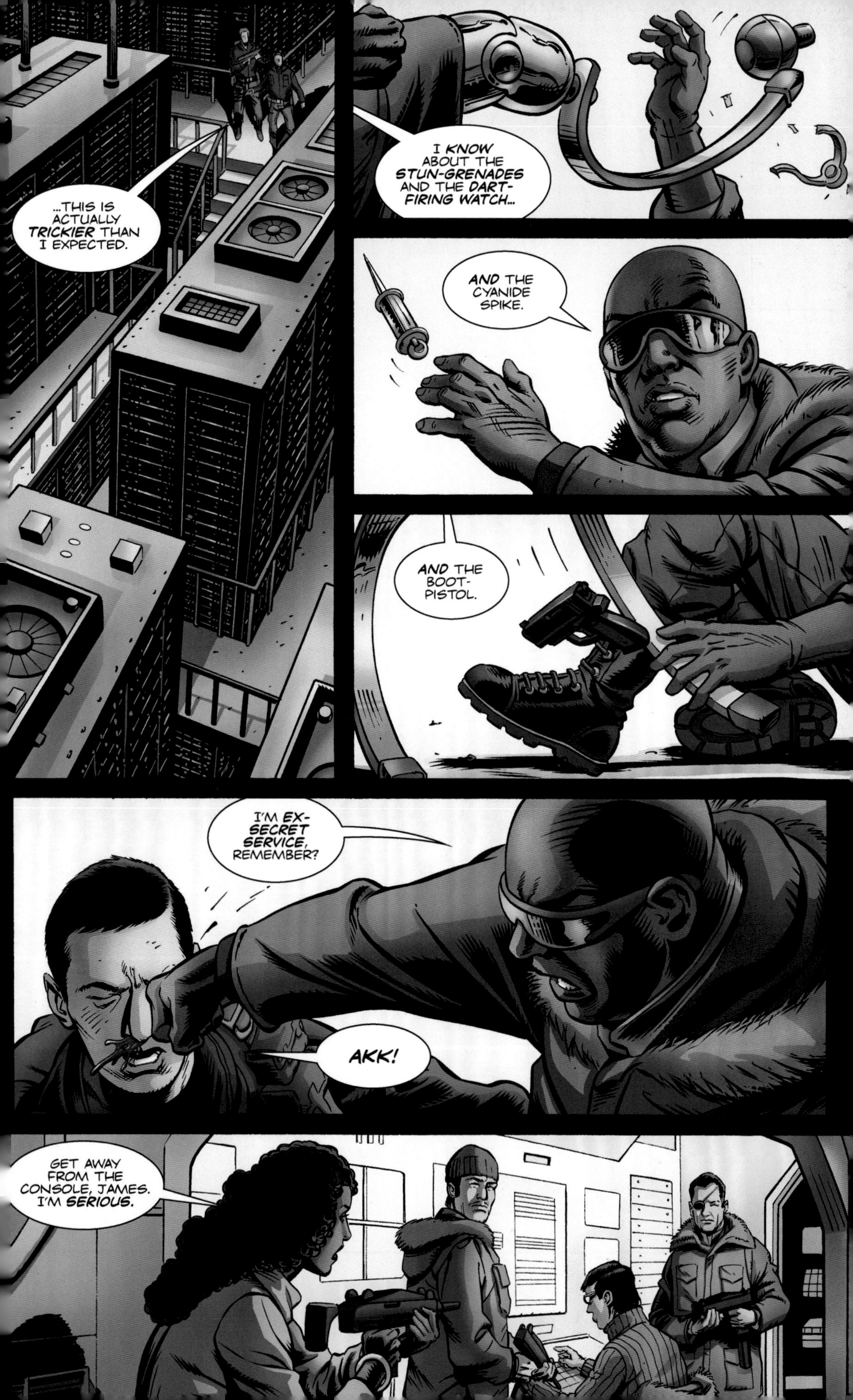
...THIS IS ACTUALLY TRICKIER THAN I EXPECTED.
I KNOW ABOUT THE STUN-GRENADES AND THE DART-FIRING WATCH...
AND THE CYANIDE SPIKE.
AND THE BOOT-PISTOL.
I'M EX-SECRET SERVICE, REMEMBER?
AKK!
GET AWAY FROM THE CONSOLE, JAMES. I'M SERIOUS.

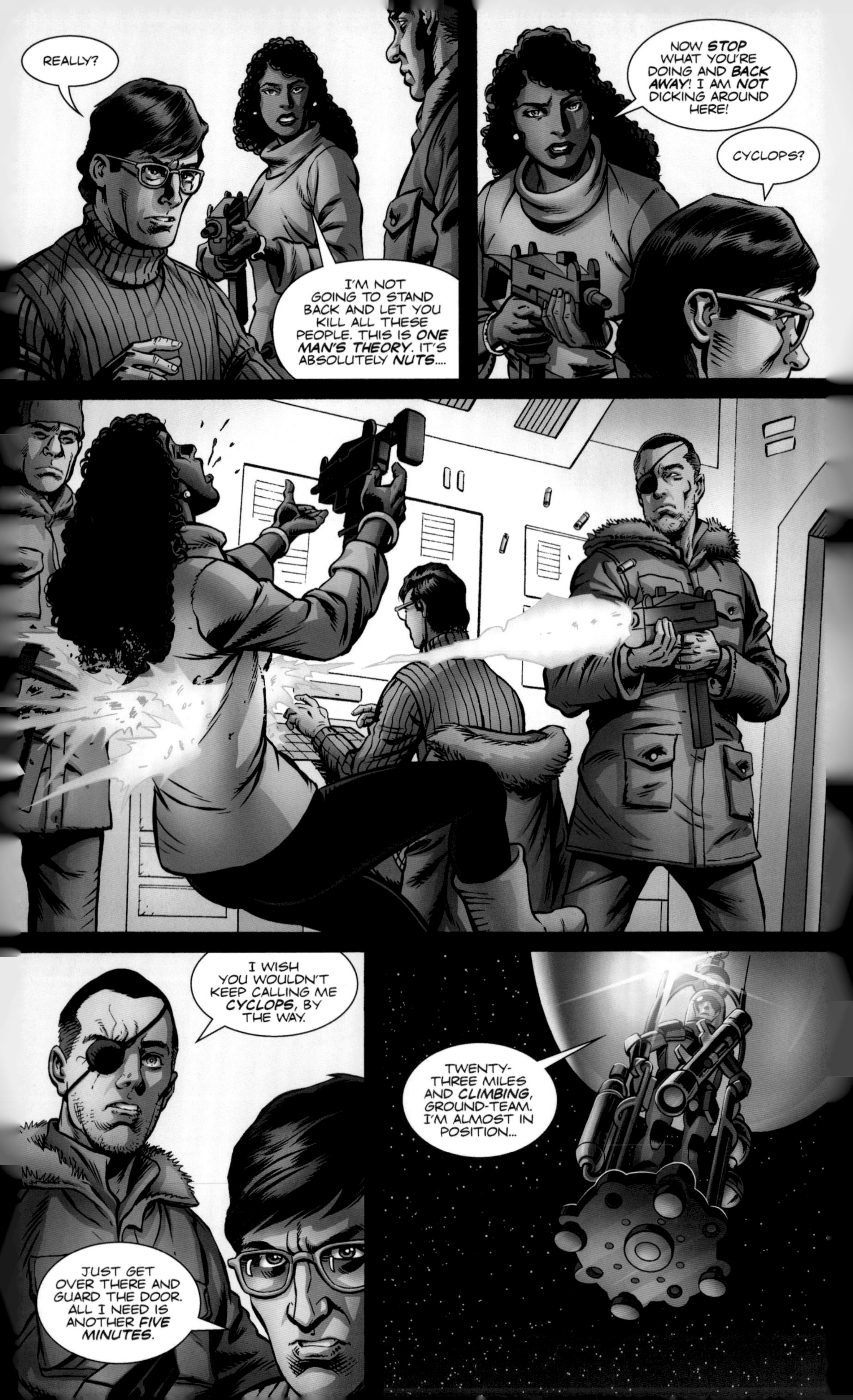
REALLY?
I'M NOT GOING TO STAND BACK AND LET YOU KILL ALL THESE PEOPLE. THIS IS ONE MAN'S THEORY. IT'S ABSOLUTELY NUTS....
NOW STOP WHAT YOU'RE DOING AND BACK AWAY! I AM NOT DICKING AROUND HERE!
CYCLOPS?
I WISH YOU WOULDN'T KEEP CALLING ME CYCLOPS, BY THE WAY.
JUST GET OVER THERE AND GUARD THE DOOR. ALL I NEED IS ANOTHER FIVE MINUTES.
TWENTY-THREE MILES AND CLIMBING, GROUND-TEAM. I'M ALMOST IN POSITION...

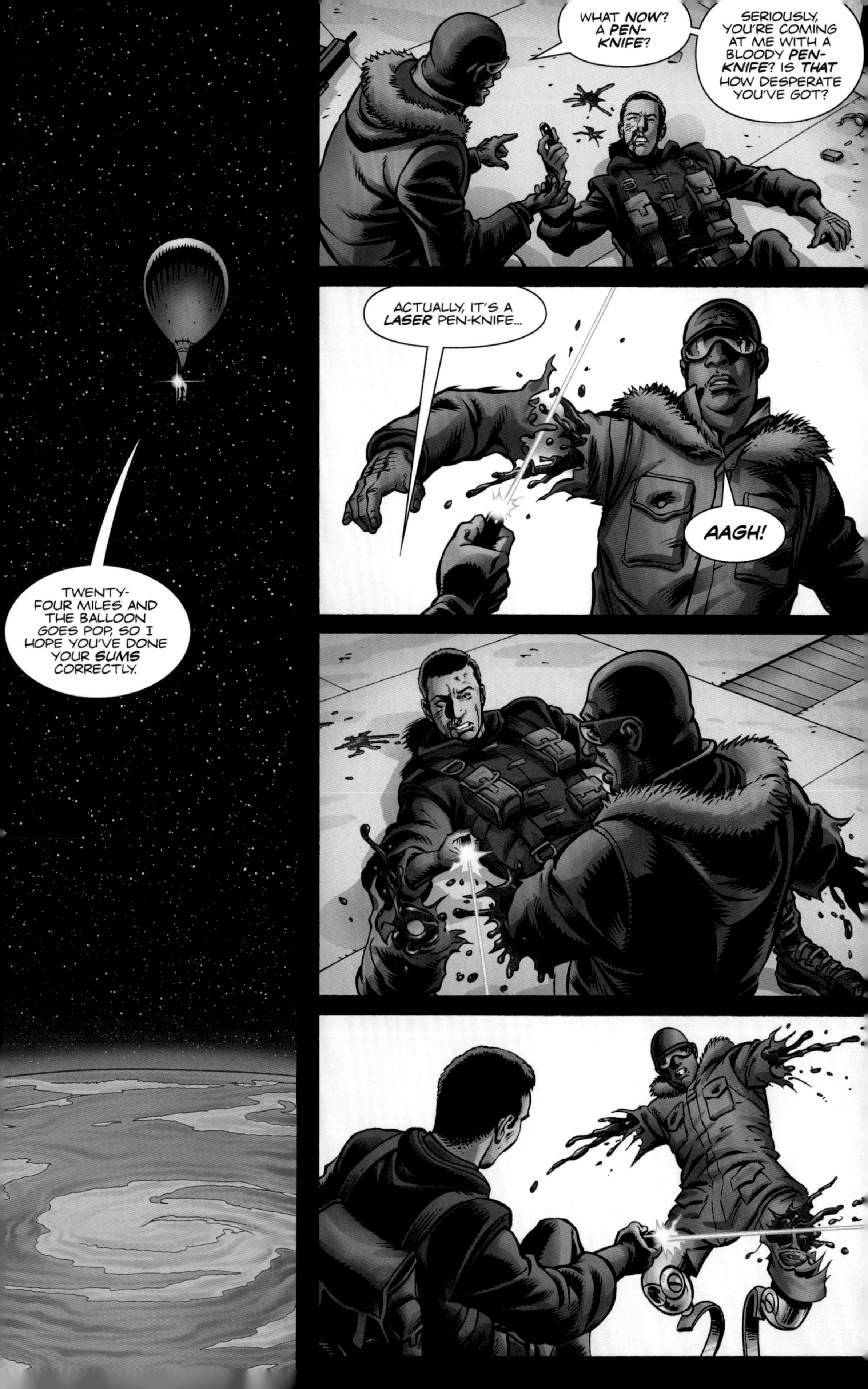
TWENTY-FOUR MILES AND THE BALLOON GOES POP, SO I HOPE YOU'VE DONE YOUR **SUMS** CORRECTLY.
WHAT **NOW**? A **PEN-KNIFE**?
SERIOUSLY, YOU'RE COMING AT ME WITH A BLOODY **PEN-KNIFE**? IS **THAT** HOW DESPERATE YOU'VE GOT?
ACTUALLY, IT'S A **LASER** PEN-KNIFE...
AAGH!

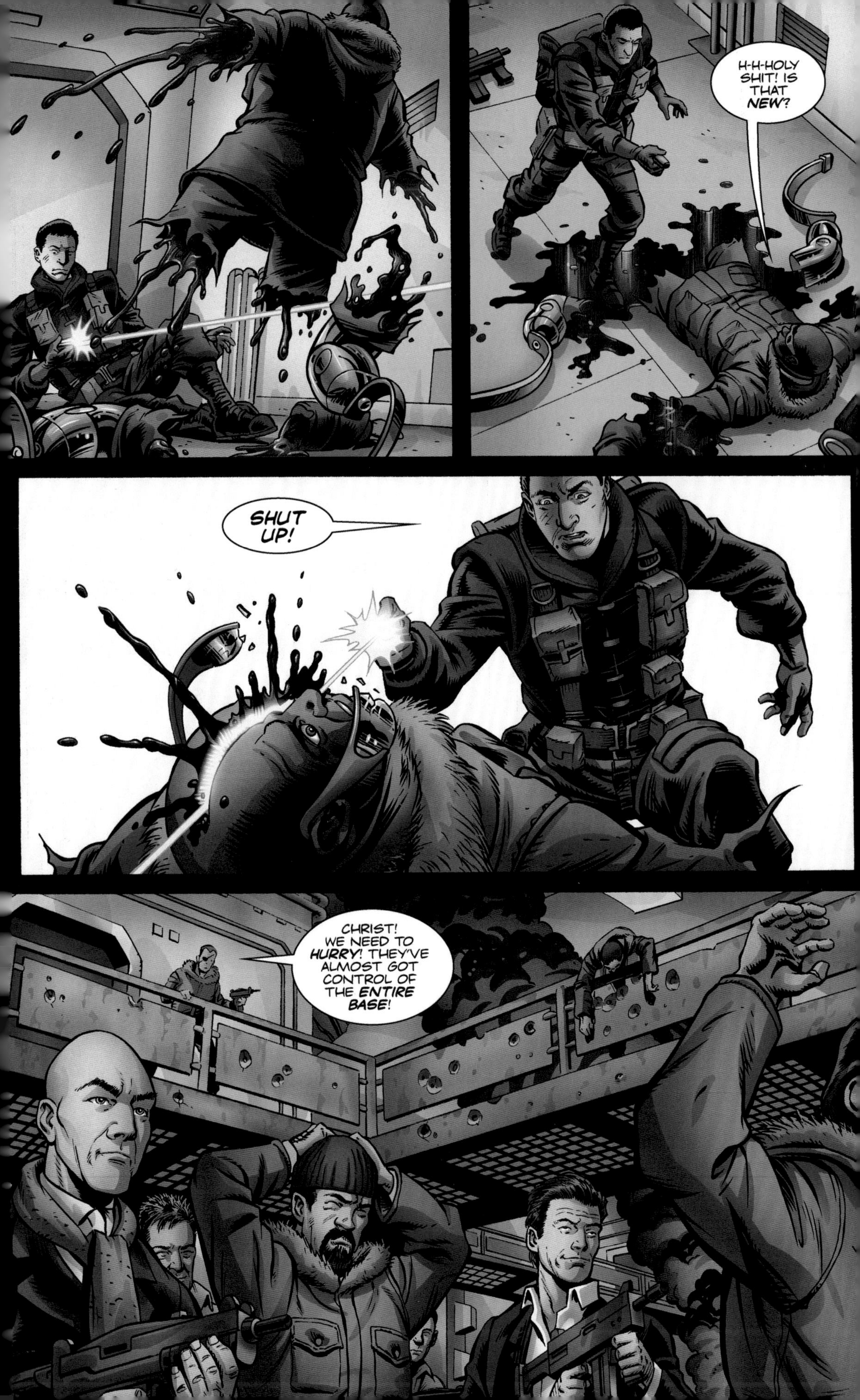
H-H-HOLY SHIT! IS THAT NEW?
SHUT UP!
CHRIST! WE NEED TO HURRY! THEY'VE ALMOST GOT CONTROL OF THE ENTIRE BASE!

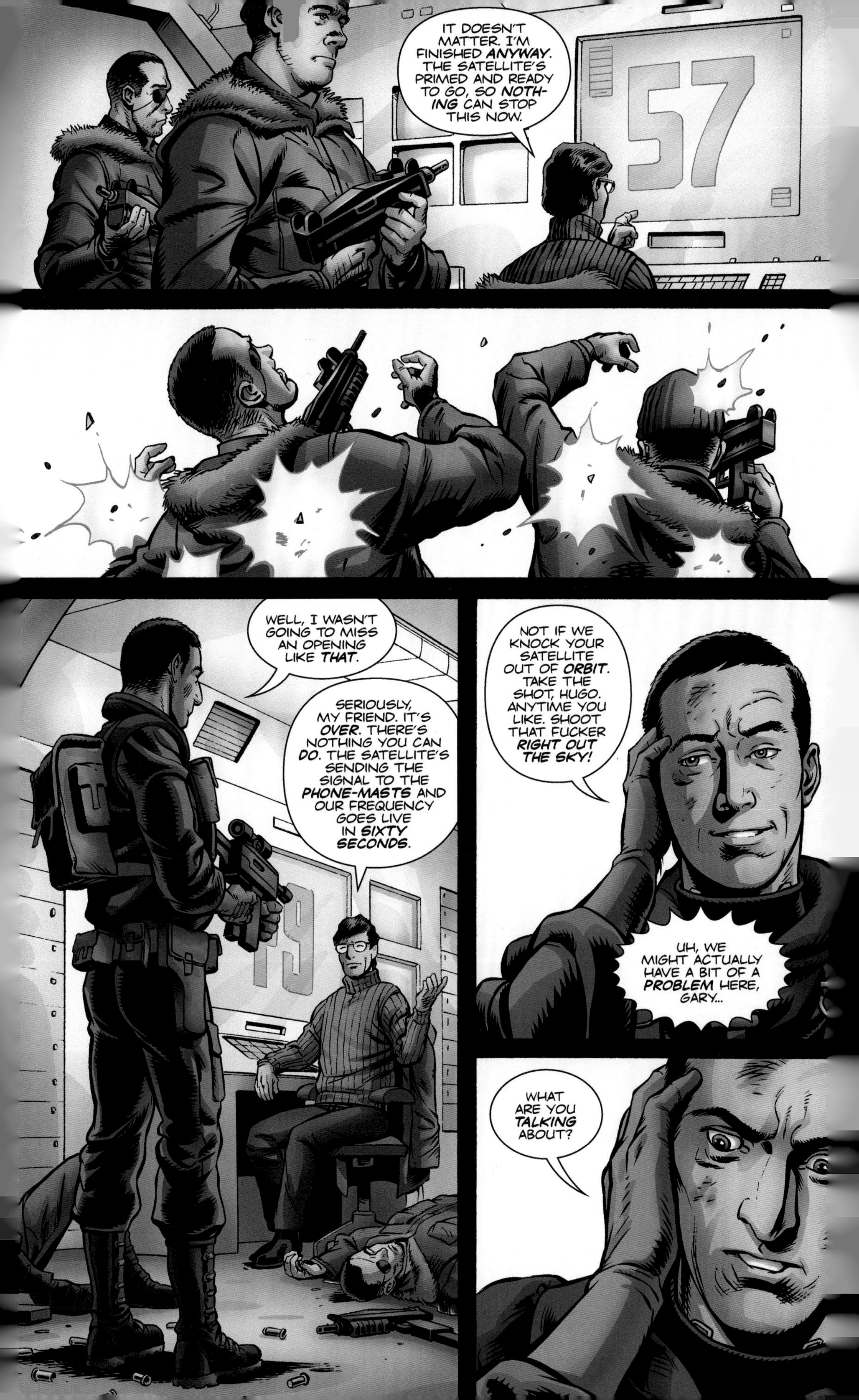
IT DOESN'T MATTER. I'M FINISHED **ANYWAY**. THE SATELLITE'S PRIMED AND READY TO GO, SO **NOTHING** CAN STOP THIS NOW.
WELL, I WASN'T GOING TO MISS AN OPENING LIKE **THAT**.
SERIOUSLY, MY FRIEND. IT'S **OVER**. THERE'S NOTHING YOU CAN **DO**. THE SATELLITE'S SENDING THE SIGNAL TO THE **PHONE-MASTS** AND OUR FREQUENCY GOES LIVE IN **SIXTY SECONDS**.
NOT IF WE KNOCK YOUR SATELLITE OUT OF **ORBIT**. TAKE THE SHOT, HUGO. ANYTIME YOU LIKE. SHOOT THAT FUCKER **RIGHT OUT THE SKY!**
UH, WE MIGHT ACTUALLY HAVE A BIT OF A **PROBLEM** HERE, GARY...
WHAT ARE YOU **TALKING** ABOUT?

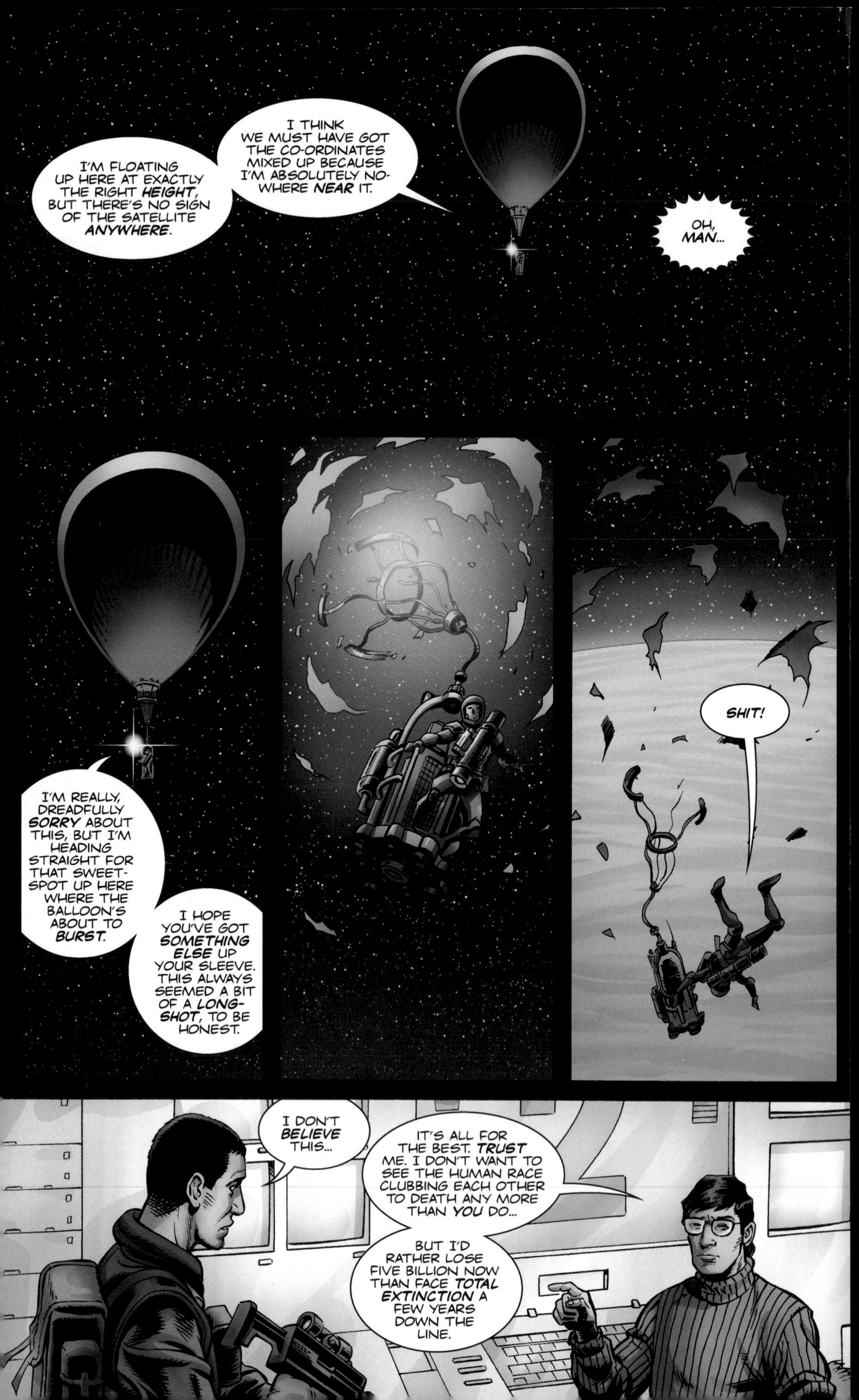

I'M FLOATING UP HERE AT EXACTLY THE RIGHT HEIGHT, BUT THERE'S NO SIGN OF THE SATELLITE ANYWHERE.
I THINK WE MUST HAVE GOT THE CO-ORDINATES MIXED UP BECAUSE I'M ABSOLUTELY NO-WHERE NEAR IT.
OH, MAN...
I'M REALLY, DREADFULLY SORRY ABOUT THIS, BUT I'M HEADING STRAIGHT FOR THAT SWEET-SPOT UP HERE WHERE THE BALLOON'S ABOUT TO BURST.
I HOPE YOU'VE GOT SOMETHING ELSE UP YOUR SLEEVE. THIS ALWAYS SEEMED A BIT OF A LONG-SHOT, TO BE HONEST.
SHIT!
I DON'T BELIEVE THIS...
IT'S ALL FOR THE BEST. TRUST ME. I DON'T WANT TO SEE THE HUMAN RACE CLUBBING EACH OTHER TO DEATH ANY MORE THAN YOU DO...
BUT I'D RATHER LOSE FIVE BILLION NOW THAN FACE TOTAL EXTINCTION A FEW YEARS DOWN THE LINE.

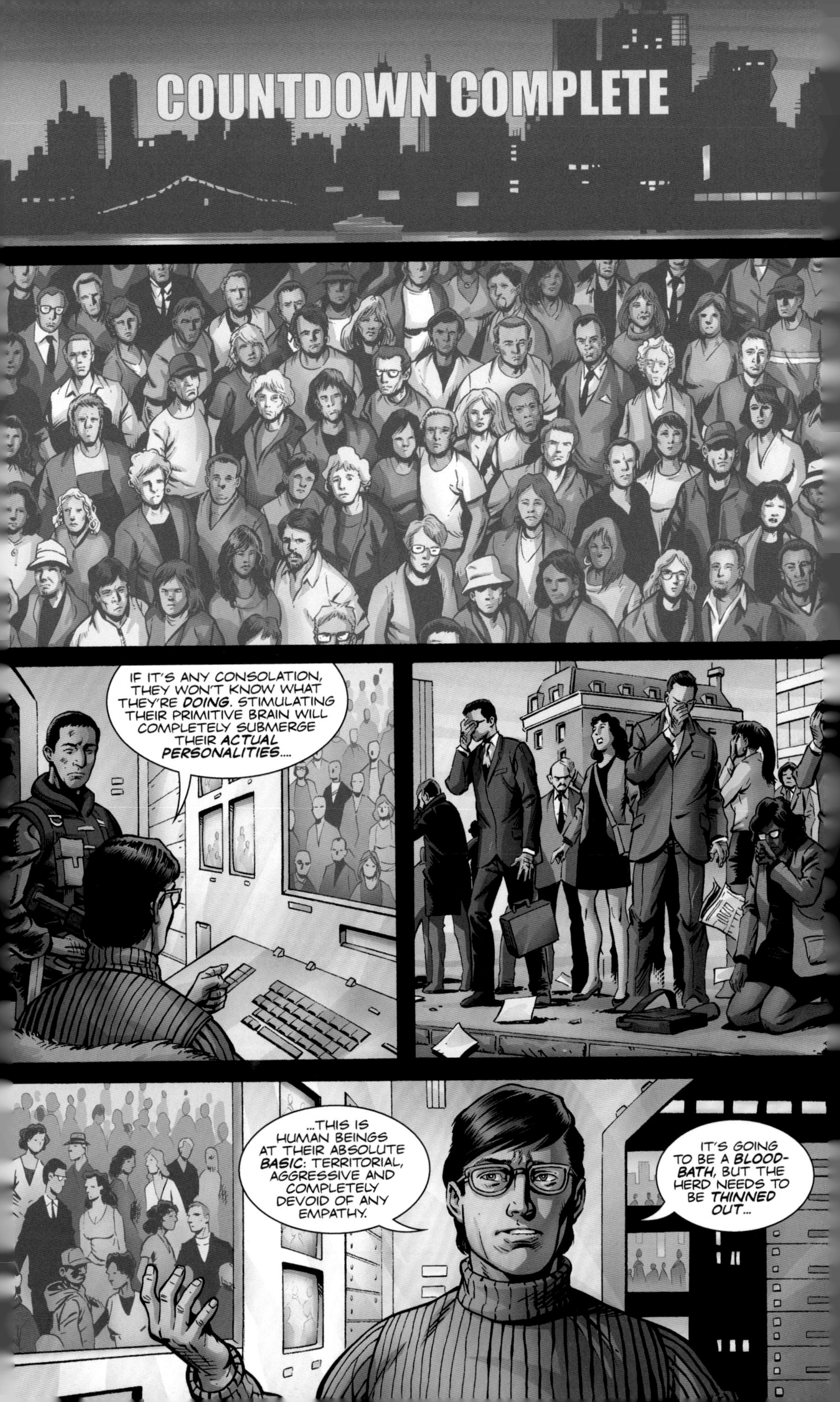
COUNTDOWN COMPLETE
IF IT'S ANY CONSOLATION, THEY WON'T KNOW WHAT THEY'RE DOING. STIMULATING THEIR PRIMITIVE BRAIN WILL COMPLETELY SUBMERGE THEIR ACTUAL PERSONALITIES....
...THIS IS HUMAN BEINGS AT THEIR ABSOLUTE BASIC: TERRITORIAL, AGGRESSIVE AND COMPLETELY DEVOID OF ANY EMPATHY.
IT'S GOING TO BE A BLOOD-BATH, BUT THE HERD NEEDS TO BE THINNED OUT...

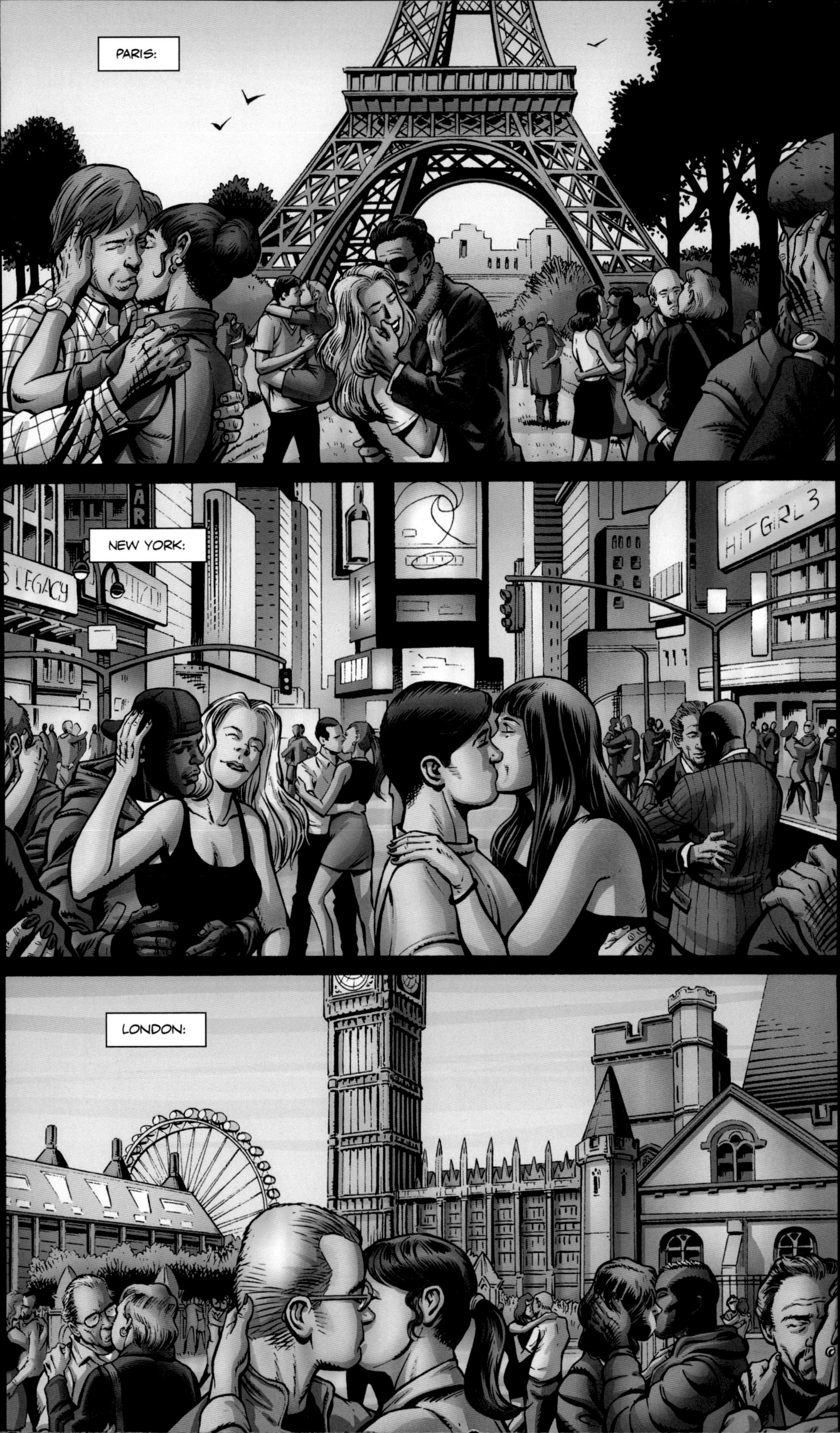
PARIS:
NEW YORK:
HITGIRL 3
LONDON:

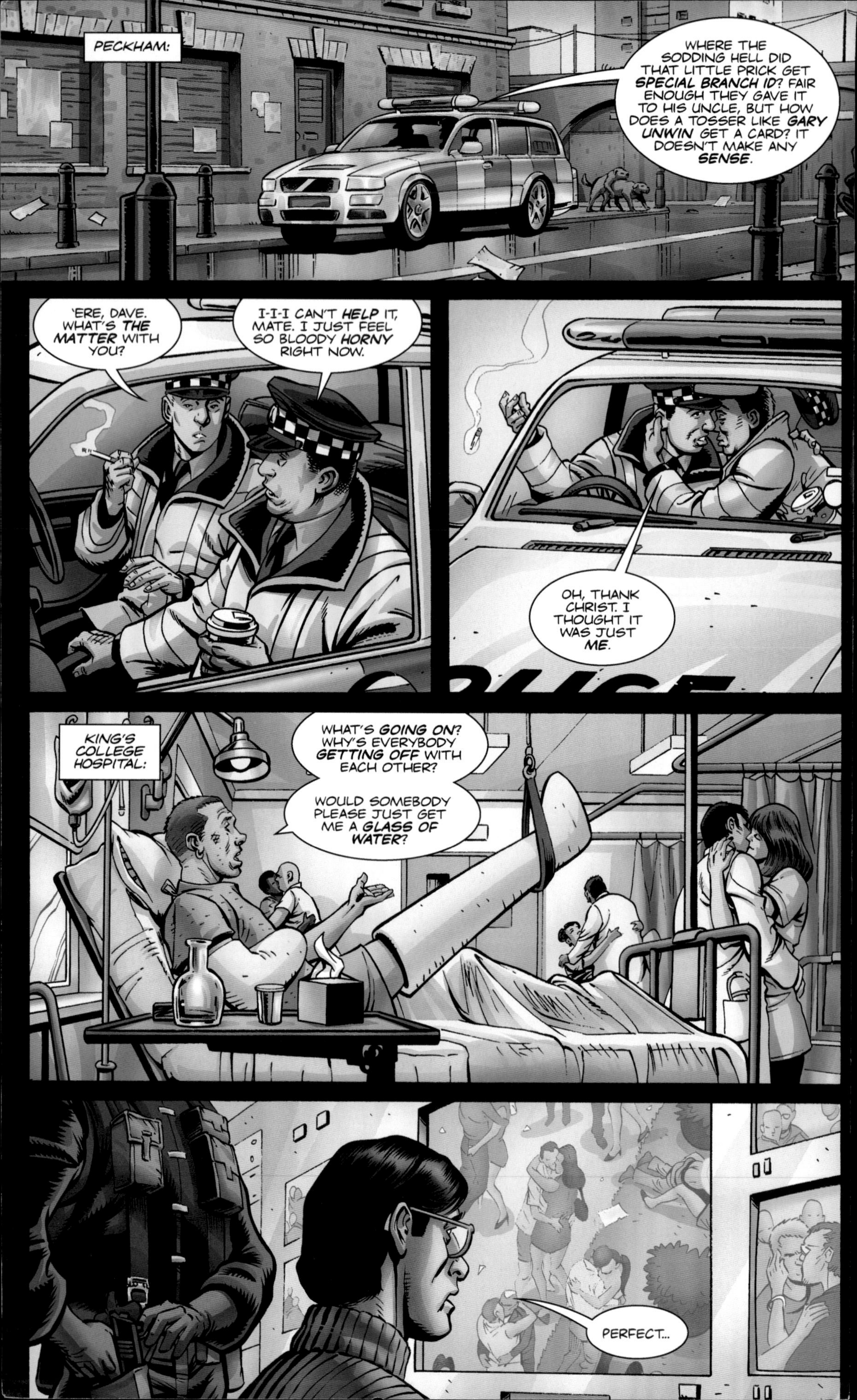
PECKHAM:
WHERE THE SODDING HELL DID THAT LITTLE PRICK GET SPECIAL BRANCH ID? FAIR ENOUGH THEY GAVE IT TO HIS UNCLE, BUT HOW DOES A TOSSER LIKE GARY UNWIN GET A CARD? IT DOESN'T MAKE ANY SENSE.
'ERE, DAVE. WHAT'S THE MATTER WITH YOU?
I-I-I CAN'T HELP IT, MATE. I JUST FEEL SO BLOODY HORNY RIGHT NOW.
OH, THANK CHRIST. I THOUGHT IT WAS JUST ME.
KING'S COLLEGE HOSPITAL:
WHAT'S GOING ON? WHY'S EVERYBODY GETTING OFF WITH EACH OTHER?
WOULD SOMEBODY PLEASE JUST GET ME A GLASS OF WATER?
PERFECT...

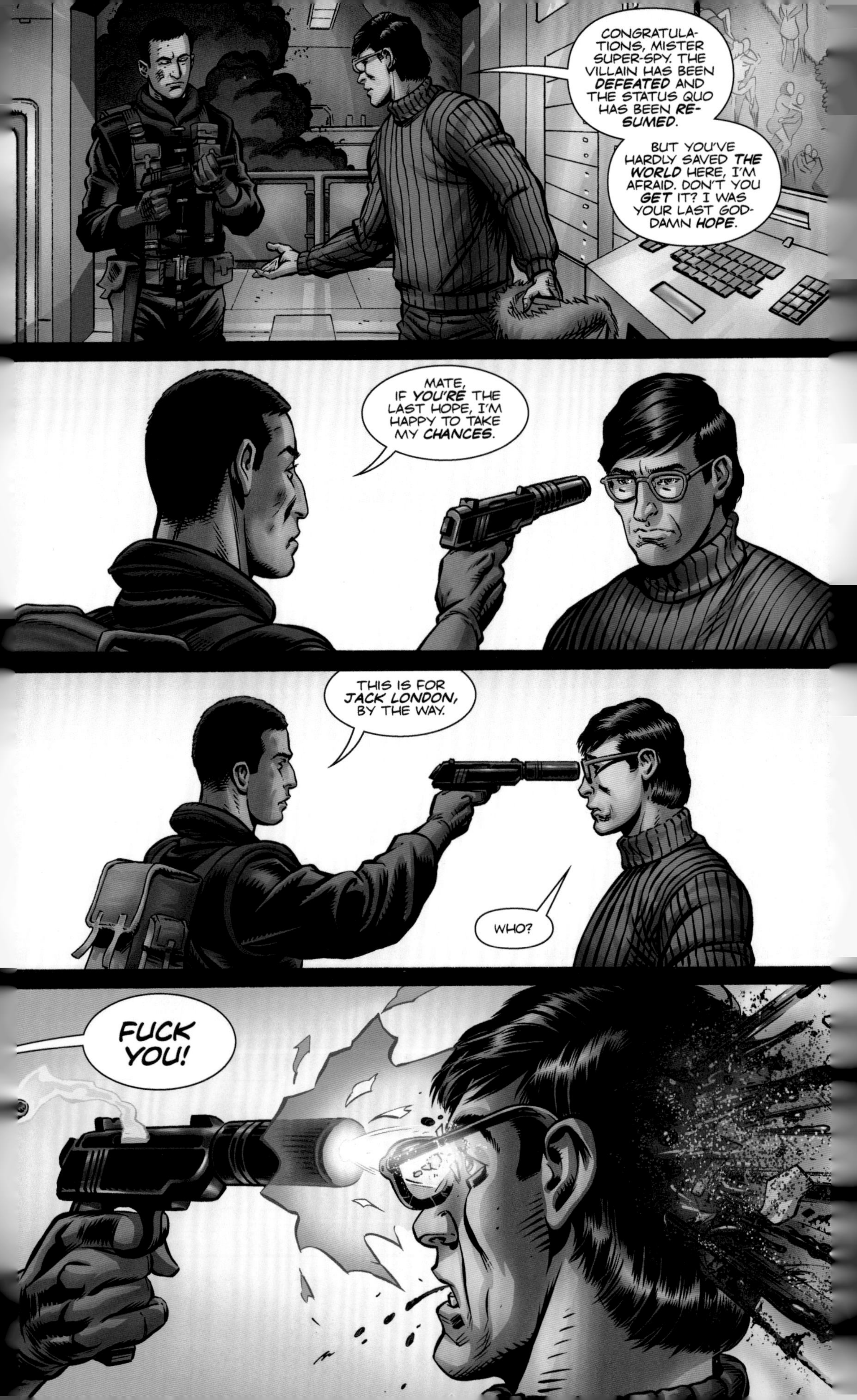
CONGRATULATIONS, MISTER SUPER-SPY. THE VILLAIN HAS BEEN ***DEFEATED*** AND THE STATUS QUO HAS BEEN ***RESUMED***.
BUT YOU'VE HARDLY SAVED **THE WORLD** HERE, I'M AFRAID. DON'T YOU ***GET*** IT? I WAS YOUR LAST GOD-DAMN ***HOPE***.
MATE, IF ***YOU'RE*** THE LAST HOPE, I'M HAPPY TO TAKE MY ***CHANCES***.
THIS IS FOR ***JACK LONDON***, BY THE WAY.
WHO?
FUCK YOU!

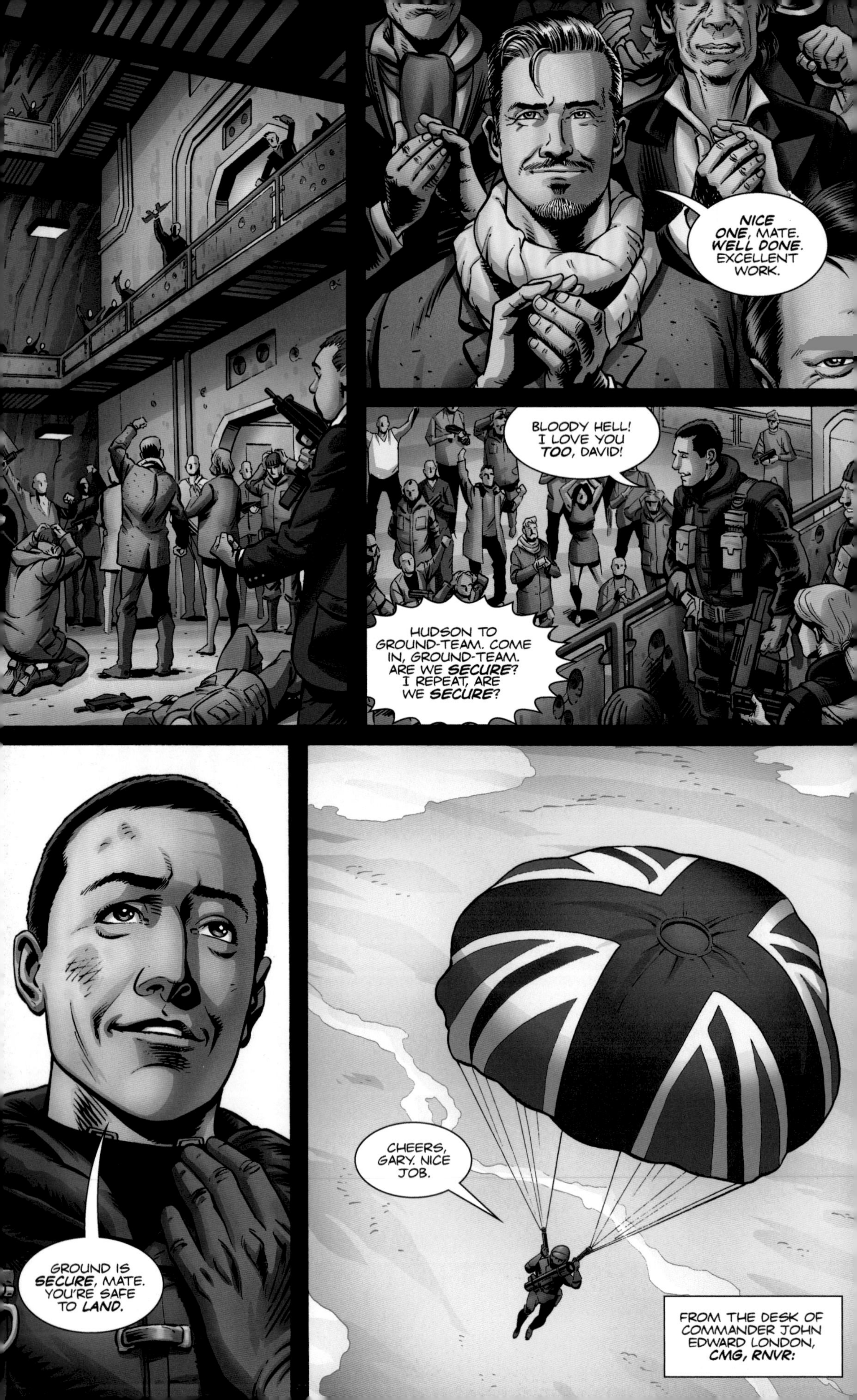
NICE ONE, MATE. WELL DONE. EXCELLENT WORK.
BLOODY HELL! I LOVE YOU TOO, DAVID!
HUDSON TO GROUND-TEAM. COME IN, GROUND-TEAM. ARE WE SECURE? I REPEAT, ARE WE SECURE?
GROUND IS SECURE, MATE. YOU'RE SAFE TO LAND.
CHEERS, GARY. NICE JOB.
FROM THE DESK OF COMMANDER JOHN EDWARD LONDON, CMG, RNVR:

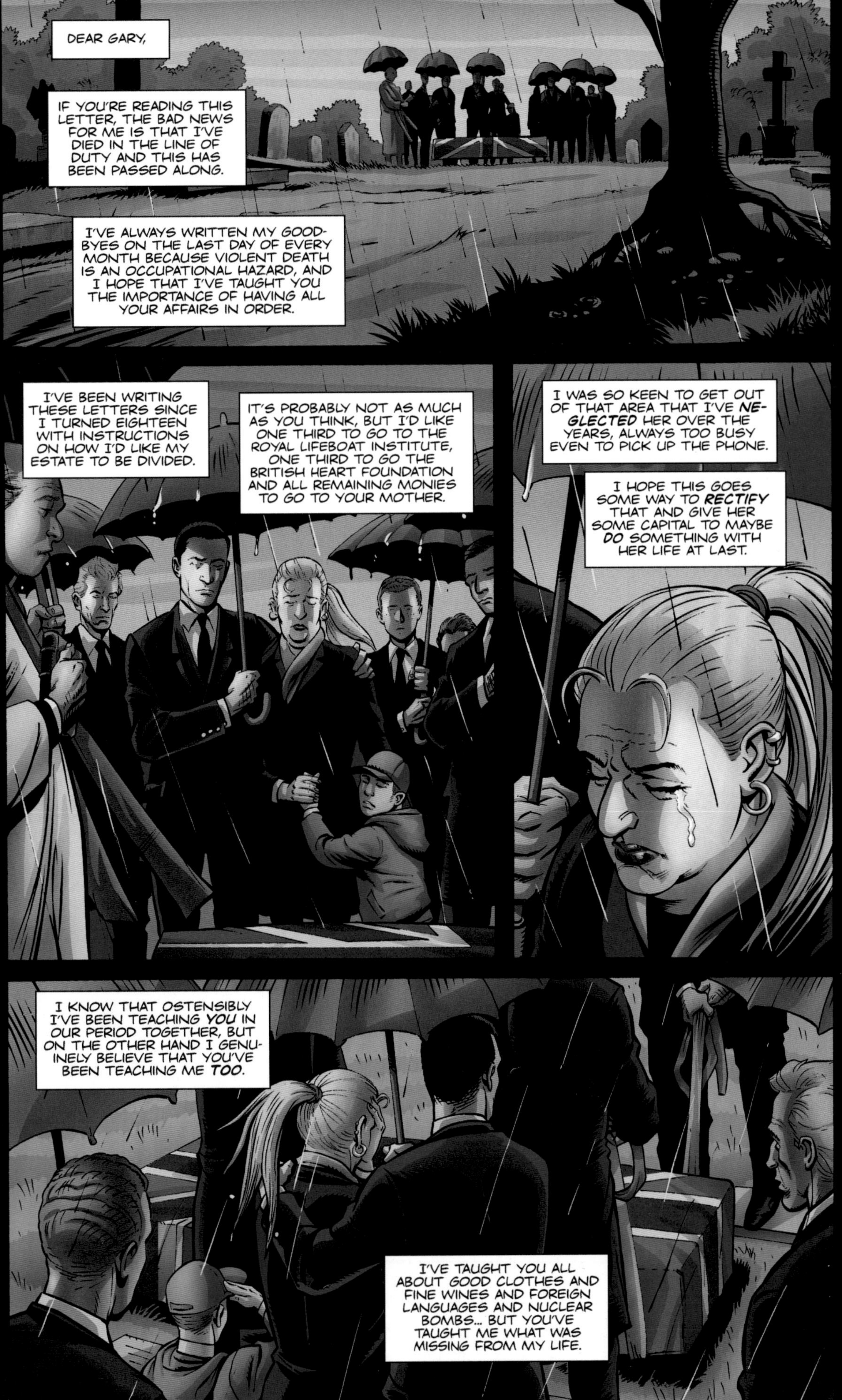
DEAR GARY,
IF YOU'RE READING THIS LETTER, THE BAD NEWS FOR ME IS THAT I'VE DIED IN THE LINE OF DUTY AND THIS HAS BEEN PASSED ALONG.
I'VE ALWAYS WRITTEN MY GOOD-BYES ON THE LAST DAY OF EVERY MONTH BECAUSE VIOLENT DEATH IS AN OCCUPATIONAL HAZARD, AND I HOPE THAT I'VE TAUGHT YOU THE IMPORTANCE OF HAVING ALL YOUR AFFAIRS IN ORDER.
I'VE BEEN WRITING THESE LETTERS SINCE I TURNED EIGHTEEN WITH INSTRUCTIONS ON HOW I'D LIKE MY ESTATE TO BE DIVIDED.
IT'S PROBABLY NOT AS MUCH AS YOU THINK, BUT I'D LIKE ONE THIRD TO GO TO THE ROYAL LIFEBOAT INSTITUTE, ONE THIRD TO GO THE BRITISH HEART FOUNDATION AND ALL REMAINING MONIES TO GO TO YOUR MOTHER.
I WAS SO KEEN TO GET OUT OF THAT AREA THAT I'VE ***NE-GLECTED*** HER OVER THE YEARS, ALWAYS TOO BUSY EVEN TO PICK UP THE PHONE.
I HOPE THIS GOES SOME WAY TO ***RECTIFY*** THAT AND GIVE HER SOME CAPITAL TO MAYBE ***DO*** SOMETHING WITH HER LIFE AT LAST.
I KNOW THAT OSTENSIBLY I'VE BEEN TEACHING ***YOU*** IN OUR PERIOD TOGETHER, BUT ON THE OTHER HAND I GENU-INELY BELIEVE THAT YOU'VE BEEN TEACHING ME ***TOO***.
I'VE TAUGHT YOU ALL ABOUT GOOD CLOTHES AND FINE WINES AND FOREIGN LANGUAGES AND NUCLEAR BOMBS... BUT YOU'VE TAUGHT ME WHAT WAS MISSING FROM MY LIFE.

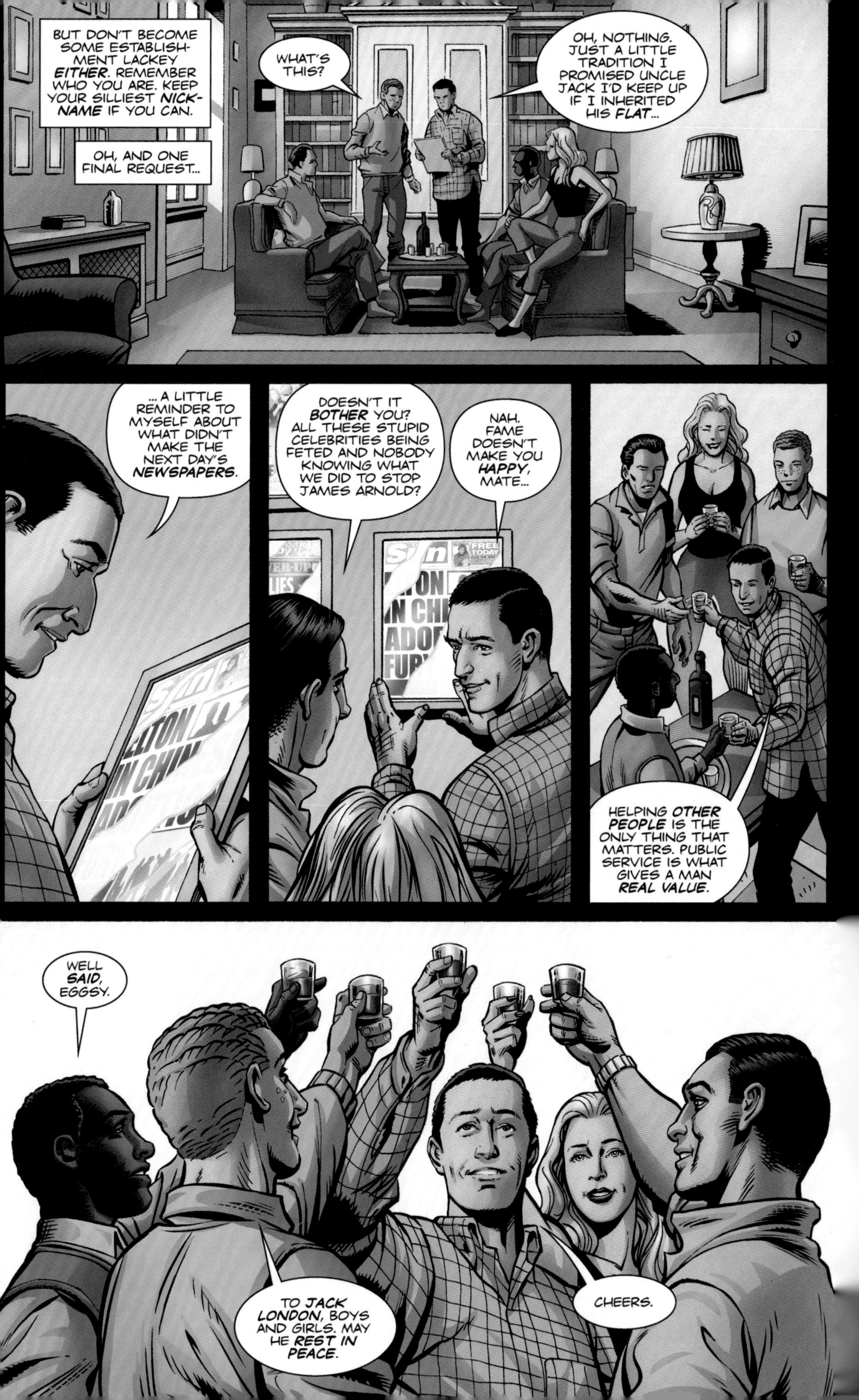
BUT DON'T BECOME SOME ESTABLISHMENT LACKEY EITHER. REMEMBER WHO YOU ARE. KEEP YOUR SILLIEST NICKNAME IF YOU CAN.
OH, AND ONE FINAL REQUEST...
WHAT'S THIS?
OH, NOTHING. JUST A LITTLE TRADITION I PROMISED UNCLE JACK I'D KEEP UP IF I INHERITED HIS FLAT...
... A LITTLE REMINDER TO MYSELF ABOUT WHAT DIDN'T MAKE THE NEXT DAY'S NEWSPAPERS.
DOESN'T IT BOTHER YOU? ALL THESE STUPID CELEBRITIES BEING FETED AND NOBODY KNOWING WHAT WE DID TO STOP JAMES ARNOLD?
NAH. FAME DOESN'T MAKE YOU HAPPY, MATE...
HELPING OTHER PEOPLE IS THE ONLY THING THAT MATTERS. PUBLIC SERVICE IS WHAT GIVES A MAN REAL VALUE.
WELL SAID, EGGSY.
TO JACK LONDON, BOYS AND GIRLS. MAY HE REST IN PEACE.
CHEERS.

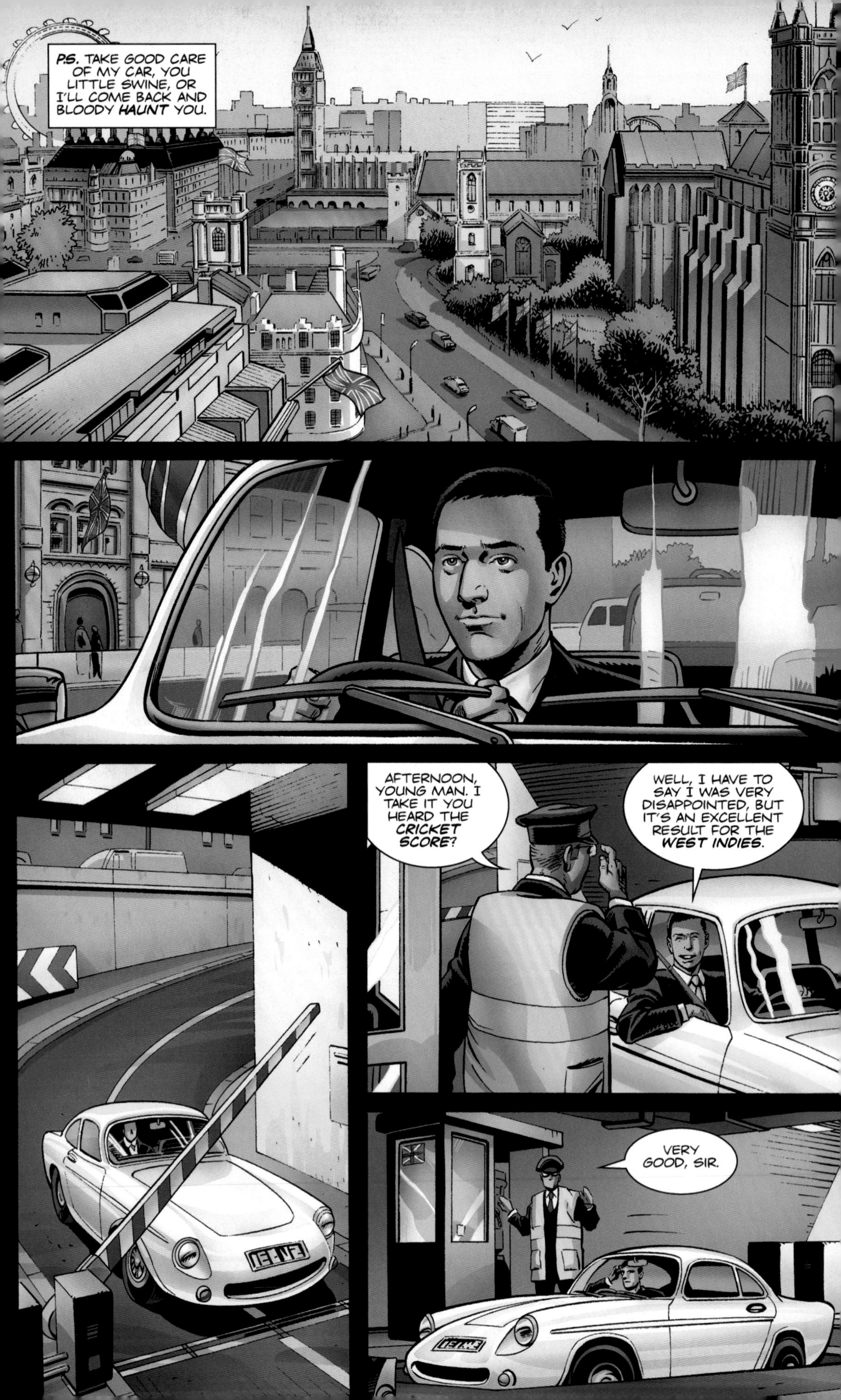
P.S. TAKE GOOD CARE OF MY CAR, YOU LITTLE SWINE, OR I'LL COME BACK AND BLOODY HAUNT YOU.
AFTERNOON, YOUNG MAN. I TAKE IT YOU HEARD THE CRICKET SCORE?
WELL, I HAVE TO SAY I WAS VERY DISAPPOINTED, BUT IT'S AN EXCELLENT RESULT FOR THE WEST INDIES.
VERY GOOD, SIR.

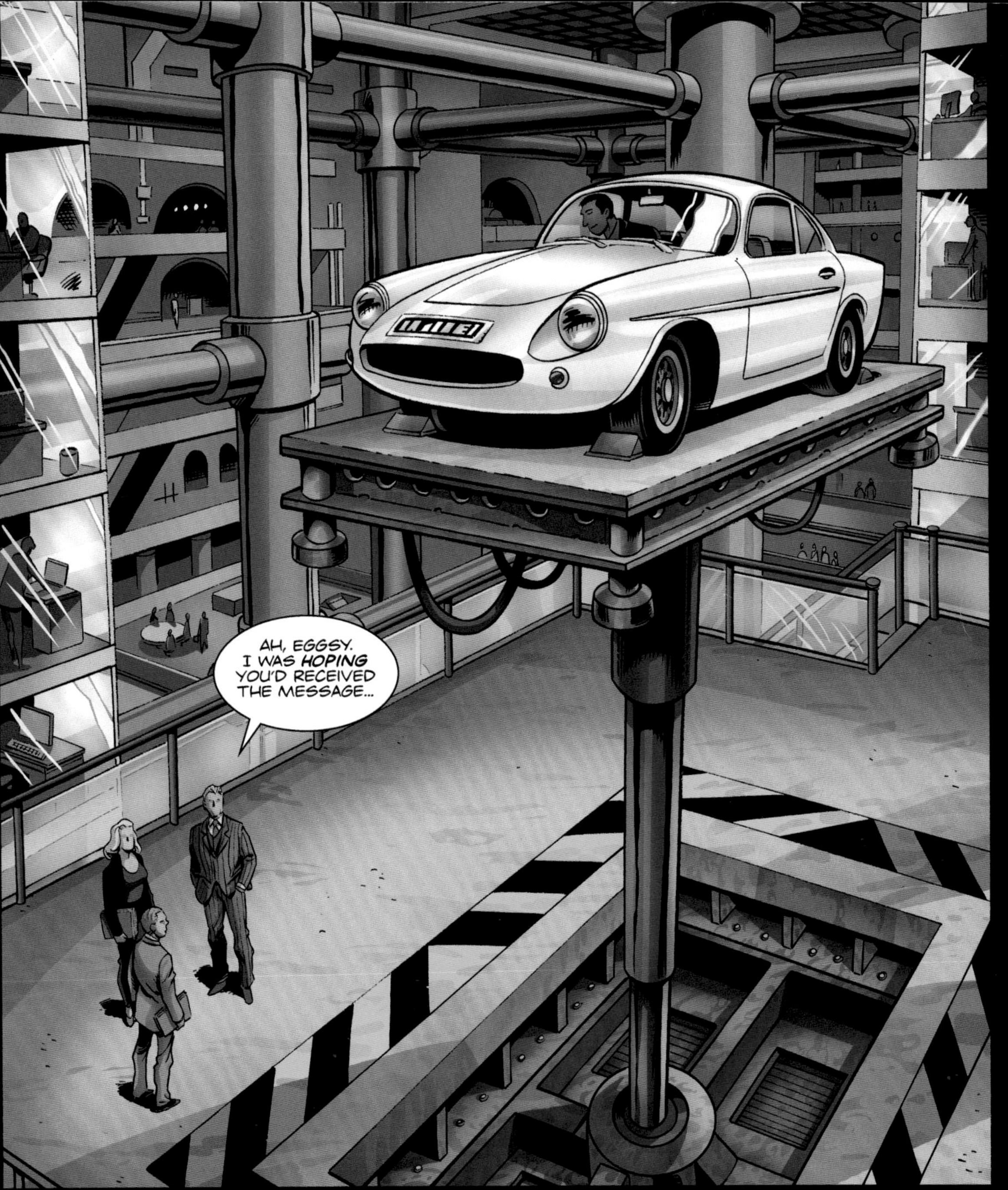
AH, EGGSY. I WAS HOPING YOU'D RECEIVED THE MESSAGE...

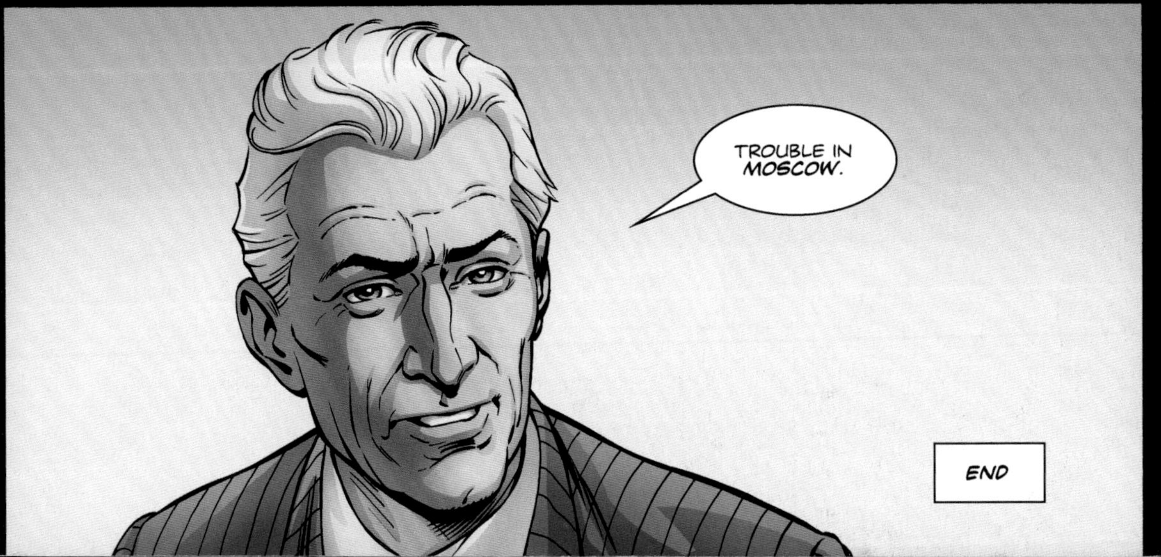
TROUBLE IN MOSCOW.
END

MILLAR

KICK-ASS
MARK MILLAR
JOHN ROMITA JR.

HIT-GIRL
MARK MILLAR
JOHN ROMITA JR.
TOM PALMER and DEAN WHITE

KICK-ASS 2
MARK MILLAR
JOHN ROMITA JR.

MARK MILLAR DUNCAN FEGREDO
MPH
NUMBER ONE
$2.99

WANTED
MARK MILLAR • JG JONES • PAUL MOUNTS
NOW A MAJOR MOTION PICTURE FROM
UNIVERSAL PICTURES
WWW.MILLARWORLD.TV

MARK MILLAR & LEINIL YU
SUPERIOR
FROM THE
WRITER OF
KICK-ASS

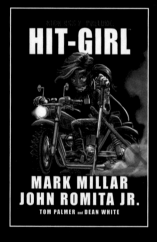

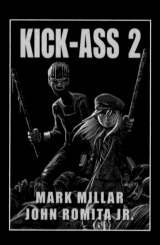

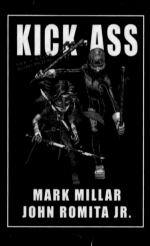

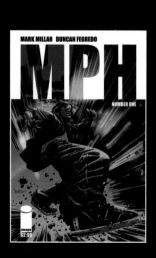

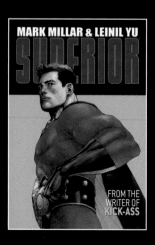

WORLD ®
THE COLLECTION

THE SECRET SERVICE
KINGSMAN

MARK MILLAR
DAVE GIBBONS
MATTHEW VAUGHN

MARK MILLAR · GORAN PARLOV
STARLIGHT

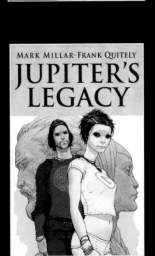

MILLAR & McNIVEN'S
NEMESIS

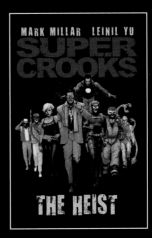

MARK MILLAR · LEINIL YU
SUPER CROOKS

THE HEIST

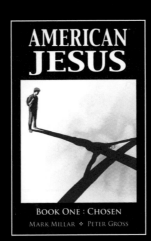

MARK MILLAR · FRANK QUITELY
JUPITER'S LEGACY

AMERICAN JESUS

BOOK ONE : CHOSEN
MARK MILLAR ✦ PETER GROSS

THE CREATORS

Mark Millar is the *New York Times* best-selling writer of Wanted, the Kick-Ass series, The Secret Service, Jupiter's Legacy, Nemesis, Superior, Super Crooks, American Jesus, MPH, and Starlight. Wanted, Kick-Ass, Kick-Ass 2, and The Secret Service (as Kingsman: The Secret Service) have been adapted into feature films, and Nemesis, Superior, Starlight, and War Heroes are in development at major studios. His DC Comics work includes the seminal Superman: Red Son, and at Marvel Comics he created The Ultimates — selected by Time magazine as the comic book of the decade — Wolverine: Old Man Logan, and Civil War — the industry's biggest-selling series in almost two decades. Mark was a producer on the past adaptations of his works and is an Executive Producer on the feature-film and television projects currently in development. He is CEO of Millarworld Productions, an advisor on motion pictures to the Scottish government, and Creative Consultant to Fox Studios.

Dave Gibbons began his career in British comics working on *2000AD* and *Dr. Who* before being recruited to America by DC Comics. His collaboration with Alan Moore, the Hugo Award-winning *Watchmen*, is the best-selling graphic novel of all time. With writer Frank Miller he created the acclaimed *Martha Washington/Give Me Liberty* series. Also a writer, his work for Marvel includes *Captain America*, *Dr. Strange,* and *The Hulk*. He is currently consulting on new storytelling technologies with a number of companies.

Matthew Vaughn produced such films as *Lock, Stock and Two Smoking Barrels* and *Snatch* in his native England before taking the director's chair for crime thriller *Layer Cake* in 2004 and fantasy epic *Stardust* in 2007. In his first collaboration with Mark Millar, Vaughn directed the film adaptation of *Kick-Ass,* before helming *X-Men: First Class* in 2011. He produced *Kick-Ass 2,* wrote and produced *X-Men: Days of Future Past,* and produced, wrote, and directed *Kingsman: The Secret Service,* the feature motion-picture adaptation of *The Secret Service.* He's a producer of the upcoming *The Fantastic Four* and *Superior.*